HEALTH CARE IN TRANSITION
VOLUME 1

HEALTH CARE IN TRANSITION
VOLUME 1

MARY N. SMYTH (EDITOR)

Nova Science Publishers, Inc.
New York

Senior Editors: Susan Boriotti and Donna Dennis
Coordinating Editor: Tatiana Shohov
Office Manager: Annette Hellinger
Graphics: Wanda Serrano
Editorial Production: Jennifer Vogt, Matthew Kozlowski, Jonathan Rose, Alexandra Columbus and Maya Columbus
Circulation: Ave Maria Gonzalez, Vera Popovich, Luis Aviles, Melissa Diaz, Nicolas Miro and Jeannie Pappas
Communications and Acquisitions: Serge P. Shohov
Marketing: Cathy DeGregory

Library of Congress Cataloging-in-Publication Data
Available Upon Request

ISBN 1-59033-272-5.

400 Oser Ave, Suite 1600
Hauppauge, New York 11788-3619
Tele. 631-231-7269 Fax 631-231-8175
e-mail: Novascience@earthlink.net
Web Site: http://www.novapublishers.com

Printed in the United States of America

CONTENTS

PREFACE

Health care is clearly in transition-but to where? Managed or unmanaged care? HMO's or not? Are insurance companies and hospitals the enemy of health care for their own patients? What about the 40,000,000 uninsured in America? Don't ask the patients, for they have become the ping pong balls in the health care game. This book examines important issues in this ever-growing maze.

Chapter 1

PUBLIC SECTOR MENTAL HEALTH SERVICES FOR MULTICULTURAL POPULATIONS: BRIDGING THE GAP FROM RESEARCH TO CLINICAL PRACTICE

Richard H. Dana, Myriam Aragon and Terry Kramer
Tri-City Mental Health Center
Pomona, CA

ABSTRACT

A history of biased mental health services for multicultural populations in the United States is being gradually replaced by increasing awareness in all concerned professions that cultural competence is essential, particularly in public sector managed care. California has assumed a leadership role nationally in demonstrating the efficacy of culturally competent services. This paper provides a case study example of agency initiative and compliance with state mandates. Some implications of using a process model to monitor feasible and effective research and service guidelines are discussed. A fusion of research and clinical practice may ultimately affirm social justice as a desirable moral consequence of managed mental health care in California.

INTRODUCTION

Multicultural populations in the United States have a history of receiving discriminatory and biased mental health services. At present, approximately 40% of mental health consumers represent this population with disproportionately more persons receiving services in the public sector. Except in culture-specific agencies, underutilization of services continued primarily because cultural differences have been minimized, ignored, and considered irrelevant. Nevertheless, during the last decade there has been an increasing awareness in all concerned professions (e.g., psychiatry, psychology, social work, counseling, nursing, and rehabilitation) that cultural issues and ethnic/racial identifications are central to the entire process of access, diagnosis, and interventions for mental health problems experienced by multicultural populations. Each of these professions now has an advocacy role in placing culture at the heart of research, services, and service delivery. Recent issues of the American Psychologist, for example, have addressed cultural incompetence and malpractice in both mental health research and clinical practices (e.g., Hall, 1997; Rogler, 1999; Strickland, 2000; S. Sue, 1999).

The plight of all mental health consumers in California is characterized by an immense gap between the magnitude of human need and available funding for services (Little Hoover Commission, 2000). It is estimated that 21% of this population, or 5,225,368 persons, have a diagnosable mental disorder each year (Department of Finance, 2000). Approximately 1.7 million of the diagnosable population currently receive no help whatsoever. Serious Mental Illness (SMI) and Severe and Persistent Mental Illness (SPMI) impacts 5.4% and 2.6%, or 1,343,646 and 646,950 persons, respectively. For those 467, 000 consumers who received treatment in the public sector during one year (Legislative Analyst's Office, 2000), the direct state and local costs exceeded 5 billion dollars annually (SGR Health Alliance, 2000). These data indicate gross under-funding of the California mental health system. As a consequence, public facilities experience excessively large caseloads and a mentality of only serving the SNI with minimal or no services to others. In addition, until recently there has been a perceived justification for inattention to cultural competence and quality care.

However, at present the political power of a non-White majority population in California (Dear, Schockman & Hise, 1996) provides the impetus for culturally competent mental health services. Gibbs (1999) described the California crucible of ethnic and racial tensions as an opportunity for national leadership toward an egalitarian multicultural society with an immediate impact on mental health systems. Mock (1999) affirmed that a partial realization of social justice is commensurate with strivings for cultural competence in California mental health systems. Managed care mental health systems, however, use cost-output calculations for therapeutic practices that have moral consequences bearing some responsibility for adverse alterations in our conventional societal understandings "about the proper ways of being human" (Cushman & Gilford, 2000, p. 985). These authors also acknowledge that managed care exists within a larger societal context "in how people live, respond to the power relations of their world, distribute resources, and conceive of and pursue the good" (p. 994). Thus, the California crucible offers a unique opportunity to demonstrate the efficacy of managed mental health care practices that are neither inherently racist nor dehumanizing in impact and outcomes for multicultural populations.

As one response to these legitimate concerns, this paper describes a profound restructuring of mental health services for multicultural populations in California, exemplified by a quest in the Tri-City Mental Health Center for cultural competence in its community and conformity with state initiatives. The intent of this description is to provide a model for culturally competent mental health care using retrospective and prospective accompanying data. Nonetheless, it is recognized that each agency represents a self-contained microcosm interfacing with a unique community client population with a mandate to provide an effective system of managed mental health care. While there are limited aspirations for interagency generality or transposability of specific agency practices, it is now feasible to employ a model providing a general structure of areas in which services can be ameliorated, systematically evaluated, and subsequently altered.

A description of these service areas within the format of the Multicultural Assessment-Intervention Process Model (MAIP) (Dana, 1997, 2000a) can serve as an impetus toward a system of care that affects the overall status of mental health within a community. MAIP has been presented in flow chart format (e.g., Dana, 1998a, b) that follows the client as consumer throughout the process of access, diagnosis, and intervention. There are steps, or points in this process, where relevant questions are asked to elicit information that facilitates subsequent steps leading to more reliable diagnostic statements and interventions that are more likely to have beneficial outcomes. Following this model, the need for client-provider match is examined initially "with regard to race, ethnicity, language, service delivery style, service setting décor, and client perception of the provider's personality and competence" (Ponterotto, Gretchen & Chauhan, 2001, p. 81). Second, acculturation assessment necessitates client self-disclosure of information relevant to an understanding of cultural identity ultimately required for a cultural formulation that can permit a more accurate and reliable clinical diagnosis. Third, this self-disclosure also fosters specification of a client's problem that leads to a fourth step, the possible selection of additional, appropriate diagnostic assessment instruments. Fifth, information from all previous steps encourages selection of an intervention with sufficient cultural content to ensure credibility and compliance by consumers in accord with personal preferences and acculturation status.

Remedies for Bias in Mental Health Services

Historically, the sources of bias have been blatant, insidious, and pervasive in their effects upon utilization of mental health services by multicultural populations (see, Dana, 1998c, 2000b, 2001a, b). Potential remedies for bias, identified in Table 1, are now available for clinical service providers, the service delivery process, psychological tests, interventions, and psychiatric diagnoses. However, Table 1 does not include the major alterations in a system of care required to reduce all the sources of bias addressed in this paper. Similarly, the awareness of cultural incompetence by service providers and the use of cultural competence measures to evaluate the effects of training are also omitted from Table 1.

A comprehensive model of 31 multicultural competencies described three counselor/service provider characteristics (i.e., awareness of own cultural values/biases and client world view as well as knowledge of credible/acceptable interventions) and beliefs, knowledge, and skills related to each of these characteristics (see, Sue, Arredondo, & McDavis, 1992). Four self-report instruments emerged from this model the Cross-Cultural Counseling Inventory-Revised (CCCI-R; La Fromboise, Coleman, & Hernandez, 1991), the Multicultural Awareness-Knowledge-and-Skills Survey (MAKSS; D'Andrea, Daniels, & Heck, 1991), the Multicultural Counseling Awareness Scale (MCAS; Ponterotto, Sanchez, & Magids, 1991), and the Multicultural Counseling Inventory (MCI; Sodowsky, Taffe, Gutkin, & Wise, 1994). Reviews of these instruments are available (Ponterotto & Alexander, 1996; Ponterotto, Rieger, Barnett & Sparks, 1994). A fifth instrument-the Multicultural Counseling Competence and Training Survey (MCCTS) -was also developed from the comprehensive model and other resources for use in a national survey of counselors (Holcomb-McCoy & Myers, 1999). These multicultural counseling instruments provide one response to national survey of predominantly White (90%) professional psychologists and counselors (Allison, Crawford, Echemendia, Robinson, & Kemp, 1994). In this survey, self-perceived competence with African Americans, Asian Americans, Hispanic Americans, and American Indians/Alaska Natives was 38%, 16%, 26%, and 8%, respectively. A second study, limited to professional counselors, suggested that the non-White counselors, one-third of the sample, perceived themselves as multiculturally competent, except in knowledge and racial identity dimensions in spite of reporting inadequate training (Holcomb-McCoy & Myers, 1999). Ethnic minority counselor identity enhanced these self-perceptions of competence. The usefulness of some of these survey instruments has been examined for continuing education workshops and other forms of limited training experiences. However, the instruments have not been applied in mental health work settings nor has there been research attention to the development of in-service training on the basis of the contents of these inventories. All of these instruments were subsequently used in the Tri-City research program.

Table 1. Bias Sources and Suggested Remedies

Locus	Source	Remedy
Clinician	Ethnocentrism	Examine own identity
	Racism	Immersion in another culture
	Prejudice	Training
	Stereotyping	Supervision
Service Delivery	Anglo style social etiquette: Impersonal, formal, task-oriented	Culture-specific styles
Tests/Techniques	Anglo emics or pseudo-etics used as etics.	Cross-cultural equivalence in language (translation), constructs, and format.
Interventions	Anglo pseudo-etic services.	Match interventions with client cultural orientation status: culture-general (Anglo), combined culture-general & culture-specific, culture-specific and identity specific.
DSM-IV	Anglo emic symptoms, syndromes, and disorders used as genuine etics.	Culture-Bound Disorders Cultural formulations

Adapted from Dana, R. H. (1998c)

STATE OF CALIFORNIA MENTAL HEALTH AGENDA

Standards for cultural competence were developed initially by the Western Interstate Commission for Higher Education (WICHE) Mental Health Program (WICHE, 1997). Implementation of these standards began on July 1, 1998 with a plan for culturally competent specialty mental health services developed by the California Cultural Competence Task Force (State of California, Department of Mental Health, 1997). The plan requirements include two general assessments, first of the population served, and second of the organization and its staff. Specific standards were also included for Access (i.e., language accessibility, linguistically appropriate written information, and responsiveness of specialty mental health services), Quality of Care (i.e., consumer and family role in service development, competent evaluation, diagnosis, treatment and referral services), and Quality Management (i.e., utilization, outcome of services, continuous quality improvement plan).

TRI-CITY MENTAL HEALTH CENTER (TCMHC)

TCMHC was established in 1960 as a Joint Powers Authority by the cities of Claremont, La Verne, and Pomona, and was included under the Community Mental Health Act (a.k.a. Short-Doyle Act) to provide outpatient mental health services as well as educational and informational services for a catchment area also including neighboring areas. These services include 24-hour emergency services, crisis stabilization, intensive day treatment, intensive case management, outpatient, dual diagnosis for adults and adolescents, alcohol and drug treatment, psychiatric medication, telepsychiatry, psychosocial rehabilitation, and vocational services for culturally, ethnically, and linguistically diverse adults who are 45% Latino, 25% Black, 26% White, 3% Asian, and 1% American Indian/Alaska Native (1990 census). Additional programs include extensive school-based services, therapeutic behavioral services, homeless outreach, and housing. These services are provided by staff who are 41% Latino (includes ¾ bilingual), 33% White, 17% Black, 8% Asian, and 1% American Indian/Alaska Native.

For 15 years, an ethnic-specific program, Casa de Esperanza, provided services to the Latino population and for three years a second ethnic-specific program provided services to Asians. These programs were consolidated in 1998 to provide more comprehensive and integrated care within a Children and Family Service Program. The Agency Cultural Competence Checklist (ACCL) (Dana, Behn & Gonwa, 1992) was used to examine TCMHC cultural competence during a two-day visit in May 1998 during which staff members were interviewed, problems were described, and suggestions were made for compliance with California Department of Mental Health standards. ACCL recommendations were also made for a research process to provide continuous aegis and examination of initiatives for increasing cultural competency. This checklist is the only currently available instrument for this purpose and has been applied in a variety of other agency settings (e.g., Dana & Matheson, 1992; Dana, 1998d).

Extrapolating from the requirements adopted by the State of California, Table 2 describes the present status of specific areas, compliance requirements for these areas, and TCMHC progress toward cultural competence standards. TCMHC has developed a cultural competency implementation plan for evaluation of agency functions including population assessment, staff recruitment and retention practices, outreach, policy and procedure reviews, and accountability.

Table 2. Status of Tri-City Mental Health Center Compliance with California Standards

Focus of Development	Recommendation for Compliance	Compliance Status
A. Population Assessment	Client demographic composition: socioeconomic, ethnic, age gender linguistic. Utilization: inpatient, outpatient, day treatment, other. Hospital; non-hospital.	Monthly and quarterly Management Information System reports of the population served.
B. Agency Assessment Policy Administration Human Resources Quality of Care	Practices acknowledging cultural and linguistic needs.	Access to Linguistic Appropriate Services Policy. Outreach Tracking/Inquiry Log. Bilingual Certification Policy. Deaf/Hearing-Impaired Services Policy. Translation Protocol. Use of AT&T Interpretation Service Protocol.
	Staff representation of client population.	Recruitment/Retention Model.
	Match staff with clients for language and ethnicity.	Ethnic and linguistic matching protocol to be developed.
	Evaluate acculturation status of clients.	Identification and implementation of acculturation measurements in process.
	Develop staff cultural competence assessment instrument.	Brief Multicultural Competency Scale in process of development.
	Accommodate clients' preferences for providers.	Disposition Screening.
	Include culture-specific treatment options.	Disposition Screening.
	Include community providers and programs.	Disposition Screening. List of services and community resources. Community Referral Protocol.
C. Accountability Data	Evaluation of Staff cultural competence evaluation.	Planned as part of core of competencies for staff performance evaluation.
	Cultural competency staff training.	Training curriculum for cultural competency in planning stage.
	Client evaluation of services and staff.	See Figure 1, Outcome Measures Client Grievance Procedure.
	Quality Assurance using outcomes measures.	See Figure 1, Outcome Measures.
	Staff satisfaction (Grievances/complaints).	Staff Grievance Procedure.
	Symptom-based, computerized assessment for matching clients with treatment options and demonstrating efficacy of interventions.	In process.
	Evaluation of acculturation status for matching clients with treatment options.	In process.

Focus of Development	Recommendation for Compliance	Compliance Status
	Cultural Formulations for DSM-IV diagnosis.	Not developed.
	Demonstrated effectiveness of treatment options for different client groups.	Planned.

RESEARCH PROGRAM

The TCMHC research program began proactively in response to the integration of Casa de Esperanza, the ACCL program evaluation, and cooperation with the University of La Verne. This program benefits from the use of the Human Service Information System (HSIS, Echo Information Group) software to capture data. Figure 1 indicates the program components conforming to the MAIP model, the process of agency adaptation to services and service delivery, and relevant outcomes to date. The first three studies in the research program were predicated on the extensive literature matching clients with providers similar in ethnicity or race (Gamst, Dana, Der Karabetian & Kramer, 2000; Gamst, Dana, Der-Karabetian & Kramer, 2001; Gamst, Dana, Kramer & Der-Karabetian, in press). This examination of the cultural/ethnic responsiveness hypothesis (Sue, Fujino, Hu, Takeuchi & Zane, 1991) was accomplished by archival studies using large samples of adults and children from the major populations served by TCMHC. A design that adjusted for as many as 12 other variables was used (i.e., age, gender, marital status, Medi-Cal, education, citizenship, primary language, trauma, referral source, language match, gender match, and diagnosis). The findings indicated that the effects of matching in this agency setting varied for different ethnic groups and with particular diagnoses. The matching effect was stronger for adults than for children. The use of Global Assessment of Function (GAF), an index of psychosocial adjustment in these studies, although consistent with earlier studies, can now be supplemented by the addition of more reliable outcome measures. Overall these initial studies not only described the complexity of relationships between ethnicity and responses to mental health services, but also indicated the need for a systematic research process.

This systematic research process will provide a program that encompasses intake, client acculturation status, client-clinician ethnicity-language matching, clinician cultural competence evaluation as well as in-service training of clinicians, a variety of relevant pre-post measures of intervention outcomes. Cultural components contained in interventions and services are also scheduled for eventual evaluation. Figure 1 juxtaposes the program components listed above with the service delivery process containing these components and the desired outcome status in conformity with the state cultural competence plan and derivative standards. It should be noted that some TCMHC objectives, listed in Table 2, are continuing to be developed at the present time. Furthermore, all child and youth outcome measures listed in Figure 1 will be supplanted within one year by a briefer set of measures designed for greater practical utility rather than primarily for research purposes (Ogles, Melendez, Davis, & Lunnen, 1999).

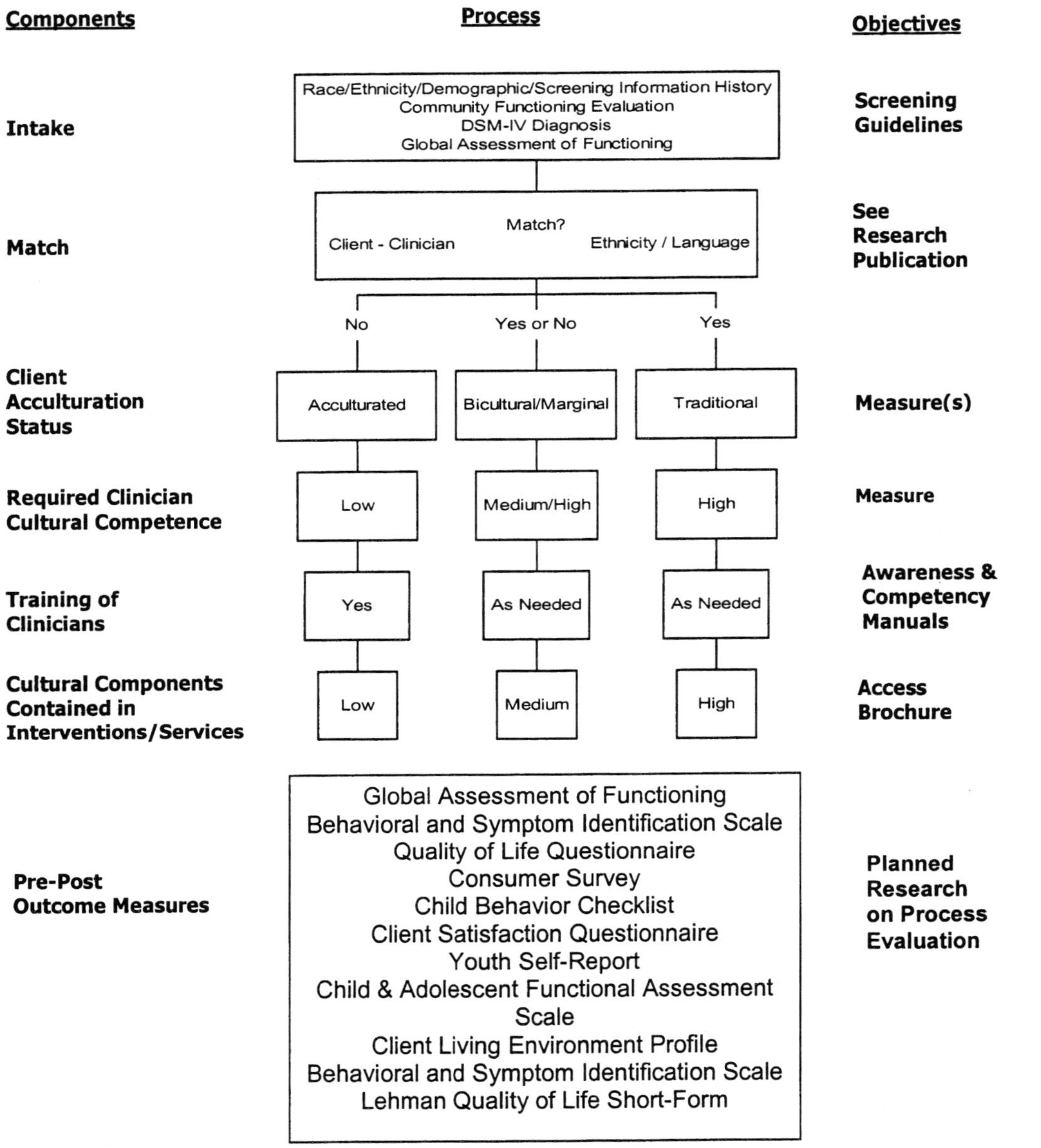

Figure 1. Tri-City Research Program

DISCUSSION

Within the public sector in California, culturally competent, quality managed mental health care is now mandatory. This is a remarkable achievement considering the gross under-funding for mental health care in the public sector. The State Department of Mental Health in California has demonstrated not merely advocacy for equivalent services to all ethnic/racial groups, but has developed a statewide plan for implementation of standards. This paper described service and research activities in one community mental health center designed to increase cultural competency. This discussion includes (a) benefits of using a process model to provide guidelines for research and practice within a system of mental health care. (b) levels of training and desirable expectations for clinical and cultural competence among service providers. (c) managed care moral obligations to facilitate increased harmony and cohesion among diverse racial/ethnic groups within an egalitarian multicultural society.

Guidelines for Systems of Multicultural Mental Health Care

A system of quality care requires a model or framework for multicultural clinical practice to provide guidelines for multiple entry points in the service delivery process where services can be examined, altered, and improved, if necessary. Five models are now available to increase the availability of quality care, including the MAIP, also referred to as the Six-Step Cultural Assessment Model by Ponterotto, Gretchen, & Chauhan, 2001. Ponterotto et al. emphasized that MAIP not only charges providers with significant and novel ethical responsibilities but also "encourages providers to recognize and understand the power differential existing between providers and their clients" on the basis of race, ethnicity, social class, education, etc. (p. 88). This power differential can only be examined by provider self-scrutiny because we lack the social mechanisms for more public monitoring. Ponterotto et al. reaffirm the premise (Dana, 1998, Chapter 4) that "it is up to the provider to replace the lost social control of his or her behavior with self control and personal ethics" (p. 89). The MAIP model forces practitioners to assume that cultural influence is present and important at each step in the service delivery process. These cultural influences can be denied only on the basis of specific information and/or empirical demonstration. This is a clinical practice analogy to what Malgady (1996, 2000) recommended for research examinations of cultural issues by reversing the Null Hypothesis.

Many persons of color in the United States receiving public sector services have an external locus of power and responsibility rather than the internal loci that describes most Whites in the United States (D. W. Sue, 1978a,b; Macaranas-Sittler, 1986). Internal control has been considered historically by clinicians as more desirable than external control. Nonetheless, this constitutes a culture-specific White perspective biasing problem conceptualization and preventing use of interventions that honor cultural beliefs or recognize realities and restrictions in everyday life (Marks, 1998). In addition, a pervasive lack of personal power among mental health system clients remains omnipresent as a result of continuing oppression. The powerlessness experienced by clients and denied, or misunderstood, by their providers may combine with the White privilege of these providers to create a lack of awareness concerning the daily and historic impact of racism on these clients (see, Clark, Anderson, Clark & Williams, 1999; Dana, 2002; Robinson & Ginter, 1999).

An overarching moral objective of the California version of managed mental health care (Cushman & Gilford, 2000) lies precisely in attempts to reaffirm humanity by making quality care available for the diverse populations within the state. Practicing of quality care can reduce the sense of frustration and experiences of discrimination that have been responsible for the failure of trust that historically compromised utilization of mental health services. If this vision of quality care were successfully implemented in public mental health agencies, many current shortcomings of managed mental health care for multicultural populations in the United States would be ameliorated (see, Dana, 1998e; Dana, Conner, & Allen, 1996).

In-Service Provider Training, Roles, Responsibilities, and Competencies

Managed mental health services are provided by a variety of providers/clinicians/ therapists who represent different levels of training and a wide variety of therapeutic competencies for patients with different diagnoses and severity of problems. Cost-containment and manpower shortages have necessitated policies maximizing the employment of providers with reduced levels of education and training (Humphreys, 1996). The issue of what constitutes relevant training requirements for specific interventions with consumers with particular diagnoses remains largely undetermined. In fact, there is a history of underutilization of Ph. D. or Psy.D. clinicians as therapists for consumers in the public sector, although these persons with these qualifications are now more likely to be found in supervisory roles. This has occurred because the California mental health system is predicated on a rehabilitation rather than a medical model, resulting in the increased use of community based teams of multidisciplinary professionals. The employment of nonprofessionals, paraprofesionals, and masters' degree professionals has always been mandatory for reasons other than cost-containment. For example, in spite of guild beliefs, there is no satisfactory research evidence that doctoral level training automatically conveys clinical competence. Only six of over 300 studies on selection, training, and therapeutic functioning of paraprofessionals described negative results in a context without evidence of harm or inferior services (Durlak, 1973). We do not possess an unequivocal, consensual lexicon of clinical skills as well as the cultural competencies required for public sector services that aspire to quality mental health care. In fact, there is now some evidence that cultural competence actually enhances clinical competence (i.e., Coleman, 1999), a finding that lends further credence to the use of the MAIP model to encourage a blurring of any distinction between clinical competencies and multicultural competencies.

In spite of these deficiencies in knowledge, it is now feasible using the MAIP research model to examine provider qualifications, efficacy, and cultural competence across interventions, diagnoses, and outcomes within a context of multicultural consumers and culturally relevant variables. It has been recommended that doctoral level psychologists employ cognitive reappraisal for adaptive coping with the changes in who does what to whom in managed mental health care settings (Humphreys, 1996). A restructuring of training within each of the mental health professions is now required to specify and document clinical competencies, although such a long-term process remains secondary to a careful examination of the effectiveness of the currently available mental health workforce.

Morality and Managed Care

As Cushman and Gilford (2000) have emphasized, it is important to be circumspect in ascribing blame to managed care for moral consequences that impact upon humanity and humanization during this new millennium in the United States. Nonetheless, a demonstration of beneficial outcomes for systematically applied relevant interventions with multicultural client populations should impact positively on racial tensions and provide an antidote to the history of bias and discrimination in mental health services. Increased acceptance among persons of color that their mental health needs are being more adequately understood and responded to can augment societal cohesion. In this regard, the ultimate objective is to ensure that racial/ethnic populations author the constructions of reality, self, health, illness and recovery that recognize and incorporate their worldviews and life circumstances. A multicultural society ultimately has to include by design multiple visions of legitimate humanity, or "the proper ways of being human" (Cushman & Gilford, 2000, p. 985) in order to survive and prosper. Managed mental health can be responsive to this societal desideratum by predicating services upon research that focuses upon an infusion and integration of cultural competencies at all levels and for all constituent groups within a system of care.

REFERENCES

Allison, K. W., Crawford, I., Echemendia, R., Robinson, L., & Knepp, D. (1994). Human diversity and professional competence: Training in clinical and counseling psychology revisited. *American Psychologist, 49,* 792-796.

Clark, R., Anderson, N. B., Clark, V. R., & Williams, D. R. (1999). Racism as a stressor for African Americans. *American Psychologist, 54,* 805-816.

Coleman, H. L. K. (1998). General and multicultural counseling competency: Apples and oranges? *Journal of Multicultural Counseling and Development, 26,* 147-156.

Cushman, P. & Gifford, P. (2000). Will managed care change our way of being? *American Psychologist, 55,* 985-996.

Dana, R. H. (1997). Multicultural assessment and cultural identity: An assessment-intervention model. *World Psychology, 3 (1/2),* 121-142.

Dana, R. H. (1998a). *Understanding cultural identity in intervention and assessment.* Thousand Oaks, CA: Sage.

Dana, R. H. (1998b) Multicultural assessment in the United States: Current realities, problems, and prospects. *European Journal of Personality Assessment, 14,* 62-70.

Dana, R. H. (1998c). Projective assessment of Latinos in the United States: Current realities, problems, and prospects. *Cultural Diversity and Mental Health, 4(3),* 165-184.

Dana, R. H. (1998d). Cultural competence in three human service agencies. *Psychological Reports, 83,* 107-112.

Dana, R. H. (1998e). Problems with managed mental health care in multicultural populations. *Psychological Reports, 83,* 107-112.

Dana, R. H. (2000a). An assessment-intervention model for research and practice with multicultural populations. In R. H. Dana (Ed.), *Handbook of cross-cultural and multicultural personality assessment* (pp. 5-16). Mahwah, NJ: Erlbaum.

Dana, R. H. (2000b). Multicultural assessment of child and adolescent personality and psychopathology. In A. L. Comunian & U. Gielen (Eds.), *International perspectives on human development* (pp. 233-258). Berlin: Pabst Science Publishers.

Dana, R. H. (2001a). Multicultural issues in assessment. In B. Bolton (Ed.), *Handbook of measurement and evaluation in rehabilitation* (3rd ed) (pp. 449-469). Gaithersburg, MD: Aspen.

Dana, R. H. (2001b). Clinical diagnosis in multicultural populations in the United States. In L. A. Suzuki, J. G. Ponterotto, & P. J. Meller (Eds.), *Handbook of multicultural assessment: Clinical, psychological, and educational applications* (2nd ed) (pp. 101-131). San Francisco: Jossey-Bass.

Dana, R. H. (2002). Mental health services for African Americans: A cultural/racial perspective. *Cultural Diversity and Ethnic Minority Psychology, 8,* 3-18.

Dana, R. H., & Matheson, L. (1992). An application of the Agency Cultural Competence checklist to a program serving small and diverse ethnic communities. *Psychosocial Rehabilitation Journal, 15(4),* 101-105.

Dana, R. H. , Behn, J. D., & Gonwa, T. (1992). A checklist for examination of cultural competence in social service agencies. *Research in Social Work Practice, 2,* 220-233.

Dana, R. H., Conner, M. G., & Allen, J. (1996). Cost containment and quality in managed mental health care: Policy, education, research, adequacy. *Psychological Reports, 79,* 1395-1422.

Department of Finance (2000). Population projections. U. S. Department of Health and Human Services, 1999. *Mental Health: A report of the U.S. Surgeon General,* 45-49.

Durlak, J. (1973). Myths concerning the nonprofessional therapist. *Professional Psychology, 4,* 300-304.

Gamst, G., Dana, R. H., Kramer, T., & Der-Karabetian, A. (in press). Ethnic match and treatment outcomes for child and adolescent mental health center clients. *Journal of Counseling & Development.*.

Gamst, G., Dana, R. H., Der-Karabetian, A., & Kramer, T. (2001). Asian American mental health clients: Effects of ethnic match and age on global assessment and visitation. *Journal of Mental Health Counseling, 23,* 57-71.

Gamst, G., Dana, R. H., Der-Karabetian, A., & Kramer, T. (2000). Ethnic match and client ethnicity effects on global assessment and visitation. *Journal of Community Psychology, 28,* 547-564.

Gibbs, J. T. (1999). The California crucible: Toward a new paradigm of race and ethnic relations. *Journal of Multicultural Social Work, 7(1/2),* 1-18.

Hall, C. C. I. (1997). Cultural malpractice: The growing obsolescence of psychology with the changing U. S. population. *American Psychologist, 52,* 642-651.

Humphreys, K. (1996). Clinical psychologists as psychotherapist: History, future, and alternatives. *American Psychologist, 51,* 190-197.

Legislative Analyst's Office (2000, April 14). *California mental health system: Selected data.* Presented to the Joint Commission on Mental Health Reform. Sacramento, CA: Author.

Little Hoover Commission (2000, November). *Geing there: Making a commitment to mental health.* Sacramento, CA: Author.

Malgady, R. G. (1996). The question of cultural bias in assessment and diagnosis of ethnic minority clients: Let's reject the Null Hypothesis. *Professional Psychology: Research and Practice, 27,* 73-77.

Malgady, R. G. (2000). Myths about the Null Hypothesis and the path to reform. In R. H. Dana (Ed.), *Handbook of cross-cultural and multicultural Personality assessment* (pp. 49-62). Mahwah, NJ: Erlbaum.

Macaranas-Sittler, N. (1986, April). *Psychological frames of reference: Cross-cultural dimensions.* Poster presented at the Southwestern Psychological Association meeting, Fr. Worth, TX.

Marks, L. I. (1998). Deconstructing locus of control: Implications for practitioners. *Journal of Counseling and Development, 76,* 251-260.

Mock, M. R. (1999). Cultural competency: Acts of justice in community mental health. *The Community Psychologist, 32(1),* 38-40.

Ogles, B. M., Melendez, G., Davis, D. C., & Lunnen, K. M. (1999, October). *The Ohio Youth Problems, Functioning, and Satisfaction Scales (Short-Form).* Athens, Ohio: Ohio University.

Ponterotto, J. G., & Alexander, C. M. (1996). Assessing the multicultural competence of counselors and clinicians. In L. A. Suzuki, P. J. Meller & J. G. Ponterotto (Eds.), *Handbook of multicultural assessment: Clinical, psychological, and educational implications* (pp. 651-672). San Francisco: Jossey-Bass.

Ponterotto, J. G., Gretchen, D., & Chanhan, R. V. (2001). Cultural identity and multicultural assessment: Quantitative and qualitative tools for the clinicians. In L. A. Suzuki, J. G. Ponterotto, & P. J. Meller (Eds.), *Handbook of multicultural assessment: Clinical, psychological, and educational applications* (2nd ed) (pp. 67-99).

Ponterotto, J. G., Rieger, B. P., Barrett,. A., Sparks, R. (1994). Assessing multicultural counseling competence: A review of instrumentation. *Journal of Counseling and Development, 72,* 316-322.

Robinson, T. L., & Ginter, E. J. (Eds.). Special issue: Racism healing its effects. *Journal of Counseling and Development, 77,* 1-108.

Rogler, L. H. (1999). Methodological sources of cultural insensitivity in mental health research. *American Psychologist, 54,* 424-433.

SRG Health Alliance (2000). *The state of the state of behavioral health in California: Alcohol, drug, and mental health services and systems.*

State of California, Department of Mental Health (1997, October 6). *Cultural Competence Plan Requirements: DMH Information Notice No. 97-14.*

Strickland, B. R. (2000). Misassumptions, misadventures, and the misuse of psychology. *American Psychologist, 55,* 331-338.

Sue, D. W. (1978a). Eliminating cultural oppression in counseling. *Journal of Counseling Psychology, 25,* 419-428.

Sue, D. W. (1978b). World views and counseling. *Personnel and Guidance Journal, 56,* 458-462.

Sue, D. W., Arredondo, P., & McDavis, R. J. (1992). Multicultural counseling competencies and standards: A call to the profession. *Journal of Counseling and Development, 70,* 477-486.

Sue, S. (1999). Science, ethnicity, and bias: Where have we gone wrong? *American Psychologist, 54,* 1070-1077.

Sue, S., Fujino, D. C., Hu, L-T., Takeuchi, D. T., & Zane, N. W. S. (1991). Community mental health services for ethnic minority groups: A test of the cultural responsiveness hypothesis. *Journal of Consulting and Clinical Psychology, 59,* 533-540.

WICHE (1997). *Cultural competence standards in managed mental health care for four underserved/underrepresented racial/ethnic groups.* Final Report from Working Groups on Cultural Competence in Managed Mental Health Care. Boulder, CO: Author.

Chapter 2

HEALTH BEHAVIOR AND PSYCHOSOCIAL HEALTH AS A HEALTH POLICY ISSUE FOR YOUTH AND ADOLESCENCE

Bettina F. Piko*

Szeged University
Department of Psychiatry
Division of Behavioral Sciences
Szeged, Hungary

Over the past several decades there has been considerable the attention paid to youth and adolescence (Fuchs and Reklis, 1992; Sells and Blum, 1996; Resnick et al., 1997). There is recognition that this is a developmental period characterized by many changes (Mechanic, 1991; Eccles et al., 1993; Jessor et al., 1993), moreover, how adolescents answer these health challenges may also have major implication for later adult morbidity and mortality (Sells and Blum, 1996). Though most adolescents and young adults are free of serious physical illness, they may experience and report considerable psychosomatic and psychological distress symptoms in which psychosocial factors may play an important role (Piko, Barabás and Boda, 1997). Psychosocial factors, due to the adjustment processes during adolescence, are extremely important in understanding health and illness in this stage of the life course.

Health is a complex concept including both biological and psychosocial dimensions. Research has found that in the relative absence of serious health problems, adolescents construct self-assessment of health and health-related quality of life based on other indices, e.g., psychosomatic symptoms, health risk behaviors and psychological well-being (Krause and Jay, 1994; Mechanic and Hansell, 1989; Piko, 2000a). Moreover, this is the time for developing a heightened introspectiveness, i.e., self-awareness of bodily experiences that influences their symptom monitoring and reporting behavior as a part of the biological and

* **Acknowledgement:** The author thanks Kevin M. Fitzpatrick (The University of Alabama at Birmingham, USA) for his useful comments on an earlier draft of the paper.

psychosocial changes they undergo (Hansell, Mechanic and Brondolo, 1986). Thus, psychosomatic symptoms and psychological well-being, beyond acute and chronic illness episodes, seem to be appropriate health indicators among youth.

While we know a great deal about the biological and psychosocial dimensions of health, e.g. the connections between health status and health risk behaviors in adulthood, we know much less about these associations among youth. Such measures, however, would be useful for health policy impications. Traditionally, a risk-focused approach was applied to identify specific risk factors for psychosocial health problems and health risk behaviors (Jessor, 1993). Recently, health policy has focused specifically on protection since prevention programs require an identification of protective factors to be addressed (Hawkins, Catalano and Miller, 1992; Resnick et al., 1997; Fitzpatrick and LaGory, 2000). Among protective factors, social support and physical activity seem to be crucial in youth and adolescence.

Physical activity is a significant preventive health behavior. Regular physical activity and physical fitness have been shown to reduce the incidence of a number of diseases, e.g., coronary heart disease, diabetes mellitus, osteoporosis or hypertension (Fentem, 1994). It has also been suggested that vigorous physical activity has positive effects on mental health, e.g., reducing both symptoms of depression and anxiety (Byrne and Byrne, 1993), increasing self-confidence and self-efficacy (Rimal, 2001). Based on a comparison of health-related data among a sporting and non-sporting population it has been argued that sports participants possessed better self-perceived health than members of the general population (Lamb et al., 1991). This relationship was also found among adolescents (Thorlindsson, Vilhjalmsson and Valgeirsson, 1990; Piko, 2000a). Adolescents' physical activity, in particular community sports, were found to be associated with social support from others (Sallis, Prochaska and Taylor, 2000). Research results, however, are somewhat controversial in terms of the relationships between phsyical activity and other health-related behaviors. For example, the frequency of substance use is often found to be positively associated with sports activity (Rooney, 1984; Thorlindsson, Vilhjalmsson and Valgeirsson, 1990; Piko, Barabás and Markos, 1996). This phenomenon can in part be explained by the fact that since the types of behavior conducive to good health arise from diverse motives and influences, they may be unrelated or even in conflict (Mechanic, 1991). Thus some sports activities as well as smoking, drinking alcohol or experimenting with illicit drugs are not only social events with peers but sometimes act as forms of risk-taking as well. Moreover, since there is a tendency with older youth to engage in less sport, the benefit from any preventive health effect of physical activity is lowered (Lee, Paffenbarger, Hsieh, 1992; Riddoch and Boreham, 1995; Leslie et al., 1999).

Similar to physical activity, considerable research has examined the beneficial effects of social support on health and well-being (Rosengren et al., 1993; Dean et al., 1994; van Oostrom et al., 1995). Social support has both a direct positive effect on health status and may serve as a 'buffer' or mediator of the effects of stress on mental and physical health (House, Landis and Umberson, 1988; Schwarzer and Leppin, 1991). It is suggested, however, that perceived, rather than received support has primary significance for health outcomes (Burleson, Albrecht and Sarason, 1994; Piko, 2000b). Measures of perceived social support usually assess availability of help and satisfaction with help provided (Cohen, Underwood and Gottlieb, 2000). However, the relationship between social support and adolescents' psychosocial health and health risk behavior is also controversial. Adolescence is an age during which social relationships undergo dramatic changes (Newcomb and Bagwell, 1995;

Bogenschneider et al., 1998; Schneider, Atkinson and Tardif, 2001). Research findings show that high engagement in peer-oriented activity and thus friend-related social support measures are often associated with an increase in health risk behaviors (Aseltine, 1995; Ary et al. 1999; Piko, 2000b; Simons-Morton et al., 2001). Moreover, certain types of social support, e.g., task-oriented guidance show a positive (non-supportive) relationship with psychosocial health among adolescent boys suggesting that social ties may generate stressful demands as well (Piko, 1998).

As literature suggests, some protective factors may have harmful effects as well, the main goal of the present paper is to categorize youths and adolescents using cluster analysis based on the interrelationships among psychosocial health variables and protective factors. A series of cluster analyses was conducted in order to explore group characteristics. Quick cluster (K means) analysis was performed. Since this analysis calls for the number of clusters to be specified a priori, a series of hierarchical cluster analyses was performed in each sample as guidance in selecting the appropriate number of clusters for the K-means analysis (Norusis, 1993). For each of the hierarchical analyses, the appropriate number of clusters was selected through examination of the squared Euclidean distance coefficients. For each case, either a four, five or six cluster solution was indicated. The final cluster solutions provide the possibility of describing different groups of youths and adolescents based on the variations of psychosocial health and protective factors.

STUDY 1

The first study focused on the patterns of psychosocial health and health risk behaviors among university students. Data were collected in conjunction with a research project of health risk behavior of the student population in Szeged, Hungary. In this sample, physical activity behavior was assessed as a measure of protection since after high school years (where physical education is compulsory) engaging in any sports activity is based on the students' choice (Piko, Barabás and Markos, 1996). Therefore, physical activity can be viewed as a critical protective factor among a university student population (Leslie et al., 1999).

Method

Subjects

The potential number of students participating in our sample was 980. The age range of the respondents was 18-31 years of age (mean = 21.0 years, S.D. = 2.3 years). Students were randomly selected and asked to participate. Of 980 questionnaires sent out, 691 were returned after 1-3 weeks giving a response rate of 70.5%: 272 (39.4%) men and 419 (60.6%) women.

Procedure

A self-administered questionnaire was used as a method of data collection. The following *health-related variables* were measured: frequency of common psychosomatic symptoms, psychological well-being, physical activity behavior, medical contacts per year related to the previous year (acute and chronic illness episodes) and health risk behaviors during the past 12 months.

Leisure-Time Physical Activity Indices

A recall questionnaire method was used to collect detailed information on physical activity behavior. The primary instrument for measuring activity was an adopted and modified form of the Minnesota Leisure Time Physical Activity Questionnaire (Taylor et al., 1978; Folsom et al., 1985). It applies a standardized interview to elicit the type, frequency and duration of physical activities performed during the previous 12 months. Given the high educational level of our subjects, a self-complete format was used. Similar to the instructions of the original questionnaire, the energy expended in a specific activity is estimated as the product of the intensity code (I) and duration of exercise in minutes per year (D). Assigning intensity codes for the various activities, we used the Activity Metabolic Indices (AMI) derived from kcal/day in energy expenditure. Four intensity activity categories were used: heavy AMI (6.0 kcal/min), moderate AMI (4.4-5.5 kcal/min), light AMI (2.0-4.0 kcal/min) and total AMI. Taylor *et al.* (1978) validated the method by comparing the activity scores with a treadmill test of work performance in 175 adult men. A clear and statistically significant relationship was observed. Though the method has limitations, i.e. it requires detailed data on frequency and duration over the full year, yet it has been suggested that the questionnaire is suitable for characterizing the leisure-time physical activity in large, young or middle-aged groups such as a student population (Montoye and Taylor, 1984).

Psychosocial Health: Psychological Well-Being and Psychosomatic Symptoms

The *psychological well-being* rating scale was an internal level variable that was coded from high levels of distress to high levels of well-being. The aim of the measure was to collect information on the general well-being of the students during the past 12 months. The 6-item scale was adopted and modified from the Langner index by Ross and Hayes (1988). Respondents were asked items such as: "During the past 12 months, how often have you felt irritable, had troubles?"...etc. Responses were coded as nearly always (4), often (3), sometimes (2), seldom (1) and never (0). The final scale with a range of 0-24 had a Cronbach's alpha of 0.80. The following self-reported *psychosomatic symptoms* have been investigated: back-pain, tension headache, sleeping problems, chronic fatigue, stomach pyrosis, tension diarrhoea and palpitation (Piko, Barabás and Boda, 1997). The aim of this measure was to obtain information on the frequency of these symptoms during the past 12 months. Respondents were asked: "During the past 12 month, how often have you had a back-pain?"... etc. Responses were coded as often (3), sometimes (2), seldom(1) and never (0). The final scale with a range of 0-21 had a Cronbach's alpha of 0.75.

Acute and Chronic Illness Episodes

Respondents were asked the following question: 'Did you have acute or chronic illness episodes with which you contacted a physician during the past 12 months? The variables were measured by the number of days that limited their activities because of acute or/and chronic illness.

Health Risk Behaviors

The frequency of four harmful habits (smoking, alcohol and coffee drinking, and illicit drug use) were measured (Piko, Barabás and Markos, 1996). Rating scales were calculated to create a composite variable of harmful habits that involve a frequency score of 0-6. The final scale with a possible range of 0-24 had a Cronbach's alpha of 0.70.

Results

Table 1 presents means, standard deviations and correlations for the study variables used in the present analysis of university students. A considerably high correlation exists between psychological well-being and the psychosomatic symptom score. While there was a positive association between the frequency of psychosomatic symptoms and health risk behaviors, physical activity was positively related to both psychological well-being and health risk behaviors.

Table 1: Desciptive Statistics and Correlations for the Study Variables in the Analysis of University Students

Variable	Mean	SD	Psychological well-being	Acute illness episodes	Chronic illness episodes	Psycho-somatic symptoms	Health risk behaviors
Psychological well-being (score: 0-24)	13.9	3.7	-	-	-	-	-
Acute illness episodes (number of days)	8.2	7.0	-0.05	-	-	-	-
Chronic illness episodes (number of days)	2.0	4.2	-0.04	-0.01	-	-	-
Psychosomatic symptoms (score: 0-18)	5.0	3.1	-0.46***	0.08*	-0.04	-	-
Health risk behaviors (score: 0-24)	3.1	3.7	-0.06	0.07	-0.02	0.08*	-
Physical activity behavior(kcal/day)	702.2	478.5	0.17***	0.02	-0.04	-0.05	0.08*

*p<0.05 **p<0.01 ***p<0.001

Table 2 shows the final 5-cluster solution for the sample of university students, that is, this solution provides the most theoretically meaningful groups without any overlap between clusters.

CLUSTER 1 characterized a high-risk group (16.6% of total sample) that showed a relatively high amount of acute illness episodes with a moderately high score on psychosomatic symptoms and chronic illness episodes, and a low level of physical activity.

CUSTER 2 characterized a healthy but symptom-prone group (28.9% of total sample) whose most significant characteristic was a relatively high score on psychosomatic symptoms.

Table 2: Means for Health Related Variable Scores by Cluster Groups of University Students (n=691)

Variables	Cluster 1	Cluster 2	Cluster 3	Cluster 4	Cluster 5
Psychological well-being	12.4	13.6	14.2	12.5	12.4
Acute illness	28.7	10.0	4.3	5.0	10.8
Chronic illness	2.1	0.6	0.2	0	38.20
Psychosomatic symptom score	5.3	6.4	5.4	2.5	6.0
Health risk behavior score	2.4	2.4	1.8	6.0	2.0
Physical activity (AMI)	200.0	651.8	765.2	1238.8	59.1
N	115	200	345	11	20
%	16.6	28.9	50.0	1.6	2.9
Cluster group	High risk group	Healthy but symptom-prone group	Healthy group	Risk-taking group	Chronically ill group

CLUSTER 3 characterized healthy students (50.0% of total sample) who showed a high level of psychological well-being, an average level of physical activity and psychosomatic symptom score, a low frequency of both acute and chronic illness episodes and health risk behaviors.

CLUSTER 4 characterized a risk-taking group (1.6% of total sample). The main characteristic of this cluster was the extremely high levels of physical activity and a considerably high score on health risk behaviors. Apart from these, students belonging to this cluster were rather healthy with the lowest score on psychosomatic symptoms and chronic illness episodes.

Finally, CLUSTER 5 was characterized a chronically ill group (2.9% of total sample). This group showed a high frequency of chronic illness episodes and psychosomatic symptoms with a moderately high frequency of acute illness and the lowest level of physical activity.

Discussion

The main goal of the study of university students has been to explore the interrelationships among the variables of psychosocial health, health risk behaviors and physical activity. The correlation matrix showed that physical activity was positively correlated with both psychological well-being and health risk behaviors. Results suggested that some students who often engaged in sports activity, also reported a higher frequency of substance use, similarly to previous studies (Rooney, 1984; Thorlindsson, Vilhjalmsson and Valgeirsson, 1990; Piko, Barabás and Markos, 1996). Cluster analysis was applied to categorize youths in terms of the associations among variables and to gain deeper insight into the relationship between physical activity (as a protective factor) and health risk behaviors.

The analysis gave a 5-cluster solution that consisted of a high-risk group, a healthy but symptom-prone group, a cluster of healthy students, a risk-taking group and a cluster of chronically ill students. The cluster of risk-taking youths was characterized by an extremely high level of physical activity and a considerably high score on health risk behaviors. These healthy students were probably driven by sensation-seeking when turned to both sports activity and substances. Sensation-seeking was also found to be associated with adolescents' physical acitvity in a previous review (Sallis, Prochaska and Taylor, 2000). Apart from this group of youths, none of the clusters showed similar activities.

It is also worth mentioning that the majority of university students showed a good health profile, there was a cluster of chronically ill students who had reported the highest frequency of chronic illness episodes and psychosomatic symptoms, and a very low level of both physical activity and health risk behaviors. Moreover, a symptom-prone group of students reported a high score on psychosomatic symptoms and acute illness episodes but they also scored relatively high on physical activity. In this case, physical activity as a protective factor might compensate the harmful effects of health problems on students' psychological well-being. In another group, on the contrary, students were characterized by a relatively high amount of acute illness episodes, a moderately high score on psychosomatic symptoms and chronic illness, and a low level of physical activity. This group can be viewed as being at high risk in terms of a close relationship between a low level of physical activity and the frequent health problems.

Results of the cluster analysis support the idea that despite the fact that most young people are free of serious health complaints, some are at high risk for certain health problems or health risk behaviors that could have profound effects on their later adult life and health.

STUDY 2

The second study focused on the patterns of psychosocial health and health risk behavior among secondary school students. Data were collected in conjunction with a research project of social support and health in the secondary school student population in Szeged, Hungary. A series of cluster analyses was conducted to explore group characteristics using similar statistical methods as those found in study 1. In this sample, social support variables were assessed as a measure of protection. Adolescence is characterized as a stage during which support structure undergoes dramatic changes as adolescents begin to move away from parents and develop peer-based orientations (Newcomb and Bagwell, 1995; Schneider, Atkinson and Tardif, 2001). Therefore, social support can be viewed as a critical protective factor in a high school student population (Piko, 2000b).

Methods

Subjects

The representative sample was stratified by gender and the type of school, the age range of the respondents was 15-19 years (mean = 17.3 years, S.D. = 1.4 years). The potential number of students participating in our sample was 1200. Of 1200 questionnaires sent out, 1039 were returned after 1-4 weeks, giving a response rate of 86.6%: 45.6% boys and 54.4% girls.

Procedure

Self-administered questionnaires were used with a standardized procedure of administration followed. Secondary school teachers distributed the questionnaires to students prior to classes after a brief explanation of the objectives of the study and instructions on how to fill out the questionnaires. The questionnaires took approximately 35-45 minutes to complete.

Psychosocial Health: Psychological Well-Being and Psychosomatic Symptoms

The well-being rating scale and the scale of psychosomatic symptoms applied to measure psychosocial health among secondary students is similar to that as described in study 1. The Cronbach's alpha coefficients based on the present data were: psychological well-being scale: 0.78, and psychosomatic symptom scale: 0.75.

Acute and Chronic Illness Episodes

The measures for acute and chronic illnesses were measured by the number of days which limited their activities because of acute or/and chronic illness as described in study 1.

Social Support

The Measures of Perceived Social Support developed by Turner and Marino (1994) was used to assess the level of satisfaction with the support experienced from mother, father and friends. Each of the three scales contained six items and coded such that higher scores indicate greater satisfaction with perceived support. Satisfaction was measured by the amount of agreement with the items e.g. "I feel very close to my mother/father/friends or I often feel really appreciated by my mother/father/friends". Responses were the following: very much like my experience (3), much like my experience (2), somewhat like my experience (1), not at all like my experience (0). The final scales had a range of 0-18 with Cronbach's alpha coefficients based on the present data: mother support 0.89, father support 0.92, and friend support 0.87.

Health Risk Behaviors

The frequency of three harmful habits (smoking, alcohol and illicit drug use) were measured. Alcohol use was assessed with a question: "During the past 12 months how often did you drink alcohol?" Response categories were never (0), occasionally (1), regularly, weekly (2), regularly, daily (3). Smoking was assessed by asking how many cigarettes per week or day the adolescents smoked in the past 12 months. Response categories were none (0), 1-2 /week (1), <10/day (2), 10-20/day (3), >20/day (4). Illicit drug use was measured by the question: "During the past 12 months, how often did you use illicit drugs (e.g. marijuana)?" The answer could be not at all (0), just tried a few times (1) and regulary (2).

Rating scales were calculated to create a composite variable of health risk behaviors. The final scale had a possible range of 0-10 with a Cronbach's alpha of 0.69.

Results

Table 3 shows descriptive statistics and correlations among study variables used in the analysis of high school students. Psychological well-being was correlated negatively with acute and chronic ilnness episodes, psychosomatic symptoms, and health risk behaviors, while positively correlated with the measures of social support. Both mother and father support were negatively correlated with health risk behaviors and the psychosomatic symptom score. Beside, father support also was negatively associated with chronic illness episodes.

Table 3: Descriptive Statistics and Correlations for the Study Variables in the Analysis of High School Students

Variable	Mean	SD	Psycho-logical well-being	Acute illness episodes	Chronic illness episodes	Psycho-somatic symptoms	Health risk behaviors	Mother support	Father support
Psychological well-being (score: 0-24)	12.1	3.9	-	-	-	-	-	-	-
Acute illness episodes (number of days)	8.2	8.6	-0.11**	-	-	-	-	-	-
Chronic illness episodes (number of days)	1.6	4.3	-0.10**	0.11**	-	-	-	-	-
Psychosomatic symptoms (score: 0-18)	6.8	4.0	-0.53***	0.22***	0.09**	-	-	-	-
Health risk behaviors (score: 0-10)	1.7	1.6	-0.11**	0.18***	0.02	0.16***	-	-	-
Mother support (score: 0-18)	13.7	3.9	0.21***	-0.05	-0.01	-0.11**	-0.17***	-	-
Father support (score: 0-18)	11.5	4.9	0.24***	-0.04	-0.08**	-0.22***	-0.13***	0.36***	-
Friend support (score: 0-18)	13.3	3.6	0.17***	0.07*	0.06	-0.01	0.06	0.09**	0.08*

*p<0.05 **p<0.01 ***p<0.001

Table 4 presents the final 4-cluster solution for the variables in high school students.

Table 4: Means for Health Related Variable Scores by Cluster Groups of High School Students (n=1039)

Variables	Cluster 1	Cluster 2	Cluster 3	Cluster 4
Psychological well-being	11.3	12.6	11.2	8.0
Acute illness	22.3	3.6	62.5	13.0
Chronic illness	0.4	0.2	2.8	62.6
Psychosomatic symptom score	7.8	6.1	8.9	9.6
Health risk behavior score	1.7	1.5	2.5	0.8
Mother support	13.8	13.7	13.3	14.8
Father support	11.1	11.7	6.4	9.0
Friend support	13.6	13.2	14.7	15.4
N	264	697	68	10
%	25.4	67.1	6.6	0.9
Cluster group	Occasionally ill group	Healthy group	High risk and risk-taking group	Chronically ill group

CLUSTER 1 characterized an occasionally ill group (25.4% of total sample) that showed a relatively high frequency of acute illness episodes and psychosomatic symptoms.

CLUSTER 2 characterized a healthy group of youths (67.1% of total sample) who showed high levels of psychological well-being, the lowest score on psychosomatic symptoms, acute and chronic illness episodes, and average levels of social support.

CLUSTER 3 characterized a high-risk and risk-taking group (6.6% of total sample) whose main characteristic was (similar to university students) a relatively high score of health risk behaviors and a very low level of father support with a relatively high score on friend support compared to the average.

Finally CLUSTER 4 characterized a chronically ill group (0.9% of total sample) showing a high frequency of chronic illness episodes and psychosomatic symptom scores, and a low score on health risk behaviors. Among social support measures, while mother and friend support was above the average, father support was relatively low.

Discussion

The main goal of the second study has been to explore the interrelationships among the variables of adolescents' psychosocial health, health risk behaviors and social support. Literature suggests that parental support is associated with positive health behaviors while high engagement in peer-oriented activities is often associated with substance use (Aseltine, 1995; Ary et al. 1999; Pikó, 2000b; Simons-Morton et al., 2001). Indeed, correlations showed that parental support was negatively correlated with health risk behaviors, though, social support from friends was not significantly related to adolescents' health risk behaviors. This finding suggests a need for further investigating the associations among social support and health-related variables.

Cluster-analysis gave 4 clusters: a healthy group of adolescents, a high risk (and risk-taking) group, an occasionally ill group of students and a chronically ill group of adolescents.

The cluster corresponding to a high risk and risk-taking group was characterized by a high score on health risk behaviors and a very low level of father support with a relatively high score on friend support. While peer social support traditionally is associated with higher scores on health risk behaviors (Aseltine, 1995; Ary et al. 1999), lacking the appropriate father support seems to be a critical factor in the engagement of health risk behaviors. Moreover, chronically ill adolescents also reported a relatively low score on father support, while this group was also characterized by the highest scores on mother and friend support and the lowest score on health risk behaviors. These findings draw attention to some differences in the relationship between social support and adolescents' health-related variables. While risk-takers could be characterized by high scores on both health risk behaviors and friend support, and a low level of father support, those who had serious chronic health problems, reported a low level of father support, a high level of both friend and mother support, and a low score on health risk behaviors.

Similar to the results of study 1, although most secondary students were free of serious health problems, some proved to be at especially high risk in terms of the association among social support and health-related variables. Furthermore, our results support the idea that attachment to fathers may have a special role in the socialization of adolescents that influence their health and health risk behaviors (Piko, 2000b; Bogenschneider et al., 1998).

CONCLUSIONS

The main goal of the present paper has been to explore the interrelationships among psychosocial health variables and protective factors in youth and adolescence. Since preventive programs require an identification of youths at high risk we believe it is paramount that efforts be made to categorize them based on these associations (Dishion and Kavanagh, 2000.

Two protective factors were used in the analyses. Among adolescents, social support was applied as a measure of protection. Social support from parents and peers previously has been found to be a critical component in adolescents' health and health risk behaviors (Bogenschneider et al., 1998; Piko, 2000b; Simons-Morton et al., 2001). Social support processes in adolescence undergo dramatic changes as they slowly move away from the parental influences and develop more peer-based activities (Newcomb and Bagwell, 1995; Schneider, Atkinson and Tardif, 2001). Moreover, this is also the age for experiencing health risk behaviors. Among university students, physical acitivity was a critical component of youths' health since after high school engagement in any sports activity becomes nonmandatory for them (Piko, Barabás and Markos, 1996; Leslie et al., 1999).

Despite the fact that both physical activity and social support have been found to be relevant protective factors, investigations often reveal an unbeneficial relationship between them and adolescents' health-related variables (Piko, 1998; Thorlindsson, Vilhjalmsson and Valgeirsson, 1990; Ary et al., 1999). We assumed, however, that these associations could be detected only in terms of specific groups of youths and adolescents. This hypothesis has been confirmed.

While the majority of adolescents and university students showed a good health profile, in both cases there were groups of chronically ill youths and those at high-risk. A specific group of university students, i.e., risk-takers, were detected characterized by an extremely high level of physical activity and a considerably high score on health risk behaviors. While physical activity was indeed found to be a relevant protective factor, it can produce an unbeneficial relationship with substance use when both of them are motivated by sensation-seeking (Rooney, 1984; Mechanic, 1991). Chronically ill adolescents were characterized by an extremely low level of sports activity that supports the relationships between ill health and the lack of physical activity. Therefore, besides emphasizing physical activity as a health policy issue we should also take into account that engagement in various sports activity can serve as a form of sensation-seeking (Sallis, Prochaska and Taylor, 2000).

Among chronically ill adolescents, father support seems to be the critical component since the low level of social support from father was associated with a high frequency of chronic illness episodes and psychosomatic symptom score. A specific group of adolescents were characterized by a relatively high score on health risk behaviors and friend support, and a very low level of father support that confirms a critical role of fathers in their children's psychosocial health development (Bogenschneider et al., 1998; Piko, 2000b). As a health policy issue, we should emphasize that children engaging in a high level of peer-oriented activities, e.g. substance abuse, and lacking the appropriate social relationship with their fathers are at especially high risk. Cluster analysis helps identify specific or high-risk groups of youths by exploring the relevant associations among health-related data. Protective factors may have unbeneficial relationships as well that could help us understand what is going on among youth and adolescence. Preventive programs can be more effective if they take into account both beneficial and unbeneficial impacts by identifying high risk youths.

REFERENCES

Ary, D.V., Duncan, T.E., Biglan, A. et al. (1999). Development of adolescent problem behavior. *Journal of Abnormal Child Psychology, 27*, 141-150.

Aseltine, R.H. (1995). A reconsideration of parental and peer influences on adolescent deviance. *Journal of Health and Social Behavior, 36*, 103-21.

Bogenschneider, K., Wu, M.Y., Raffaelli, M. and Tsay, J.C. (1998). Parent influences on adolescent peer orientation and substance use: the interface of parenting practices and values. *Child Development, 69*, 1672-1688.

Burleson, B.R., Albrecht, T.L. and Sarason, I.G. (1994). *Communication of social support.* Sage Publications, Thousand Oaks, Calif.

Byrne, A. and Byrne, D.G. (1993). The effect of exercise on depression, anxiety and other mood states: a review. *Journal of Psychosomatic Research, 37*, 565-574.

Cohen, S., Underwood, L. and Gottlieb, B.H. (2000). *Social support measurement and intervention: A guide for health and social scientists.* Oxford University Press, New York.

Dean, K., Holst, E., Kreiner, S., Schoenborn, C. and Wilson, R. (1994). Measurement issues in research on social support and health. *Journal of Epidemiology and Community Health, 48*, 201-206.

Dishion, T.J. and Kavanagh, K. (2000). A multilevel approach to family-centered prevention in schools: process and outcome. *Addictive Behaviors, 25*, 899-911.

Eccles, J.S., Midgley, C., Wigfield, A. et al. (1993). Development during adolescence. *American Psychologist, 48*, 90-101.

Fentem, P.H. (1994). Benefits of exercise in health and disease. *British Medical Journal, 308*, 1291-1295.

Fitzpatrick, K. and LaGory M. (2000). *Unhealthy places. The ecology of risk in urban landscape*. Routledge, New York.

Folsom, A.R., Caspersen, C.J., Taylor, H.L., et al. (1985). Leisure-time physical activity and its relationship to coronary risk factors in a population-based sample. The Minnesota Heart Survey. *American Journal of Epidemiology, 121*, 571-579.

Fuchs, V. and Recklis, D. (1992). The status of American children. *Science, 255*, 41-46.

Hansell, S., Mechanic, D. and Brondolo, E. (1986) Introspectiveness and adolescent development. *Journal of Youth and Adolescence, 15*, 115-132.

Hawkins, J.D., Catalano, R.F. and Miller, J.Y. (1992). Risk and protective factors for alcohol and other drug problems in adolescence and early adulthood: Implications for substance abuse prevention. *Psychological Bulletin, 12*, 64-105.

House, J.S., Landis, K.R. and Umberson, D. (1988). Social relationships and health. *Science, 241*, 540-545.

Jessor, R. (1993). Successful adolescent development among youth in high-risk settings. *American Psychologist, 48*, 117-126.

Krause, N.M. and Jay, G.M. (1994). What do global self-rated health items measure? *Medical Care, 32*, 930-942.

Lamb, K.L., Brodie, D.A., Minten, J.H. et al. (1991). A comparison of selected health-related data from surveys of a general population. *Social Science and Medicine, 33*, 835-839.

Lee, I.-M., Paffenbarger, R.S. and Hsieh, C.-C. (1992). Time trends in physical activity among college alumni, 1962-1988. *American Journal of Epidemiology, 135*, 915-925.

Leslie, E., Owen, N., Salmon, J., Bauman, A., Sallis, J.F. and Lo, S.K. (1999). Insufficiently active Australian college students: perceived personal, social, and environmental influences. *Preventive Medicine, 28*, 20-27.

Mechanic, D. (1991). Adolescents at risk. *Journal of Adolescent Health, 12*, 638-643.

Mechanic, D. and Hansell, S. (1989). Adolescent competence, psychological well-being, and self-assessed physical health. *Journal of Health and Social Behavior, 28*, 364-374.

Montoye, H.J. and Taylor, H.L. (1984). Measurement of physical activity in population studies: a review. *Human Biology, 56*, 195-216.

Newcomb, A. and Bagwell, C.L. (1995). Children's friendship relations: A meta-analytic review. *Psychological Bulletin, 117*, 306-347.

Norusis, M.J. (1993). SPSS for Windows Professional Statistics. SPSS Inc., Chicago, Il.

Piko, B. (1998). Social support and health in adolescence: A factor analytical study. *British Journal of Health Psychology, 3*, 333-344.

Piko, B. (2000a). Health-related predictors of self-perceived health in a student population: the importance of physical activity. *Journal of Community Health, 25*, 125-137.

Piko, B. (2000b). Perceived social support from parents and peers: which is the stronger predictor of adolescent substance use? *Substance Use and Misuse, 35*, 617-630.

Piko, B., Barabás, K. and Boda, K. (1997). The frequency of common psychosomatic symptoms and its effect on self-perceived health in a Hungarian student population. *European Journal of Public Health, 7*, 243-247.

Piko, B., Barabás, K. and Markos, J. (1996). Health risk behaviour of a medical student population. Report on a pilot study. *Journal of the Royal Society of Health, 116*, 97-100.

Resnick, M.D., Bearman, P.S., Blum, R.W. et al. (1997). Protecting adolescents from harm. Findings from the National Longitudinal Study on adolescent health. *Journal of the American Medical Association, 278*, 823-832.

Riddoch, C.J. and Boreham, C.A. (1995). The health-related physical activity of children. *Sports Medicine, 19*, 86-102.

Rimal, R.N. (2001). Longitudinal influences of knowledge and self-efficacy on exercise behavior: Tests of a mutual reinforcement model. *Journal of Health Psychology*, 6, 31-46.

Rooney, JF. (1984). Sports and clean living: a useful myth? *Drug and Alcohol Dependence, 13*, 75-87.

Rosengren, A., Orth-Gomér, K., Wedel, H. and Wilhelmsen, L. (1993). Stressful life events, social support, and mortality in men born in 1933. *British Medical Journal, 307*, 1102-1105.

Ross, C.E. and Hayes, D. (1988). Exercise and psychologic well-being in the community. *American Journal of Epidemiology, 27*, 762-771.

Sallis, J.F., Prochaska, J.J. and Taylor, W.C. (2000). A review of correlates of physical activity of children and adolescents. *Medicine and Science in Sports and Exercise, 32*, 963-975.

Schneider, B.H., Atkinson, L. and Tardif, C. (2001). Child-parent attachment and children's peer relations: a quantitative review. *Developmental Psychology, 37*, 86-100.

Schwarzer, R. and Leppin, A. (1991). Social support and health: a theoretical and empirical overview. *Journal of Social and Personal Relationships, 8*, 99-127.

Sells, C.W. and Blum, R. (1996). Morbidity and mortality among US adolescents: an overview of data and trends. *American Journal of Public Health, 86*, 513-519.

Simons-Morton, B., Haynie, D.L., Crump, A.D., Eitel, S.P. and Saylor, K.E. (2001). Peer and parents influences on smoking and drinking among early adolescents. *Health Education and Behavior, 28*, 95-107.

Taylor, H.L., Jacobs, Jr. D.R., Schucker, B., et al. (1978). A questionnaire for the assessment of leisure time physical activities. *Journal of Chronic Disease, 31*, 741-755.

Thorlindsson, T., Vilhjalmsson, R. and Valgeirsson, G. (1990). Sport participation and perceived health status. A study of adolescents. *Social Science and Medicine, 31*, 551-556.

Turner, R.J. and Marino, F. (1994). Social support and social structure: a descriptive epidemiology. *Journal of Health and Social Behavior, 35*, 193-212.

van Oostrom, M.A., Tijhuis, M.A.R., de Haes, J.C.J.M., Tempelaar, R. and Kromhout, D. (1995). A measurement of social support in epidemiological research: the social experiences checklist tested in a general population in The Netherlands. *Journal of Epidemiology and Community Health, 49*, 518-524.

Chapter 3

To Treat or Not to Treat: Can Richard McCormick's Moral Criterion Serve as a Model for Neonatal Decision-Making Today?

Peter A. Clark
St. Joseph's University

Dramatic advances in neonatal medical information and technology occur daily and these advances are being implemented almost immediately. Despite the dramatic technological advances, diagnostic and prognostic certainty for many neonatal conditions remains illusive. As a result, the appropriate decision-makers are having to decide whether some handicapped newborns, such as those with congenital anomalies, low-birth-weights, and genetic defects, should be treated aggressively or not at all. This uncertainty has led to many handicapped newborns with serious congenital anomalies being treated aggressively. This treatment prolongs the lives of many newborns when in the past they would have been allowed to die. Such life-prolonging treatment decisions have far-reaching ramifications. One thing that is clear to serious observers in the field is that the implementation of medical advances and technology for some newborns is a mixed blessing at best. Despite proposed federal regulations (1984 Child Abuse Law)[1] and medical guidelines (American Academy of Pediatrics)[2] that have helped to clarify treatment issues, there is still no consensus among responsible decision-makers on a moral criterion to assist parents and health care professionals on treatment decisions. There is general agreement within the medical, legal,

---

[1] For a more detailed analysis of the 1984 Child Abuse Law, see Department of Health and Human Services, "Child Abuse and Neglect: Prevention and Treatment," reprinted from *The Federal Register* 50 (April 15, 1985), no. 72: Rules and Regulations, part 1340, 14887-14892.

[2] For a more detailed analysis of the guidelines of the American Academy of Pediatrics, see American Academy of Pediatrics, "Joint Policy Statement: Principles Of Treatment Of Disabled Infants," *Pediatrics* 73 (1984): 559-560; and American Academy of Pediatrics, "Guidelines For Infant Bioethics Review Committees," *Pediatrics* 74 (1984): 306-310.

and ethical professions that there are some handicapped newborns, in particular situations, whose lives need not be saved. Consensus ends, however, when an attempt is made to determine which specific newborns should receive or not receive medical treatment. This diversity of opinions has brought to the forefront the urgent need for a normative moral criterion to assist decision-makers in their discernment of treatment decisions for these never-competent patients.[3]

Today, parents and health care professionals are often forced to draw lines between newborns who will be treated and those who will not be. If these lines are being drawn, then ethicist Richard A. McCormick argues, "it is of public importance that we find out the criteria by which they are being drawn. My attempt is to search our tradition on the meaning of life and so forth and see if we couldn't develop criteria."[4] Realizing the magnitude of this problem, McCormick has established a moral criterion for treatment decisions regarding handicapped newborns as a "revised" natural-law ethicist in the Roman Catholic tradition.[5]

As a "revised" natural-law ethicist, McCormick has always sought a balanced middle course between extreme positions--a course that he understands as characteristic of the Judaeo-Christian tradition.[6] McCormick believes that few, if any, physicians are willing to make substantive criteria when it comes to treatment decisions for handicapped newborns. On the other hand, moral theologians, in their concern to avoid total normlessness and arbitrariness, can easily become quite dogmatic.[7] Between the two extremes of the physician's lack of concrete criteria and the theologian's dogmatism, McCormick argues that there is a middle course that entails substantive criteria to assist decision-makers regarding treatment decisions for handicapped newborns. He has proposed a patient-centered, quality-of-life criterion that can be used by appropriate decision-makers in determining treatment decisions for handicapped newborns. This author contends that the significance of McCormick's quality-of-life criterion is that it offers the appropriate decision-makers, for

[3] There is an ethical distinction regarding competent, noncompetent and never-competent patients. A competent patient is one who can make decisions regarding health care for him or herself. A noncompetent patient is one who was once competent, but now lacks that decision-making capacity. A never-competent patient is one who never had this decision-making capacity and never will have it in the future.

[4] James Castelli, "Richard A. McCormick, S.J., And Life/Death Decisions," *St. Anthony Messenger* 83 (August 1975): 34. McCormick, as interviewed by Castelli.

[5] Natural law in the Catholic tradition is based on the premise of "reason informed by faith." McCormick's understanding of natural law methodology has developed over the years from the more classicist view of natural law to the more revisionist view that is based in a historically conscious worldview. Despite this revisionist view of the natural law it is clear that McCormick remains true to a very basic commitment that underlies the Roman Catholic tradition of moral teaching: moral values and obligations are grounded in a moral order known by human reason reflecting on experience.

[6] McCormick uses as an example the traditional obligation to preserve life. He argues that the Christian tradition "has always strived to maintain a middle course between two extremes: medical-moral utopianism, i.e., sustaining life at all costs and with all means because when life is over everything is over and death is an absolute end, and its opposite, medical-moral pessimism, i.e., there is no point in sustaining life if it is accompanied by suffering, lack of function, etc. Both of these extremes are basic devaluations of human life because they remove life from the context which gives it its ultimate significance. The middle path is a recognition of the facts that human life is a basic value, the most basic value, because it is the foundation for all other values and achievements, but that life is not the absolute good and death the ultimate and absolute evil." McCormick, "A Proposal For 'Quality Of Life' Criteria For Sustaining Life," *Hospital Progress* 56 (September 1975): 76.

[7] Richard A. McCormick, "To Save Or Let Die," *How Brave A New World?: Dilemmas In Bioethics*, (Garden City, N.Y.: Doubleday, 1981), 342.

never-competent newborns, a practical, beneficial, and appropriate moral criterion that is not only reasonable and coherent but is grounded in a tradition that promotes the "best interests" of handicapped newborns.

The purpose of this article is threefold: first, to examine McCormick's quality-of-life criteria as it applies to treatment decisions for handicapped newborns; second, to apply his quality-of-life criterion to five diagnostic treatment categories, established by this author, which span the spectrum of neonatal defects; third, to assess whether McCormick's quality-of-life criterion is a practical, beneficial, and appropriate moral criterion for parents of handicapped newborns.

McCormick's Quality-of-Life Criterion

McCormick will determine how treatment decisions are made for handicapped newborns by proposing his normative understanding of best interests which evolves gradually into his quality-of-life criterion. This is a patient-centered, teleological assessment, which is based on a normative understanding of what reasonable persons ought to choose in a particular situation for the never-competent patient.[8] It appears that McCormick's quality-of-life criterion is nothing more than a further specification of his normative understanding of "best interests."[9] McCormick has a normative understanding of "best interests" because, "as social beings, our good, our flourishing (therefore, our best interests) is inextricably bound up with the well-being of others."[10] McCormick's "best interests" category is a composite category that involves quality-of-life considerations, benefit-burden considerations, and the use of proportionate reason as a tool for establishing what is promotive or destructive for the good of

[8] The structure and individual components that makeup McCormick's moral criterion for decision-making are normative; they center on what "ought" to be the case, not what "is" the case. By normative McCormick means what the never-competent patient would want because he or she "ought" to want it. The never-competent patient "ought" to make this choice because it is in his/her "best interests." For a more detailed analysis of McCormick's position on a normative understanding of his patient-centered approach, see McCormick, "The Rights Of The Voiceless," *How Brave A New World?*, 99-113.

[9] Ethicist Robert Weir disagrees with McCormick on this point. Weir argues that the quality-of-life criterion and best interests criterion are distinct and separate. McCormick responds to Weir by stating: "I believe Weir is wrong when he asserts that for those who use quality-of-life assessment, 'it is not necessary to consider the best interest of the neonate.' It is precisely because one is focused on best interests that qualitative considerations cannot be ignored but indeed are central. Weir is clearly afraid that quality-of-life considerations will be unfair. But they need not be. It all depends on where the line is drawn. I am all the more convinced of the inseparable unity and general overlap of best interests and quality-of-life considerations when I study Weir's clinical applications of his ethical criteria." McCormick, review of *Selective Nontreatment Of Handicapped Newborns*, by Robert Weir, in *Perspectives In Biology And Medicine* 29 (Winter 1986): 328.

[10] McCormick, "The Rights Of The Voiceless," *How Brave A New World?*, 101. It should be noted that McCormick's understanding of "best interests" is grounded in his "revised" natural law position. "I believe we do have reasons for assuming we know in many cases what an incompetent would want. We may assume that most people are reasonable, and that being such they would choose what is in their best interest. At least this is a safe and protective guideline to follow in structuring our conduct toward them when they cannot speak. The assumption may be factually and *per accidens* incorrect. But I am convinced that it will not often be. . . . I believe most of us want to act reasonably within parameters that are objective in character, even though we do not always do so. Or at least I think it good protective policy to assume this." Ibid., 104-105.

the person "integrally and adequately considered."[11] McCormick understands "quality of life" to be an elusive term whose meaning varies according to context. However, at a more profound level, when the issue is preserving human life, the term assumes a more basic meaning. "Just as life itself is a condition for any other value or achievement, so certain characteristics of life are the conditions for the achievement of other values. We must distinguish between two sets of conditions: those that allow us to do things well, easily, comfortably, and efficiently, and those that allow us to do them at all."[12] McCormick's quality-of-life criterion is ethically significant for parents and health care professionals, because it represents not only the value of the whole person, but it affirms that respect for the human person entails considering all the relevant factors and circumstances that are involved in any situation.

There are real difficulties in trying to establish a perfectly rational criterion for making quality-of-life judgments. To make his quality-of-life criterion more concrete, McCormick will establish two guidelines and four norms that will further specify his criterion. The first guideline developed for dealing with never-competent patients focuses on the potential for human relationships associated with the infant's condition. By relational potential McCormick means "the hope that the infant will, in relative comfort, be able to experience our caring and love."[13] Specifically, he proposes that "if a newborn baby had no potential for such relationships or if the potential would be totally submerged in the mere struggle to survive, then that baby had achieved its potential and further life-prolonging efforts were not mandatory, that is, would no longer be in the best interests of the baby."[14] Therefore, according to this guideline, when a never-competent patient, even with treatment, will have no potential for human relationships, the appropriate decision-makers can decide to withhold treatment and allow the patient to die.[15] McCormick claims this quality-of-life approach has its foundation in the traditional ordinary-extraordinary means distinction that was later clarified by Pius XII.[16] This is not an easy guideline to apply, especially in the case of never-competent patients. In essence, this guideline requires that the appropriate decision-makers

---

[11] It should be noted that when McCormick refers to benefits in his "best interests" category it is not restricted to medical benefits. Benefits also apply to social and familial benefits. This notion of "benefit" originates in Pellegrino's four components of "best interests" that McCormick has incorporated into his "best interests" category. For a more detailed analysis of Pellegrino's position, see Edmund Pellegrino, M.D., "Moral Choice, The Good Of The Patient And The Patient's Good," in *Ethics And Critical Care Medicine*, eds. J. C. Moskop & L. Kopelman (Dordrecht, Netherlands: D. Reidel, 1985), 117-138.

[12] McCormick, "A Proposal For "Quality Of Life" Criteria For Sustaining Life," 77-78.

[13] McCormick, "To Save Or Let Die," 351.

[14] McCormick, "The Best Interests Of The Baby," *Second Opinion* 2 (1986): 23.

[15] This does not mean that once a decision has been made to forego or discontinue treatment, that the dying person is not treated with dignity and respect. For McCormick, even though a person has reached his or her potential and no treatment is recommended, as members of society we still have a moral obligation to give comfort to the person while he or she is in the dying process. That comfort would consist in palliative care. Palliative care is aimed at controlling pain, relieving discomfort, and aiding dysfunction of various sorts.

[16] McCormick quotes Pius XII as saying that an obligation to use any means possible "would be too burdensome for most men and would render the attainment of the higher, more important good too difficult." Pius XII, "The Prolongation Of Life," *Acta Apostolicae Sedis* 49 (1957): 1,031-1,032. McCormick understands Pius XII to say that certain treatments may be refused because it would lead to a life that lacks the proper quality. Leonard J. Weber, *Who Shall Live?: The Dilemma Of Severely Handicapped Children And Its Meaning For Other Moral Questions*, (New York: Paulist Press, 1976), 69.

must be able to determine if a minimally accepted "quality of life" can be expected. This determination ought to be made on the basis of the never-competent's "best interests" understood normatively. This guideline does not depreciate the value of the never-competent individual but affirms that a genuine respect for the person demands attention to the prospects held out by continued life.[17]

This guideline of the potential for human relationships has been criticized for being too general and open to possible abuse.[18] McCormick himself stated when he advanced this guideline that it was "general and rather vague. But this is the way it is with all moral norms.[19] Despite being convinced that this guideline is fundamentally sound, McCormick understood that he must further concretize it. Specifically, there are those circumstances when the never-competent patient has the potential for human relationships, but the underlying medical condition is critical and will result in imminent death, or after treatment has been initiated it becomes apparent that the treatment is medically futile.[20] In these two situations it is clear that, besides the potential for human relationships, McCormick must incorporate an additional guideline that can weigh the benefits and burdens of certain treatments.

The second guideline of McCormick's quality-of-life criterion is the benefit-burden calculus. "Where medical procedures are in question, it is generally admitted that the criterion to be used is a benefits-burdens estimate . . . The question posed is: Will the burden of the treatment outweigh the benefits to the patient? The general answer: If the treatment is useless

[17] Lisa Sowle Cahill, "On Richard McCormick: Reason And Faith In Post-Vatican II Catholic Ethics," in *Theological Voices In Medical Ethics* eds. Allen Verhey & Stephen Lammers (Grand Rapids, MI.: William B. Eerdmans Publishing Co., 1993): 91. The potential for human relationships is based in the Catholic tradition. McCormick bases this potential for human relationships in the Catholic tradition. The Christian story does not yield concrete answers and fixed rules, but it does yield various perspectives and insights that inform human reasoning. One such insight is that human life is a basic good but not an absolute good. Since human life is a relative good, and the duty to preserve it is a limited one, then it is not always morally obligatory to use all means to preserve human life if a person cannot attain the higher more important good. For McCormick, the "higher" more important good is the capacity for relationships of love. The core of this guideline is developed from the love commandment found in the New Testament.

[18] Both Leonard Weber and John Connery have criticized McCormick's quality-of-life criterion. For a more detailed analysis, see Weber, *Who Shall Live?: The Dilemma Of Severely Handicapped Children And Its Meaning For Other Moral Questions* (New York: Paulist Press, 1976) and John Connery, "Quality Of Life," *Linacre Quarterly* 53 (February 1986): 26-33.

[19] "They really root in general assertions that must be fleshed out by experience, modified by discussion and consultation, propped up and strengthened by cautions and qualifications. It is in the process of their application that moral norms take on added concreteness."McCormick, "To Save Or Let Die: State Of The Questions," *America* 131 (October 5, 1974): 171.

[20] It should be noted that the term "medically futile" is an elusive and ambiguous term. There are four major types of medical futility. First, physiological futility--an intervention cannot lead to the intended physiological effect. Second, imminent demise futility--an intervention may be futile if despite that intervention the patient will die in the very near future (this is sometimes expressed as the patient will not survive to discharge, although that is not really equivalent to dying in the near future). Third, lethal condition futility--an intervention may be futile if the patient has an underlying lethal condition which the intervention does not affect and which will result in death in the not too far future (weeks, perhaps months, but not in years) even if the intervention is employed. Fourth, qualitative futility--an intervention may be futile if it fails to lead to an acceptable quality of life. For a more detailed analysis of medical futility, see Baruch A. Brody and Amir Halevy, "Is Futility A Futile Concept?" *Journal Of Medicine And Philosophy* 20 (April 1995): 126-129.

or futile, or it imposes burdens that outweigh the benefits, it may be omitted."[21] As is the case with his first guideline, McCormick claims the benefit-burden calculus emerges out of the "ordinary-extraordinary means" distinction.

McCormick believes that his notion of benefit-burden calculus within his quality-of-life criterion is a logical development of the "ordinary-extraordinary means" distinction, or what he refers to as an extension of the tradition into new problem areas.[22] McCormick believes that the "ordinary-extraordinary means" distinction has an honorable history and an enduring validity. However, he argues that these terms "summarize and promulgate judgments drawn on other grounds. It is these 'other grounds' that cry out for explication."[23] To further explain these "other grounds," McCormick reformulates the "ordinary-extraordinary means" distinction by advancing his benefit-burden calculus. An extraordinary means is one that offers the patient no real benefit, or offers it at a disproportionate cost. For McCormick, one is called to make a moral judgment: Does the benefit of a proposed medical intervention really outweigh the harm it will inevitably produce? This is a quality-of-life judgment. The benefit-burden interpretation is not a departure from the Catholic tradition. It is a reformulation of the tradition in order to deal with contemporary bioethical problem areas.[24]

The reason for this reformulation of the tradition is that over the centuries the "ordinary-extraordinary means" distinction has become less objective and more relative because medicine and technology have become more sophisticated. The medical profession is committed to curing disease and preserving life. Today, we have the medical technology to make this commitment a reality. However, McCormick argues that "this commitment must be implemented within a healthy and realistic acknowledgment that we are mortal."[25] Therefore, there is a need to reformulate the basic value of human life under new circumstances. For many contemporary ethicists the traditional terminology of ordinary-extraordinary means has outlived its usefulness and could take us only so far, especially in the case of handicapped

---

[21] Richard A. McCormick, S.J., "Technology And Morality: The Example Of Medicine," *New Theology Review* 2 (November 1989): 26.

[22] McCormick writes: "A basic human value is challenged by new circumstances, and these circumstances demand that imagination and creativity be employed to devise new formulations, a new understanding of this value in light of these new circumstances while retaining a basic grasp upon the value. For example, in-vitro fertilization poses questions about the meaning of sexuality, parenthood, and the family because it challenges their very biological roots." McCormick, "A Proposal For 'Quality Of Life' Criteria For Sustaining Life," 76.

[23] McCormick, "The Best Interests Of The Baby," 19. McCormick further states: "We must admit that the terms 'ordinary' and 'extraordinary' are but code words. That is, they summarize and are vehicles for other judgments. They do not solve problems automatically. Rather they are emotional and mental preparations for very personal and circumstantial judgments that must take into account the patient's attitudes and value perspectives, or 'what the patient would have wanted.' 'Ordinary' and 'extraordinary' merely summarize other underlying judgments. They say very little in and of themselves." McCormick, "A Proposal For 'Quality Of Life' Criteria For Sustaining Life," 77.

[24] McCormick further states that: "It must be remembered that the abiding substance of the Church's teaching, its rock bottom so to speak, is not found in the ordinary means-extraordinary means terminology. It is found in a basic value judgment about the meaning of life and death, one that refuses to absolutize either. It is *that judgment* that we must carry with us as we face the medical decisions that technology casts upon us." McCormick, "Technology And Morality: An Example Of Medicine," 29. Emphasis in the original.

[25] Richard McCormick, *The Critical Calling: Moral Dilemmas Since Vatican II* (Washington, D.C.: Georgetown University Press, 1989), 365.

newborns.[26] Focusing on the value of human life, McCormick sought to reformulate the "ordinary-extraordinary means" distinction without abandoning the tradition. Contemporary medical problems no longer only concern newborns for whom biological death is imminent. Modern medicine and technology have the ability to keep almost anyone biologically alive. Therefore, a gradual shift has occurred from the means to reverse the dying process to the quality of life sustained and preserved as the result of the application of medical technology.[27] Today, because of the advancements in medicine and technology, the focus is on the quality of life thus saved that establishes a means as extraordinary.

To address this shift in the problem from means to quality of life preserved, McCormick has reformulated the "ordinary-extraordinary means" distinction to mean the "benefit-burden calculus."[28] For McCormick, "it is clear that the judgments of burden and benefit are value judgments, moral choices. They are judgments in which, all things considered, the continuance of life is either called for or not worthwhile to the patient."[29] In making these moral judgments one can see how proportionate reason is used as a tool for determining whether a particular life-sustaining treatment is a benefit or a burden, that is, in the "best interests" of the never-competent patient and those involved in the decision-making process.

The benefit-burden calculus was also proposed by the Sacred Congregation for the Doctrine of the Faith in its *Declaration On Euthanasia* and by the President's Commission For The Study Of Ethical Problems In Medicine And Biomedical And Behavioral Research in its *Deciding To Forego Life-Sustaining Treatment.*[30] The issuance of the *Declaration On Euthanasia* in 1980 by the Magisterium gave McCormick further justification for incorporating the benefit-burden calculus into his quality-of-life criterion.[31] It also gave him

---

[26] McCormick argues there are two reasons for this: First, the terminology too easily hides the nature of the judgment being made. The major reference point in factoring out what is "reasonable" (benefit) and "excessive" (burden) is the patient--his or her condition, biography, prognosis, and values. The terminology, however, suggests that attention should fall on the means in an all too mechanical way. Second, many people misinterpret the terms to refer to "what physicians ordinarily do, what is customary." This is not what the term means. In their ethical sense, they encompass many more dimensions of the situation McCormick, *Health And Medicine In The Catholic Tradition*, 145.

[27] McCormick, "To Save Or Let Die," *How Brave A New World?*, 345.

[28] Besides McCormick's benefit-burden calculus, other ethicists have suggested various terms to reformulate the ordinary-extraordinary means distinction. Paul Ramsey suggests that the morally significant meaning of ordinary and extraordinary medical means can be reduced almost without remainder to two components--a comparison of treatments to determine if they are "medically indicated" and a patient's right to refuse treatment. See Paul Ramsey, *Ethics At The Edges Of Life: Moral And Legal Intersections*, (New Haven, CT.: Yale University Press, 1978), 153-160. Robert Veatch maintains that the terms "ordinary" and "extraordinary" are "extremely vague and are used inconsistently in the literature." Beneath this confusion he finds three overlapping but fundamentally different uses of the terms: usual versus unusual, useful versus useless, imperative versus elective. See Robert Veatch, *Death, Dying And The Biological Revolution*, (New Haven, CT.: Yale University Press, 1976), 110-112. For further examples, see McCormick, "The Quality Of Life, The Sanctity Of Life," *How Brave A New World?*, 393-405.

[29] McCormick and John Paris, "Saving Defective Infants," *How Brave A New World?*, 360.

[30] See President's Commission For The Study Of Ethical Problems In Medicine And Biomedical And Behavioral Research, "Deciding To Forego Life-Sustaining Treatment: Ethical, Medical And Legal Issues In Treatment Decisions," (Washington, D.C., U.S. Printing Office, March 1983): 218-219.

[31] The Congregation concludes that, "it will be possible to make a correct judgment as to the means by studying the type of treatment being used, its degree of complexity or risk, its cost and possibilities of using it, and comparing these elements with the result that can be expected, taking into account the state of the sick person and his or her

further proof to anchor his guideline and thus his criterion for treatment decisions in the benefit-burden calculus. Medical treatments are not morally mandatory if they are either gravely burdensome or useless for the patient.[32] McCormick has a normative understanding of medical futility, which considers whether the agreed on potential effect is of any value and benefit to the newborn, that is, in the newborn's "best interests" normatively understood. For McCormick, a medical treatment might be successful in achieving an effect (physiologically effective), but the effect might not be beneficial to the patient (qualitatively effective). Since the goal of medical treatment is to benefit the patient, it follows that nonbeneficial treatment is medically futile.[33] This entails making a value judgment, and the evaluation of whether a treatment is a benefit or a burden can be open to personal interpretation. That means these evaluations can be "borderline and controversial."[34]

The two guidelines of McCormick's quality-of-life criterion, even though he argued they were both reformulations of the "ordinary-extraordinary means" distinction, continued to be criticized by ethicists Leonard Weber, John Connery and Warren Reich for being too relative, subjective, and consequential in nature. To address this criticism McCormick, along with ethicist John Paris, S.J., proposed the following norms that would further specify the capacity for human relationships and the benefit-burden evaluation:

(1) Life-saving intervention ought not to be omitted for institutional or managerial reasons. Included in this specification is the ability of this particular family to cope with a badly disabled baby.

---

physical and moral resources." Congregation for the Doctrine of the Faith, "Declaration On Euthanasia," *Origins* 10 (August 1980): 263.

[32] Ethicists Warren Reich, John Connery, S.J., Leonard Weber, and Donald McCarthy disagree with McCormick's interpretation of the tradition on the benefit-burden distinction. Ethicist Richard Sparks writes: "For Reich, Weber, Connery, and McCarthy the limiting factor is the quality of life, which, if judged to be excessively burdensome, can make the presumably beneficial treatment extraordinary and optional, [sic] must be caused by or directly related to the use of the means contemplated. In other words, 'the burden must be the burden of medical treatment, not the burden of handicapped existence.'" Richard Sparks, *To Treat Or Not To Treat?: Bioethics And The Handicapped Newborn*, (New York: Paulist Press, 1988), 110; see also Donald G. McCarthy, "Treating Defective Newborns: Who Judges Extraordinary Means?" *Hospital Progress* 62 (December 1981): 45-50; John Connery, S.J., "Prolongation Of Life: A Duty And Its Limits," *Linacre Quarterly* 47 (May 1980):, 151-165; Leonard Weber, *Who Shall Live?*, 88-98; and Warren Reich, "Quality Of Life And Defective Newborn Children: An Ethical Analysis," in *Decision-Making And The Defective Newborn*, ed. Chester A. Swinyard (Springfield, IL.: Thomas, 1978), 488 -511.

[33] For McCormick, medical futility is determined by the parents in consultation with the health care professionals, because a determination must be made of the patient's medical status and an evaluation must be made of the medical intervention. The determination of medical futility entails balancing the values of patients, the values of medicine, and the fact that there is much uncertainty in making "predictive medical judgments." McCormick's notion of medical futility is also rooted in his understanding of the principles of beneficence and nonmaleficence--do no harm to the patient. For a more detailed analysis of medical futility, see James F. Drane and John L. Coulehan, "The Concept Of Futility: Parents Do Not Have The Right To Demand Medically Useless Treatment," *Health Progress* 74 (December 1993): 32; Robert Veatch and Carol Mason Spicer, "Futile Care: Physicians Should Not Be Allowed To Refuse To Treat," *Health Progress* 74 (December 1993): 22-27 and Glenn G. Griener, "The Physician's Authority To Withhold Futile Treatment," *Journal Of Philosophy And Medicine* 20 (April 1995): 209..

[34] McCormick and Paris, "Saving Defective Infants," *How Brave A New World?*, 358.

(2) Life-sustaining interventions may not be omitted simply because the baby is retarded. There may be further complications associated with retardation that justify withholding life-sustaining treatment.
(3) Life-sustaining intervention may be omitted or withdrawn when there is excessive hardship on the patient, especially when this combines with poor prognosis.
(4) Life-sustaining interventions may be omitted or withdrawn at a point when it becomes clear that expected life can be had only for a relatively brief time and only with continued use of artificial feeding.[35]

These norms or rules do not mandate certain decisions, nor do they replace the role of prudence and eliminate conflicts and decisions. They are simply attempts to provide outlines of the areas in which prudence should operate.[36]

McCormick further specified his quality-of-life criterion to help enlighten medical situations for the appropriate decision-makers. However, guidelines, even specified by concrete norms, cannot cover all circumstances and every possible situation. McCormick's quality-of-life criterion assists the appropriate decision-makers by giving them a range of choices. As rational persons, it is up to the appropriate decision-makers to examine each situation using proportionate reason, and the guidelines advanced by McCormick in his quality-of-life criterion, to determine what is in the "best interests" of the never-competent patient and those involved in the decision-making process. McCormick makes clear that no criterion can cover every instance where human discretion must intervene to decide. There is always the possibility of human error because we are finite and sinful people. For McCormick, "the margin of error tolerable should reflect not only the utter finality of the decision (which tends to narrow it), but also the unavoidable uncertainty and doubt (which tends to broaden it)."[37] With the assistance of these guidelines and norms, McCormick believes that the appropriate decision-makers will be given the necessary guidance to act responsibly.

APPLICATION OF MCCORMICK'S MORAL CRITERION TO FIVE DIAGNOSTIC TREATMENT CATEGORIES OF HANDICAPPED NEWBORNS

This section will address the application of McCormick's quality-of-life criterion to five specific diagnostic treatment categories of handicapped newborns. These categories attempt to encompass, as far as possible, the entire spectrum of handicapped newborns. They are based on McCormick's moral criterion of the potential for human relationships. One example of a congenital anomaly has been selected that is representative of each particular diagnostic category.

McCormick has plotted the two extreme positions on this spectrum of handicapped newborns, but has left the "conflictual middle," to be filled in by health care professionals and

[35] Ibid., 358-359.
[36] Ibid., 359.
[37] McCormick and Paris, "Saving Defective Infants," *How Brave A New World?*, 360.

bioethicsts.[38] This section will attempt to complete the "conflictual middle." The "conflictual middle" pertains to those neonatal anomalies that fall into the "gray area" of treatment decisions.[39] I have arranged these diagnostic treatment categories in a way that demonstrates the application of McCormick's "best interests" category. There is a logical progression on the spectrum from the newborn who does not warrant medical treatment to the newborn who does warrant medical treatment.

Establishing a full set of diagnostic treatment categories is not a panacea for determining treatment decisions for handicapped newborns. Not all medical conditions can be placed in specific categories; there is a marked difference in the severity of conditions within each category. Not all health care professionals or even bioethicists could or would agree to these specific categories. Nevertheless, as McCormick argues, "we ought to attempt, as far as possible, to approach neonatal disabilities through diagnostic categories, always realizing that such categories cannot deflate important differences and that there will always remain gray areas."[40] The establishment of these five diagnostic treatment categories is an attempt to meet the challenge McCormick set before health care professionals and bioethicists to assist parents and health care professionals in making treatment decisions for handicapped newborns.

Before applying McCormick's moral criterion of quality-of-life, it is important to note that for McCormick the newborn's life lacks any personal perspectives and thus life-sustaining decisions cannot be individualized.[41] This implies two general stipulations that will impact on McCormick's moral criteriology:

> First, the criteria used in determining to save or let die where an infant is concerned are generalizable to all infants. Secondly, and as a consequence, the criteria used must be the strictest possible. That is, the very minimum potential for human experiencing or relationships must be seen as sufficient warrant for attempting to save. Any other view would be racism of the adult world, and would unjustly deprive not simply one but (by logical generalizability) many infants of their chance at life.[42]

---

[38] McCormick writes: "It is the task of physicians to provide some more concrete categories or presumptive biological symptoms for this human judgment. For instance, nearly all would likely agree that the anencephalic infant is without relational potential. On the other hand, the same cannot be said for the mongoloid infant. The task ahead is to attach relational potential to presumptive biological symptoms for the gray areas between such extremes." McCormick, "To Save Or Let Die," *How Brave A New World?*, 349-350.

[39] This would include anomalies in which the newborn has the potential for human relationships, but the potential is utterly submerged in the mere struggle for survival, or the medical condition will result in imminent death, or it has been determined that further treatment is medically futile. Certain anomalies that would fall within this category would be spina bifida, hypoplastic left heart syndrome, trisomy 13, trisomy 18, Lesch-Nyhan syndrome, etc.

[40] McCormick, "The Best Interests Of The Baby," 24.

[41] This is in contrast to individuals who are competent or who were once competent. For these individuals life-sustaining decisions can be individualized to the person. McCormick writes: "That is, the notion of 'benefit to the patient' can be individualized. The adult has a past, perspectives on life and its meaning, aspirations and achievements. All these things can be weighed by the patient making life-sustaining decisions or by those who know the patient best and presumably have his best interests at heart." McCormick, "The Preservation Of Life," *Linacre Quarterly* 43 (May 1976): 100.

[42] Ibid.

This author will add a third stipulation, which is McCormick's position on infanticide. In making treatment decisions for handicapped newborns McCormick argues that "there is no proportionate reason for directly dispatching a terminal or dying patient."[43] McCormick makes a clear distinction between allowing to die and direct termination. This means that even the most handicapped newborns, those who experience extreme pain and suffering, can never be denied dignity and respect by being terminated.[44] These three general stipulations will undergird McCormick's moral criterion as it is applied to treatment decisions for handicapped newborns.

This section will be structured so that the diagnostic treatment category is presented. The representative anomaly will be examined from a medical point of view by giving a brief description of the anomaly and then the diagnosis and prognosis. Finally, McCormick's quality-of-life criterion will be applied to each anomaly to determine whether parents should decide to treat the handicapped newborn representative of the particular diagnostic category.

Category 1: The Handicapped Newborn Whose Potential for Human Relationships is Completely Nonexistent

An anomaly that would be representative of this category would be anencephaly. Anencephaly is a developmental abnormality of the central nervous system that results in the congenital absence of a major portion of the brain, skull, and scalp. Because anencephalic newborns lack functioning cerebral hemispheres, they never experience any degree of consciousness. They never have thoughts, feelings, sensations, desires, or emotions. There is no purposeful action, social interaction, memory, pain, or suffering. However, anencephalic newborns do have fully or partially functioning brain stem tissue. Consequently, they are able to maintain at least some of the body's autonomic functions (i.e., unconscious activity), including the functions of the heart, lungs, kidneys, and intestinal tract, as well as certain reflex actions. They may be able to breathe, suck, engage in spontaneous movements of the eyes, arms, legs, respond to noxious stimuli with crying or avoidance maneuvers, and exhibit facial expressions typical of healthy infants. While all of this activity gives the appearance that the anencephalic newborn has some degree of consciousness, there is none. Anencephalic newborns are totally unaware of their existence and the environment in which they live.[45]

The cause of anencephaly is usually not known. The appearance of a newborn with anencephaly is unique, and the diagnosis can be made with virtual certainty when specific criteria is met.[46] Some rare newborns fall into a "gray zone" in which it is unclear whether the diagnosis of anencephaly is proper.

---

[43] Richard McCormick, "The New Medicine And Morality," *Theology Digest* 21 (Winter 1973): 316.

[44] This is an important safeguard because there are a number of bioethicists and health care professionals who argue that there is no moral difference between direct termination and allowing to die. See Joseph Fletcher, "Ethics And Euthanasia," *American Journal Of Nursing* 73 (1973): 670-765. This article also appears as a chapter in *To Live And To Die*, ed. Robert H. Williams (New York: Spinger-Verlag, 1973), 113-124. Paul Ramsey also offers a critique of this view in *Ethics At The Edges Of Life*, 212-227.

[45] American Medical Associations's Council of Ethical and Judicial Affairs, "The Use Of Anencephalic Neonates As Organ Donors," *Journal Of The American Medical Association* 273 (May 24-31, 1995): 1615.

[46] (1) A large portion of the skull is absent. (2) The scalp, which extends to the margin of the bone, is absent over the skull defect. (3) Hemorrhagic, fibrotic tissue is exposed because of defects in the skull and scalp. (4)

The prognosis for an anencephalic newborn is that the life span is very short. Many die within a few hours, less than half survive more than a day, and fewer than 10% survive more than a week.[47] However, because anencephalic newborns do not receive aggressive treatment their potential life span is probably longer than their actual life span.[48]

The first guideline that specifies McCormick's quality-of-life criterion is the potential for human relationships associated with the infant's condition. According to medical authorities, the anencephalic newborn has no potential for human relationships because this newborn lacks functioning cerebral hemispheres, and therefore the neonate will never experience any degree of consciousness. For McCormick, when a person never had or no longer has the potential for human relationships--which are the very possibility for growth in love of God and neighbor--then parents are no longer morally required to preserve that life by all human means.[49] To preserve human life in this situation would be to replace the "higher, more important good." "Physical life" would become the ultimate value. When this happens, the value of human life has been distorted. When human life is devoid of the possibility of experiencing human love, that is, no experience or interrelation is possible, then life has achieved its potential.[50] The anencephalic newborn has no potential for human relationships and has achieved its potential.

In conclusion, when the handicapped newborn's potential for human relationships is completely nonexistent, and further treatment will be of no benefit to the newborn, parents in consultation with health care professionals ought to decide morally, in the newborn's "best interests," to forego medical treatment for a newborn in this diagnostic category. This is a moral judgment in which, all things considered, the parents decide that further treatment is of no benefit to the newborn. However, once this decision has been made, the anencephalic newborn should be cared for and treated with dignity and respect during the dying process.[51]

Recognizable cerebral hemispheres are absent David A. Stumpf, M.D. *et al.*, "The Infant With Anencephaly,"*The New England Journal Of Medicine* 322 (March 8, 1990): 670.

[47] It should be noted that there is one case where Stephanie Keene, known as "Baby K," lived for two and one half years before dying. Many question if anencephaly was the proper diagnosis in this case. For a more detailed analysis of this case, see Mark A. Bonano, "The Case Of Baby K: Exploring The Concept Of Medical Futility," *Annals Of Health Law* 4 (1995): 151.

[48] For a more detailed analysis of anencephaly, see A.D. Abbattista, F. Vigevano, G. Catena, and F. Parisi, "Anencephalic neonates And Diagnosis Of Death," *Transplant Process* 8 (December 29, 1997): 3634-3635; C. Lantz, "The Anencephalic Infant As Organ Donor," *Health Law Journal* 4 (1996): 179-195; D. A. Shewmon, "Anencephaly: Selected Medical Aspects," *Hastings Center Report* 18 (1988): 11-19; P. A. Baird and A. D. Sadovnick, "Survival In Infants With Anencephaly," *Clinical Pediatrics* 23 (1984): 268-271; Malcolm Levene and David Tudehope, *Essentials Of Neonatal Medicine* (Oxford: Blackwell Scientific Publications, 1993), 278-281; and Gordon Avery, Mary Ann Fletcher and Mhairi MacDonald, *Neonatology: Pathophysiology And Management Of The Newborn*, 4th ed. (Philadelphia, PA.: Lippincott Co., 1994), 1155-1156.

[49] McCormick, "The Judaeo-Christian Tradition And Bioethical Codes," *How Brave A New World?*, 14.

[50] McCormick, "The Quality Of Life, The Sanctity Of Life," *How Brave A New World?*, 405.

[51] Weber criticizes McCormick's quality-of-life criterion in regards to "once McCormick has made the claim that we must decide to treat or not on the basis of the child's condition, will people really be able to pay much attention to his insistence that every life is valuable regardless of condition?" Weber, *Who Shall Live?*, 82. McCormick argues that even though an anencephalic newborn has reached his or her potential and no treatment is recommended because it is of no benefit to the newborn, as members of society we have a moral obligation to care for this newborn while he or she is in the dying process. McCormick bases this position on the fact that every human life is sacred, is of incalculable worth, and deserves to be treated with dignity and respect, which is rooted

Category 2: The Handicapped Newborn Who Has a Potential for Human Relationships but Whose Potential is Utterly Submerged in the Mere Struggle for Survival

An anomaly that would be representative of this diagnostic treatment category would be a preterm neonate with a Grade IV massive intraventricular hemorrhage (IVH) of the brain[52] and hydrocephalus.[53] Hemorrhage in or around the brain is a major problem in newborns, especially when premature. Hypoxia (lack of oxygen supply), pressures exerted on the newborn's head during labor, and the presence of the germinal matrix (a mass of embryonic cells lying over the caudate nucleus and present only in the fetus) in premature newborns are three major causes of intraventricular hemorrhage. The overall incidence of IVH has decreased in recent years from 40-60% to 20% or less in neonates weighing less than 1500 grams at birth. The incidence and severity are inversely proportional to gestational age.[54] Although there has been a reduction in incidence during the past decade, IVH remains a major concern, principally because of the improved survival rates of very low-birth-weight infants (<1000g), who are the highest risks for the development of IVH.[55]

Ultrasonography is the procedure of choice for screening and diagnosis. Sonograms are usually obtained via the anterior fontanelle. In the presence of normally sized ventricles, scanning through the posterior fontanelle may increase the rate of detection of IVH.[56] The diagnosis of IVH may be suspected on the basis of clinical signs alone in approximately 50%

---

in the Christian story. McCormick, "The Judaeo-Christian Tradition And Bioethical Codes," *How Brave A New World?*, 10-11.

[52] There are four grades of severity of Intraventricular Hemorrhage by ultrasound scan. Grade I-- the germinal matrix hemorrhage with no or minimal intraventricular hemorrhage; Grade II--intraventricular hemorrhage without dilatation; Grade III--intraventricular hemorrhage with ventricular dilatation; and Grade IV--intraventricular hemorrhage with parenchymal involvement. Tricia Lacy Gomella, M. Douglas Cunningham, Fabien Eyal and Karin Zent, *Neonatology* 4th edition (Stamford, CT.: Appleton & Lange, 1999), 462. See also, Joseph Volpe, M.D., "Intraventricular Hemorrhage And Brain Injury In The Premature Infant: Diagnosis, Prognosis, And Prevention," *Clinics In Perinatology* 16 (June 1989): 388-389.

[53] Hydrocephalus is caused by a pathological obstruction along the pathway of cerebrospinal fluid circulation, this condition is a progressive enlargement of the head from increased amounts of cerebrospinal fluid into the ventricles of the brain. Newborns with IVH usually experience progressive hydrocephalus and show evidence of irreversible damage of the brain or other major organs (i.e., multiple congenital anomalies and cerebral atrophy secondary to meningitis). In this group, prognosis is uniformly poor, and shunting operations have little to offer. For a more detailed analysis, see Avery *et al., Neonatology*, 1145.

[54] The incidence of major IVH (large IVH or any intraparenchymal hemorrhage) was 5.2% (versus 13-28% in earlier studies) in infants of less than 1500 grams who did not receive any prenatal or postnatal pharmacotherapy for the prevention of IVH other than antenatal steroids administered to accelerate pulmonary maturity. Major IVH occurred in 16% of infants born at < 25 weeks and in only 2.1% of infants born at >25 weeks of gestation. The risk period is during the first 3-4 postnatal days: 50% of IVH occurs in the first 6-12 hours of life, 75% by the second day, and 90% by the third day. Ten percent to 65% of newborns with early IVH have progression of the hemorrhage, with maximal extent occurring within 3-5 days of the initial diagnosis. Gomella et al., 460-461. See also R.D. Sheth, "Trends In Incidence And Severity Of Intraventricular Hemorrhage," *Journal of Child Neurology* 13 (June 1998): 261-264.

[55] Avery *et al., Neonatology*, 1127.

[56] Gomella et al., 462. Although CT scanning and magnetic resonance imaging (MRI) are acceptable alternatives, they are more expensive and require transport from the intensive care unit to the imaging device. Ibid.; See also, A. Hill, "Intraventricular Hemorrhage: Emphasis On Prevention," *Seminar in Pediatric Neurology* 5 (September 1998): 152-160.

of newborns. The severity of clinical features range from an asymptomatic state through a saltatory neurologic deterioration over several days to a catastrophic presentation with coma, apnea, tonic extensor posturing, brain stem dysfunction, and flaccid quadriparesis. Associated systemic abnormalities may include hypotension, metabolic acidosis, bradycardia, serum glucose, and electrolyte disturbances. Bloody or xanthochromic cerebrospinal fluid (CSF) supports a diagnosis of intraventricular hemorrhage.[57]

The prognosis for newborns with a Grade IV massive intraventricular hemorrhage is poor, especially if the hemorrhage extends into the parenchyma.[58] The short-term outcome of IVH is related principally to the size of the hemorrhage and may be considered in terms of mortality or hydrocephalus among survivors. Newborns with a Grade IV massive intraventricular hemorrhage and parenchymal involvement have a high mortality rate (50%-80%), and post-hemorrhagic hydrocephalus often develops (65%-100%). The most critical determinant of long-term outcomes is the extent of parenchymal involvement.[59] Major IVH occurs frequently in the context of hypoxic-ischemia cerebral insult, and long-term neurological outcome depends on concomitant or preceding hemorrhagic or nonhemorrhagic hypoxic-ischemic cerebral injury.[60]

A newborn with a Grade IV massive intraventricular hemorrhage and hydrocephalus has the potential for human relationships, but because the intraventricular hemorrhage is so severe and there is the associated complication of progressive hydrocephalus the potential for human relationships is utterly submerged in the mere struggle for survival.[61] Applying McCormick's quality-of-life criterion to this newborn with a Grade IV massive intraventricular hemorrhage, one can see that McCormick would base his decision to withdraw or forgo medical treatment on the Christian tradition that human life is a basic good but a good to be preserved as the condition of other values. Since these other values cluster around and are rooted in human relationships, it follows that when the relational potential is utterly submerged in the mere

---

[57] Ibid., 1128.

[58] Parenchyma is the distinctive tissue characteristic of an organ and responsible for its functioning.

[59] In a study by F. Guzzetta, M.D. *et al.*, it was determined that newborns with a massive intraventricular hemorrhage and periventricular parenchymal injury, identified on ultrasound scan as intraparenchymal echodensity (IPE) greater than 1cm, was unfavorable. Thus, newborns with extensive IPE (that is, IPE that included fronto-parieto-occipital regions), 30 of 37 (81%) died, and of the seven survivors, all had subsequent motor deficits. For a more detailed analysis, see F. Guzzetta, M.D. *et al.*, "Periventricular Intraparenchymal Echodensities In The Premature Newborn: Critical Determinant Of Neurological Outcome," *Pediatrics* 78 (1986): 995.

[60] For a more detailed analysis of IVH, see Avery *et al., Neonatology*, 1132. See also B. Vohr, W.C. Allan, D.T. Scott et al, "Early-Onset Intraventricular Hemorrhage In Preterm Neonates: Incidence Of Neurodevelopmental Handicap," *Perinatology* 23 (June 1999): 212-217; L. Barton, J.E. Hodgman, and Z. Pavlova, "Causes Of Death In The Extremely Low Birth Weight Infant," *Pediatrics* 103 (February 1999): 446-451; Joseph J. Volpe, M.D., A. Ernest, M.D., and Jane G. Stein, M.D., "Intraventricular Hemorrhage And Brain Injury In The Premature Infant," *Clinics In Perinatology* 16 (June 1989): 387-411; John J. Paris and Kevin O'Connell, "Withdrawal Of Nutrition And Fluids From A Neurologically Devastated Infant: The Case Of Baby T," *Journal Of Perinatology* 11 (1991): 372-373; Michael Jellinek, Elizabeth Catlin, I. Davis Todres, and Edwin Cassem, "Facing Tragic Decision With Parents In The Neonatal Intensive Care Unit: Clinical Perspectives," *Pediatrics* 89 (January 1992): 119-122.

[61] To clarify what McCormick means by the potential for human relationships being utterly submerged in the mere struggle for survival, he writes: "Something other than the 'higher, more important good' would occupy first place. Life, the condition for other values and achievements, would usurp the place of these and become itself the ultimate value. When that happens, the value of human life has been distorted out of context." McCormick, "To Save Or Let Die," *How Brave A New World?*, 347-348.

struggle for survival, that life can be said to have achieved its potential.[62] If the meaning and consummation of life is to be found in love of neighbor, then clearly such meaning is inseparable from human relationships.[63] Therefore, when the potential to love one's neighbor is no longer possible, one does not have a moral responsibility to continue medical treatment.

McCormick grounds his position in the traditional ordinary/extraordinary means distinction. If the means used to preserve the newborn's life will bring about a grave hardship for the newborn and those responsible for his or her care, then this means to preserve life is considered extraordinary and nonobligatory, that is to say not beneficial to the newborn. To continue treatment on the newborn with a Grade IV massive intraventricular hemorrhage and hydrocephalus would not be in the "best interests" of the newborn because it would cause a grave hardship and would be of little or no benefit for the newborn and those responsible for his or her care. The medical facts presented confirm that there is no proportionate reason for prolonging the life of a newborn with a Grade IV massive intraventricular hemorrhage and progressive hydrocephalus. This newborn has irreversible damage to the brain and other major organs and the newborn's prognosis is extremely poor with a high mortality rate. This newborn's ability to relate to others is completely or almost nearly lost in the mere struggle for physical survival. Human relationships would no longer function as the heart and meaning of this newborn's life as they should.[64] To continue treatment on a newborn in this diagnostic category would only devalue the life of the newborn. This is because it would remove the newborn's life from the Christian context and story that is the source of its ultimate value.

In support of McCormick's position regarding not treating a newborn with a Grade IV massive intraventricular hemorrhage is the third norm of his quality-of-life criterion. The third norm used to specify the capacity for human relationships states: "Life sustaining interventions may be omitted or withdrawn when there is excessive hardship, especially when this combines with poor prognosis." The prognosis for a newborn with a Grade IV massive intraventricular hemorrhage is very poor. The mortality rate is between 50% to 90%. According to neonatologists, to initiate or continue medical treatment would do harm to the well-being of this newborn. McCormick's quality-of-life judgments must avoid doing harm to all patients.[65] To treat a newborn in this situation would violate the basic principle of bioethics: "*non nocere*" (do no harm). However, even though a decision has been made to forgo or withdraw medical treatment, newborns in this category should continue to receive humane and necessary palliative care that will relieve pain and suffering, because every human life is sacred, is of incalculable worth, and deserves to be treated with dignity and respect.

In conclusion, when the handicapped newborn has the potential for human relationships but this potential is utterly submerged in the mere struggle for survival, parents can decide in the newborn's "best interests" not to seek medical treatment. Parents can reasonably determine that treatment is not in the "best interests" of this newborn, because it offers no

---

[62] McCormick, *Health And Medicine In The Catholic Tradition*, 54.

[63] McCormick, "The Best Interests Of The Baby," 23.

[64] McCormick, "To Save Or Let Die," *How Brave A New World?*, 347.

[65] For McCormick, the well-being of a patient consists generally in a life prolonged beyond infancy, without excruciating pain, and with the potential for participating, to at least a minimal degree, in human experience. For a more detailed analysis of this position, see McCormick, "A Proposal For 'Quality Of Life' Criteria For Sustaining Life," 79.

benefit to this newborn "integrally and adequately considered." McCormick believes this moral judgment is not only reasonable but is firmly grounded in the Catholic theological tradition.

Category 3: The Handicapped Newborn Who Has the Potential for Human Relationships but the Underlying Medical Condition will Result in Imminent Death

An anomaly that is representative of the newborn who has a potential for human relationships but the underlying medical condition will result in imminent death is a newborn with hypoplastic left heart syndrome. Hypoplastic left heart syndrome encompasses a variety of specific cardiovascular malformations producing similar hemodynamic and clinical manifestations, including aortic atresia, mitral atresia, permanent closure of the foramen ovale, and aortic stenosis. The left heart chamber is usually very small, and endocardial fibroelastosis is common.[66] Hypoplastic left heart syndrome occurs in 10.2% of infants with severe heart disease and is one of the most common lesions presenting in the first week of life. It is less common in very premature newborns (<1.85kg). It is usually an isolated lesion, although it has been described in association with autosomal trisomy syndromes and in infants of diabetic mothers (10.9%). Familial cases occur.[67] The etiology is unknown. However, it is postulated that the cause is premature closure of foramen ovale, abnormally large ductus arteriosus, and autosomal recessive.[68]

---

[66] Endocardial fibroelastosis is the thickening of the endocardium into a fibroelastic layer of tissue which may occur in the left ventricle of the hypoplastic heart. For a more detailed analysis, see Avery *et al.*, *Neonatology* , 551-552.

[67] Ibid., 551. It should be noted that a study performed by Marvin Natowicz, M.D. *et al.*, found that as in other complex congenital heart lesions, the prevalence of underlying genetic causes of and major extra cardiac anomalies associated with hypoplastic left heart syndrome is substantial--28% in this study. Natowicz writes: "For many of the genetic disorders we identified, the association with hypoplastic left heart syndrome that we observed is not unexpected. Thus, the association of the syndrome with the chromosomal disorders that we found in our series is not surprising because all of these chromosomal syndromes are associated with high incidence of congenital heart disease. An association between hypoplastic left heart syndrome and trisomy 13, trisomy 18, trisomy 21, and Turner syndrome has, in fact, been noted previously, as has an association with duplication 12p, duplication 16q, monosomy 4p, and monosomy 11q syndromes. Similarly, an association between Smith-Lemli-Opitz, Apert, and Holt-Oram syndromes and hypoplastic left heart syndrome is probably not fortuitous in that each is frequently associated with congenital heart disease." Marvin Natowicz, M.D. *et al.*, "Genetic Disorders And Major Extra Cardiac Anomalies Associated With Hypoplastic Left Heart Syndrome," *Pediatrics* 82 (November 1988): 702-704. This is an important point because in addition to the anomaly of hypoplastic left heart syndrome there is usually associated with this anomaly other serious genetic disorders. These associated genetic disorders will play a major role in the decision-making process of whether such newborns should receive medical treatment.

[68] The foramen ovale is a normal feature of the heart allowing blood to flow between atria. A ductus arteriosus is a normally occurring shunt between the aorta and the pulmonary artery. In utero, the ductus arteriosus allows blood flow to be diverted from the high-resistance pulmonary circulation to the descending aorta and the low-resistance placental bed. Functional closure of the ductus arteriosus occurs soon after birth but can be delayed in premature infants and in certain situations. Finally, autosomal has to do with any of the 22 chromosome pairs not associated with sex determination. For a more detailed analysis, see Avery *et al.*, *Neonatology*, 551-553; see also Denise Kirsten, "Patent Ductus Arteriosus In The Preterm Infant," *Neonatal Network* 15 (March 1996): 19-26.

The diagnosis can be made with echocardiography by demonstrating a very small or unrecognizable left ventricle.[69] The ascending aorta is small with retrograde flow in cases of aortic atresia, and there is frequently a discrete juxtaductal coarctation. Newborns become symptomatic within the first week of life. It is estimated that 40% are diagnosed in the second day of life, 75% in the sixth day of life and 86% in the thirteenth day of life. The clinical picture of hypoplastic left heart syndrome may be simulated by respiratory distress syndrome, interrupted aortic arch, severe complex coarctation, early neonatal myocarditis, isolated critical valvar aortic stenosis, sepsis or some inherited metabolic disorders. Within the first few days of life the newborn will develop congestive heart failure and a shocklike picture may develop precipitously. The newborn becomes ashen gray with poor peripheral perfusion, and all pulses are weak. Ductal constriction may be intermittent, with femoral pulses intermittently palpable. Symptoms and signs of congestive heart failure are associated with hypotension and, terminally, with bradycardia.[70] The chest radiograph shows cardiac enlargement and pulmonary plethora, and the electrocardiogram (ECG) usually demonstrates right axis deviation, right atrial hypertrophy, right ventricular hypertrophy, and markedly diminished or absent left ventricular forces.[71]

The prognosis for a newborn with hypoplastic left heart syndrome is very poor. Without surgery, the mortality rate is 98% by one year of age. The mean age of survival is four to twenty-three days. There are few survivors with mitral atresia or hypoplastic left ventricle with severe aortic and mitral stenosis. Therefore, three options are given. The first option is surgical correction, which is done in two or three stages. This technique has variable results; survival is only fair after both procedures.[72] Neonatal cardiac transplantation is a second option with good results at some centers, but the shortage of donors is a problem. Palliative care (keeping the newborn comfortable until death) is the third option. The two main methods of treatment have high fiscal and emotional costs.[73]

---

[69] Echocardiography is examination of the structures and movements of the heart with reflected pulsed ultrasound. As a non-invasive investigation employing non-ionizing energy, it has become established as a useful additional method of evaluating heart disease. For a more detailed analysis, see Avery *et al.*, *Neonatology*, 552-553.

[70] Bradycardia is an abnormally slow rate of heart beat (usually taken as 60 per minute or less). For a more detailed analysis, see Ibid., 1361-1362.

[71] Avery et al., *Neonatology*, 552.

[72] The first is palliation (the Norwood procedure), redirecting the blood flow so that the right ventricle serves as the "systemic ventricle," and is high risk intervention. The second stage (Fontan procedure) directs the systemic venous return directly to the pulmonary circulation and the atrial septal defect is closed. The Fontan procedure may be done in two stages. Ibid.

[73] For a more detailed analysis of hypoplastic left heart syndrome, see Gomella et al., 339-340; D. L. Williams, A.C. Gelijns, A.J. Moskowicz et al., "Hypoplastic Left Heart Syndrome: Valuing The Survival," *Journal of Thorascic Cardiovascular Surgery* 19 (April 2000): 720-731; S.H. Daebritz, G.D. Nollert et al., "Results of Norwood Stage I Operation: Comparison of Hypoplastic Left Heart Syndrome With Other Malformations," *Journal of Thorascic Cardiovascular Surgery* 119 (February 2000): 358-367; S. Weinstein G.W. Gaynor, N.D. Bridges et al., "Early Survival of Infants Weighing 2.5 Kilograms or Less Undergoing First-Stage Reconstruction For Hypoplastic Left Heart Syndrome," *Circulation* 100 (November 9, 1999): Supplement III-167-170; W. A. Long, *Fetal And Neonatal Cardiology* (Philadelphia, PA.: W. B. Sanders, 1990); J. H. Moller and W. A. Neal, *Fetal, Neonatal, And Infant Cardiac Disease* (Norfolk, CT.: Appleton and Lange, 1989); M.B. Munn, "Prenatally Diagnosed Hypoplastic Left Heart Syndrome--Outcomes After Postnatal Surgery," *Journal of Maternal Fetal Medicine* 8 (July-August 1999): 147-150; and Leonard L. Bailey *et al.*, "Cardiac Allotransplanation In Newborns As Therapy For Hypoplastic Left Heart Syndrome," *The New England Journal Of Medicine* 315 (October 9, 1986): 949-951.

In this third diagnostic treatment category, since the potential for human relationships is present, McCormick will use the second guideline of his quality-of-life criterion--the benefit-burden calculus--to determine whether newborns ought to be treated. What is to be determined is whether the burden of the treatment will outweigh the benefit to the newborn. If the parents in consultation with the health care professionals determine that further medical treatment would not improve the newborn's prognosis, or benefit the overall well-being of the newborn, then, all things considered, parents should decide that further treatment would not be in the "best interests" of the newborn.

In examining the newborns in this category as applied to hypoplastic left heart syndrome, what must remain at the forefront are the "best interests," normatively defined, of the newborn and those involved in the decision-making process. In the case of the newborn with hypoplastic left heart syndrome it appears that further medical treatment would not be in the "best interests" of these newborns. Any benefit obtained would be outweighed by the burdens. A newborn diagnosed with hypoplastic left heart syndrome has the additional complication of a high incidence of chromosomal disorders. This is a major factor that must be taken into consideration. Without surgery the mortality rate for this newborn is 98%. Heart transplantation is a possible medical option, but it must be remembered that there are very few hearts available for transplantation and heart transplantation is an experimental procedure. Even with surgery, which has a high fiscal and emotional cost, the mortality rate remains high.[74] Any possible medical benefits obtained by this type of surgery would be outweighed by the social and familial burdens.[75]

McCormick's notion of a normative understanding of "best interests" considers not only the relevant medical facts but also the relevant social and familial factors. Financial and emotional costs ought to be considered. That means, if the social factors are excessive, then the newborn should not and would not want to be treated, because it would place excessive burdens on those who must care for the newborn's existence. What the newborn "ought" to want should encompass the needs of those who will care for this child. This anomaly entails extensive surgeries, long-term hospitalization, long-term home care, and there are serious genetic disorders associated with hypoplastic left heart syndrome that will entail additional treatment and serious financial and emotional burdens for the family. Both social and familial factors ought to play a proportionate role in determining the benefit/burden calculus.[76]

[74] It should be remembered that Avery *et al.* believe that neither reconstructive surgery leading to a Fontan procedure or cardiac transplantation can be viewed as curative. See Avery *et al.*, *Neonatology*, 552. For a more detailed analysis of heart transplantation in newborns, see Leonard L. Bailey *et al.*, "Cardiac Allotransplantation In Newborns As Therapy For Hypoplastic Left Heart Syndrome," *New England Journal Of Medicine*, 949-951.

[75] In McCormick's notion of "best interests" the benefits are not restricted to medical benefits. Benefits also apply to social and familial factors. This can be seen in how McCormick has incorporated Pellegrino's four components of "best interests" into his interpretation. For a more detailed analysis of Pellegrino's four components, see Pellegrino, "Moral Choice, The Good Of The Patient And The Patient's Good," in *Ethics And Critical Care Medicine*, 117-138.

[76] It should be noted that McCormick's position on social and familial factors has been criticized for being too restrictive and deviating from both the Catholic tradition and from his own normative understanding of "best interests." McCormick claims that his restrictive notion of social and familial factors, as they pertain to treatment decisions for handicapped newborns, is due to the fact that a broader interpretation could lead to social utilitarianism. This caution is certainly relevant because the possibility of potential abuse is always present. However, the safeguards McCormick has built into his quality-of-life criterion--guidelines and norms--should

In conclusion, when a handicapped newborn has the potential for human relationships but the underlying medical consdition will result in imminent death, parents in consultation with health care professionals are not morally obliged to initiate treatment or continue medical treatment. It is clear that the burdens out weight the benefits to the newborn. Therefore, it is in the best interest of the newborn and all concerened to withdraw or forego medical treatment for a newborn in these circumstances.

Category 4: The Handicapped Newborn Has the Potential for Human Relationships but after Medical Treatment Has Been Initiated, It Becomes Apparent that the Treatment May Be Medically Futile

An anomaly that is representative of a newborn who has the potential for human relationships but after initiating treatment, it becomes apparent that the treatment may be medically futile, is a newborn with full length small and large bowel Necrotizing Enterocolitis (NEC) with perforation. It is a major cause of mortality and morbidity in newborns with birth weights less than 1,500 gms.[77] NEC is a condition predominantly seen in premature newborns, which is characterized by partial- or full-thickness intestinal ischemia, usually involving the terminal ileum.[78] NEC is probably the most serious gastrointestinal disorder occurring in newborns. Because NEC appears predominantly in sick, low-birth-weight newborns, the incidence has increased in recent years as the mortality rate for very low-birth-weight newborns has decreased. It has been estimated that 90% of cases occur in preterm newborns with an incidence of 8 to 12% in newborns < 1.5 kg.[79] Thus, the more premature the newborn, the longer the duration of risk. The etiology is not fully known. Multiple factors appear to be involved, including hypoxia, acidosis, and hypotension, which may lead to ischemic damage of the mucosal barrier of the small intestine. Secondary bacterial invasion of the mucosa may be involved in the pathogenesis of pneumatosis intestinalis. Other factors considered to increase the risk of NEC are umbilical artery catheterization, infection with certain types of bacteria, and hypoalbuminemia.[80] Although the cause is uncertain, the histopathology is well established.[81]

---

help to alleviate the possibility of such abuse. In addition, health care professionals serve as a safeguard in that they can act as the newborn's advocate should they suspect abuse.

[77] NEC is the most common surgical emergency in newborns; the mortality exceeds that of all gastrointestinal tract congenital malformations combined. It is the third leading cause of neonatal death, with a 30 to 50 percent mortality rate. For a more detailed analysis, see Leslie A. Parker, "Necrotizing Enterocolitis," *Neonatal Network* 14 (September 1995): 17.

[78] The ileum is the part of the small intestine between the jejunum (the second part of the small intestine extending from the duodenum to the ileum) and the caecum (the first part of the large intestine, situated in the right lower quadrant of the abdomen, which forms a pouch-like cavity connecting the terminal ileum to the ascending colon and the vermiform appendix). For a more detailed description, see *The Oxford Medical Companion*, eds. John Walton, Jeremiah Barondess, and Stephen Lock (Oxford: Oxford University Press, 1994), 397.

[79] The incidence increases with decreasing gestational age. Sixty percent to 80% of cases occur in high-risk premature newborns, while 10-25% occur in low-risk and full-term newborns. Newborns with NEC represent 2-5% of NICU admissions. Gomella et al., 452.

[80] It can be noted that NEC has been observed to occur in epidemics in neonatal intensive care units, further supporting the role of microbial agents in pathogenesis. For a more detailed analysis, see Avery *et al.*, *Neonatology*, 614. It should also be noted that another risk factor for NEC that is gaining acceptance is maternal

The diagnosis of NEC is based on both clinical assessment and x-ray studies. The onset of NEC occurs most commonly between day three and day ten of life but may occur as early as the first twenty-four hours of life or as late as three months. Clinical presentations vary widely. Abdominal distension is one of the earliest and most consistent clinical signs, along with an intolerance of feeding with vomiting. The vomitus of about one-half of the newborns is bile stained. Other symptoms include bloody stools, apnea, bradycardia, lethargy, shock, and retention of gastric contents due to poor gastric emptying. Hematest-positive stools help confirm the diagnosis, but blood may be absent or a late finding. Abdominal wall erythema and a palpable abdominal mass are commonly late findings and signify more extensive disease. Radiographic findings in early NEC may show only separated loops of distended intestine, suggesting bowel wall thickening. A persistent large loop of intestine seen on a series of x-ray films has been used by some as an indication of surgery, but these newborns may also be treated medically.[82]

The prognosis for NEC depends on the severity of the disease. Initial management of the newborn with NEC without pneumoperitoneum is standardized.[83] The newborn receives nothing orally, the stomach is decompressed with a gastric sump tube, and intravenous antibiotics are begun. Indications for surgery include pneumoperitoneum, persistent acidosis (i.e., pH less than 7.2), rapidly worsening pulmonary status, and unremitting neutropenia or thrombocytopenia.[84] Mortality is higher in newborns who have perforated before surgery, and it is therefore better to operate before perforation has occurred. Surgery in newborns with perforation should be expeditious and conservative. The frankly necrotic or perforated intestine should be removed and ileostomies formed.[85] When massive resection is necessary, the chance for the newborn's survival is limited, but the premature newborn's intestine still has the potential for growth and adaption, and rarely is the entire intestine involved in the

cocaine use. Leslie Parker writes: "Cocaine may cause mesenteric ischemia via two mechanisms: (1) Cocaine causes maternal vasoconstriction, which decreases uterine blood flow and leads to fetal hypoxia. (2) Cocaine crosses the placenta and causes fetal vasoconstriction and subsequent hypoxia. Cocaine exposed neonates with NEC tend to be more critically ill than other infants with NEC. Because the bowel is more necrotic, these infants have an increased need for surgical intervention, and their overall mortality is increased." For a more detailed analysis, see Parker, "Necrotizing Enterocolitis," 20.

[81] Initially, the disease begins as mucosal ischemia, with resultant sloughing of this layer. As the disease progresses, gas develops within the muscular layers and may be seen on x-ray films as pneumatosis cystoides intestinalis. If full-thickness necrosis occurs, perforation and peritonitis develop. The rapidity of disease progression differs in each newborn, but those who perforate usually do so within the first days of the disease. Avery *et al.*, *Neonatology*, 614-615; 937-938.

[82] Elizabeth H. Thilo, M.D., Raul Lazarte, M.D., and Jacinto Hernandez, M.D., "Necrotizing Enterocolitis In The First Twenty-Four Hours Of Life," *Pediatrics* 73 (April 1984): 476-480; and Avery *et al.*, *Neonatology*, 937-938.

[83] Pneumoperitoneum is air in the peritoneal cavity. Artificial pneumoperitoneum is sometimes induced in order to assist radiological diagnosis; it was formally a common procedure in the treatment of pulmonary tuberculosis, to help in immobilization of the lung. For a more detailed analysis, see *The Oxford Medical Companion*, 775.

[84] Thrombocytopenia results from either decreased platelet production or increased peripheral platelet destruction or sequestration. A bone marrow examination is usually required to make this distinction. Normally, bone spicules contain 3-10 megakaryocytes per low-power field. Normal or increased numbers of megakaryocytes imply increased platelet consumption. Decreased numbers suggests decreased platelet production. For a more detailed analysis, see William Claiborne Dunagan, M.D. and Michael L. Ridner, M.D., eds., *Manual Of Medical Therapeutics* 26th ed. (Boston, MA.: Little, Brown and Company, 1986), 330.

[85] An ileostomy is a surgically created opening of the ileum on to the abdominal surface. For a more detailed description, see *The Oxford Medical Companion*, 397.

disease.[86] The long-term success rate for treatment for NEC has been good, despite long hospitalization for gastrointestinal adaption when massive resection is necessary. The quoted survival rate for newborns with medically treated NEC is now more than 80%, and the mortality rate for those requiring surgery is 20-40%.[87]

In this fourth diagnostic treatment category, since the potential for human relationships is present, McCormick's second guideline of his quality-of-life criterion--the benefit-burden calculus--would be applied to determine whether these newborns ought to be treated. What is to be determined is whether the burden of the treatment will outweigh the benefit to the newborn. If the parents in consultation with the health care professionals determine that further medical treatment would not improve the newborn's prognosis, or benefit the overall well-being of the newborn, then, all things considered, parents should decide that further treatment would not be in the "best interests" of the newborn. A newborn diagnosed as having full-length small and large bowel NEC with perforation has a high mortality rate and according to medical authorities, further medical treatment is qualitatively futile, that is, any possible medical effect is of no benefit to the newborn. Therefore, it appears that further treatment for newborns in this diagnostic category is not morally obligatory.

It should be noted that in this category of anomalies, the medical facts regarding diagnosis and prognosis are extremely pertinent. There are less severe cases of NEC that can be treated successfully. Each medical anomaly contains individual differences and "gray areas" are always a reality. This is an example of why McCormick argues that consultation with health care professionals is essential for parents in making these treatment decisions. Neonatologists have the medical knowledge and the expertise of comparative judgments of newborns with similar anomalous conditions that can assist parents in the decision-making process. They will be able to assist the parents in making a determination of the effectivenss and burdens of such treatment. The health care professionals can also serve as a check and

---

[86] If an extensive amount of necrotic bowel is resected, there may be an insufficient amount of bowel remaining for digestion. This could result in short gut syndrome and possibly be incompatible with life. See Parker, "Necrotizing Enterocolitis," 21.

[87] For a more detailed analysis of NEC, see Gomella et al., 452-456; Avery *et al.*, *Neonatology*, 614-616; 937-939. M.D. Kamitsuka, M.K. Horton, and M.A. Williams, "The Incidence Of Necrotizing Enterocolitis After Introducing Standardized Feeding Schedules For Infants Between 1250 and 2500 Grams And Less Than 35 Weeks Of Gestation," *Pediatrics* 105 (February 2000): 379-384; J. Neu and M.D. Weiss, "Necrotizing Enterocolitis: Pathophysiology And Prevention," *Journal of Parenteral Enteral Nutrition* 23 (September-October 1999): Supplement 1--3-7; J. Sonntag, M.H. Wagner, J. Waldschmidt et al., "Multisystem Organ Failure And Capillary Leak Syndrome In Severe Necrotizing Enterocolitis Of Very Low Birth Weight Infants," *Journal of Pediatric Surgery* 33 (March 1998); 484-484; R.C. Holman, B.J. Stoll, M.J. Clark et al., "The Epidemiology Of Necrotizing Enterocolitis Infant Mortality In The United States,"*American Journal of Public Health* 87 (December 1997): 2026-2031; C. L. Snyder, G.K. Gittes, J.P. Murphy et al., "Survival After Necrotizing Enterocolitis In Infants Weighing Less Than 1,000 Grams: 25 Years' Experience At A Single Institution," *Journal of Pediatric Surgery* 32 (March 1997): 434-437; E. Tallo-Martinez, N. Claure and E. Bancalari, "Necrotizing Enterocolitis In Full Term And Near-Term Infants: Risk Factors," *Biological Neonate* 71 (1997): 292-298; W. A. Ballance *et al.*, "Pathology Of Neonatal NEC: A Ten Year Experience," *Journal Of Pediatric Medicine, Supplement 1, Pt. 2* 117 (1990); and D. Anderson, and R. M. Kliegman, "The Relationship Of Neonatal Alimentation Practices To The Occurrence Of Endemic Necrotizing Enterocolitis," *American Journal Of Perinatology* 8 (1991).

balance to ensure the best interests of the newborn are being protected.[88] In this category, as in the previous one, social and familial factors ought to be considered. These factors play an appropraite role in moral decision-making.

In conclusion, when a handicapped newborn has the potential for human relationships but after initiating treatment, it becomes apparent that the treatment is medically futile, parents in consultation with health care professionals are not morally obliged to continue medical treatment. This is a value judgment that is based on McCormick's guidelines of relational potential and benefit/burden calculus. McCormick's quality-of-life criterion sets basic parameters and enlightens the particular medical situation. Ultimately, the parents will use prudence to examine the medical facts and to weigh, all things considered, whether the burdens of treatment outweigh the benefits to the newborn. In this diagnostic treatment category, the burdens and benefits need to be weighed carefully. With the severity of this particular medical anomaly the burdens frequently outweigh the benefits to the newborn. Therefore, in the "best interests" of the newborn, and all concerned, parents in consultation with health care professionals have the moral obligation to forgo or withdraw treatment for a newborn in these circumstances.

Category 5: The Handicapped Newborn who has the Potential for Human Relationships and has a Correctable or Treatable Condition

An anomaly that is representative of this diagnostic treatment category is a newborn with trisomy 21 (Down syndrome) and the complication of esophageal atresia with tracheoesophageal fistula. Trisomy 21 or Down syndrome is caused by a faulty chromosome distribution. In about 95% of cases of Down syndrome, there is an extra chromosome 21. The overall incidence is about 1/700 live births, but there is a marked variability depending on maternal age.[89] The extra chromosome 21 comes from the father in one-fourth to one-third of the cases.

Esophageal atresia occurs approximately in 1 of 3000 to 4500 births. In the most common form of esophageal anomaly (86% of newborns), the blind-ending upper esophageal segment usually extends into the upper portion of the thorax, and the lower portion of the esophagus is connected to the trachea at or just above the tracheal carina. This connection is usually 3 to 5 mm in diameter and easily admits air or, in a retrograde fashion, acidic gastric secretions.[90]

The clinical diagnosis of a newborn with Down syndrome would be a newborn who tends to be placid, rarely cries, and demonstrates muscular hypotonicity. Nuchal lymphedema, similar to that seen in Turner's syndrome, also occurs in Down syndrome and is being

---

[88] To serve as an advocate for these neonates, time should be allowed for the clinical picture to emerge, consultation and confirmation with other colleagues must be sought, there should be frequent assessment of the neonate's prognosis, and neonatologists should not categorize neonates too early or change their categories too late.

[89] In the early childbearing years, the incidence of Down syndrome is about 1/2000 live births; for mothers over 40 years of age, it rises to about 1/40 live births. Just over 20% of newborns with Down syndrome are born to mothers > 35 years of age, yet these older mothers have only 7% to 8% of the children. However, the number of women having babies after age 35 has been rising rapidly in the last few years. For a more detailed analysis, see Robert Berkow, M.D., *The Merck Manual*, 2299.

[90] Avery *et al.*, *Neonatology*, 923.

detected with increasing frequency prenatally by fetal ultrasonography.[91] Physical and mental development are retarded; the mean IQ is about 50. Microcephaly, brachycephaly, and a flattened occiput are characteristic. The eyes are slanted, and epicanthal folds are present. Congenital heart disease is found in about 35% of patients; atrioventricular canal defects and ventricular septal defects are most common.[92]

The diagnosis of esophageal atresia may not be obvious on the initial examination of a newborn unless an attempt is made to pass a tube into the stomach. The earliest clinical sign is excessive oral secretions, regurgitation of saliva, and cyanosis. The saliva collects in the blind-ending esophagus and then accumulates until it is apparent around the lips as excessive mucus. The first feeding is followed by choking, coughing, and regurgitation. Abdominal distention is a prominent feature, occurring as inspired air is transmitted through the fistula and distal esophagus into the stomach. Gastric juice may pass upward in the distal esophagus, transversing the tracheoesophageal fistula and spilling into the trachea and lungs, leading to chemical pneumonia. A contrast x-ray film confirms the diagnosis of atresia; a lateral projection with 1 ml of dilute barium or an isoosmolar contrast agent (e.g., metrizamide) shows the length of the upper pouch, defines its precise extension into the chest, and demonstrates the rare upper pouch fistula. Esophageal atresia has become more frequently recognized during maternal ultrasonography. Failure to visualize a fetal stomach in a mother who has polyhydramnios suggests esophageal atresia. Prenatal diagnosis permits a search for associated problems and allows a comprehensive, coordinated approach to the family and newborn in the prenatal period.[93]

The prognosis for a Down syndrome newborn who has esophageal atresia with tracheoesophageal fistula is excellent.[94] The aim of preoperative management is to prevent aspiration pneumonia that makes surgical correction more hazardous. Oral feedings are withheld. A double lumen suction catheter is inserted into the upper esophageal pouch and attached to continuous suction to prevent aspiration of swallowed saliva. When the newborn is stable, immediate primary repair is undertaken. If unstable, surgery is delayed until the clinical status is stabilized, the impact of associated anomalies is determined, and the newborn can be anesthetized and operated on safely. When the newborn is stable, a thoracotomy can be done to repair the esophageal atresia and close the tracheoesophageal

---

[91] Lymphedema is the accumulation of excessive lymph fluid and swelling of subcutaneous tissues due to obstruction, destruction, or hypoplasia of lymph vessels. For a more detailed analysis, see Robert Berkow, M.D., *The Merck Manual*, 593. Turner's syndrome, also known as Gonadal Dygenesis or Bonnevie-Ullrich syndrome, is a complete or partial absence of one of the two X chromosomes in the female. Its incidence is about 1/3000 live female births. For a more detailed analysis, see Ibid., 2305.

[92] In addition, Brushfield's spots (gray to white spots resembling grains of salt around the periphery of the iris) usually are visible in the neonatal period and disappear during the first twelve months of life. The bridge of the nose is flattened, the mouth is often held open because of a large, protruding tongue that is furrowed and lacks the central fissure, and the ears are small with down-folded helixes. The hands are short and broad, with single palmar crease (simian crease); the fingers are short, with clinodactyly (incurvature) of the fifth finger, which often has two phalanges. The feet have a wide gap between the first and the second toes, and a plantar furrow extends backward. Hands and feet show characteristic dermal prints (dermatoglyphics). Ibid., 2299-2301.

[93] Avery *et al*., *Neonatology*, 923-924.

[94] It should be noted that the life expectancy of a Down syndrome newborn without major heart defects is about 45-50 years of age. Robert Berkow, M.D., *The Merck Manual*, 2301-2302.

fistula.[95] Occasionally, the gap between the esophageal segments is too great for a primary repair. Gentle stretching of the esophageal segments before later anastomosis may be beneficial, or repair by interposing a segment of colon or forming a gastric tube between the esophageal segments may be required. The most common acute complications are leakage at the site of anastomosis and stricture formation. If there is no leakage feedings are begun and quickly advanced.[96] The survival rate for newborns who were classified as stable and had primary repair is 100%. Survival in the unstable group who had staged repair is 57%. The deaths were due to associated anomalies, including congenital diaphragmatic hernia and hypoplastic left heart syndrome.[97]

To determine whether a Down syndrome newborn who has esophageal atresia with tracheoesophageal fistula ought to be treated, both guidelines of McCormick's quality-of-life criterion will be applied. In this situation the handicapped newborn has the potential for human relationships. This newborn will in relative comfort be able to experience our caring and love. Thus, both the parents and the newborn will be able to share in the higher, more important good. Continued physical existence will offer this newborn hope of sharing those values for which physical life is a fundamental condition.[98] Secondly, the benefits of proper medical treatment clearly outweigh the burdens. According to the medical authorities, a newborn with Down syndrome associated with esophageal atresia and tracheoesophageal fistula has an excellent chance of living a productive life with corrective surgery. Therefore, all things considered, there is a proportionate reason to seek corrective surgery in this situation, because it is in the "best interests" of the newborn and those involved in the decision-making process.

The decision to treat is also supported by the second norm established by McCormick and John Paris as a further specification of the capacity for human relationships as a summary of the benefit/burden calculus. The norm states: "Life-sustaining interventions may not be

---

[95] The fistula is identified and carefully divided from the trachea. The tracheal opening is closed with several sutures, with care to avoid narrowing the tracheal lumen. The circumference of the lower esophageal fistula is usually small and is enlarged by trimming and spatulating its open end. The tip of the upper pouch is mobilized extensively and cut across to expose the lumen. For a more detailed analysis, see Avery *et al.*, *Neonatology*, 924-925.

[96] It should be noted that in the early 1900's, virtually all newborns born with esophageal atresia and tracheoesophageal fistula died. In 1941 Haight and Towsley were the first to bring a newborn with esophageal atresia and tracheoesophageal fistula through the rigors of primary transthoracic reconstruction. This landmark accomplishment occurred before antibiotics, respiratory support, or sophisticated intravenous nutrition were available. This surgical approach formed the basis of modern operative and postoperative care of newborns with this anomaly. Fifty years after the first survivor was announced, every newborn born with atresia of the esophagus who is spared coexisting fatal anomalies and is offered appropriate care has an excellent chance of leading a normal life. In a study done at Children's National Medical Center in Washington, D.C. 118 patients with blind upper esophageal pouch and a fistula arising from the bifurcation of the trachea were treated between 1966 and 1989. Eighty-eight percent of the patients survived. For a more detailed analysis, see Ibid., 923-926.

[97] Ibid., 923-927; Gomella, 533-534, and Berkow, *The Merck Manual*, 2065-2067. For a more detailed analysis of esophageal atresia with tracheoesophageal fistula, see L. Spitz, E. Keily, R. J. Brereton, "Esophageal Atresia: A Five Year Experience With 148 Cases," *Journal Of Pediatric Surgery* 22 (1987): 103-106; J. G. Randolph, K. Newman, K. D. Anderson, "Current Results And Repair Of Esophageal Atresia With Tracheoesophageal Fistula Using Physiologic Status As A Guide To Therapy," *Annals Of Surgery* 209 (1989): 520-526; and E. C. Pohlson, R. Schaller, and D. Trapper, "Improved Survival With Primary Anastomosis In The Low-Birth-Weight Neonate With Esophageal Atresia And Tracheoesophageal Fistula," *Journal Of Pediatric Surgery* 24 (1988): 415-420.

[98] McCormick, "To Save Or Let Die," *How Brave A New World?*, 351.

omitted simply because the baby is retarded. There may be further complications associated with retardation that justify withholding life-sustaining treatment." In this situation, all things considered, there is a proportionate reason to treat this Down syndrome newborn because the complication associated with the retardation can be corrected with a very high probability of success. As long as the medical condition is treatable or correctable and the corrected condition will result in improvement of the newborn's prognosis, comfort, and well-being or general state of health, then this is looked upon as a beneficial treatment and under the benefit/burden calculus it ought to be made available to this newborn. Failure to treat a Down syndrome newborn with a correctable condition would be allowing a cultural bias to distort the basic value of human life.

In conclusion, when a handicapped newborn has the potential for human relationships and an associated medical condition that is treatable or correctable, and thus there is a great benefit to the patient, parents have a moral obligation to treat this newborn. The guidelines and norms advanced by McCormick's quality-of-life criterion assist parents in consultation with health care professionals to examine the range of moral choices and to determine what is in the "best interests" of this newborn normatively understood.

Critical Assessment of McCormick's Moral Criterion

Complex bioethical dilemmas challenge society to search for answers and to formulate policies regarding issues ranging from the first moments of life to the last moments before death. Contemporary theologians have been challenged to address these issues from a theological perspective; but there has been little clarity about how this should be done and what impact this will have on reasonable people. Alasdair MacIntyre has attempted to make this challenge more clear. "What ought we to expect from contemporary theologians in the area of medical ethics? First--and without this everything else is uninteresting--we ought to expect a clear statement of what difference it makes to be a Jew or a Christian or a Moslem rather than a secular thinker."[99] McCormick has attempted to answer MacIntyre's challenge from a Christian perspective. He has stipulated in his moral criterion what it means to be a Christian and how the Christian story impacts on the decision-making process in bioethics. After applying his moral criterion to the five diagnostic treatment categories of handicapped newborns, this author will now assess whether his moral criterion is practical, beneficial, and appropriate for Christian decision-makers.

McCormick believes and this author concurs that his moral criterion is practical, beneficial, and appropriate for Christian decision-makers in making treatment decisions for handicapped newborns, because it is reasonable and is grounded in the Judaeo-Christian tradition. Before making an assessment on this statement it is first necessary to examine what these terms mean. The term "practical" means useful. In this context it refers to whether McCormick's moral criterion is capable of being used or put into effect by Christian decision-makers. Specifically, when it is applied to neonatal anomalies, does it assist Christian decision-makers in coming to a well-reasoned conclusion? Does his moral criterion give

[99] Alasdair MacIntyre, "Theological Ethics And The Ethics Of Medicine And Health Care," *Journal Of Medicine And Philosophy* 4 (1979): 435.

Christian decision-makers various choices within given parameters? "Beneficial" refers to promoting the well-being of the handicapped newborn. When applied to neonatal anomalies, does McCormick's moral criterion promote the "best interests," normatively understood, of the handicapped newborn and all concerned in the decision-making process? "Appropriate" refers to suitability. Is McCormick's moral criterion fitting for the needs of particular handicapped newborns? That is, does it adequately consider the relevant medical data, the pertinent circumstances of the situation, the religious and cultural values of the family, and other applicable factors that should be considered in the process of decision-making? These questions will have to be addressed in order to give McCormick's moral criterion a proper assessment.

As a "revised" natural law ethicist, McCormick believes that reason is shaped by faith, and this shaping takes the form of perspectives, themes, and insights associated with the Christian story. Rooted in "revised" natural law, McCormick believes his moral criterion is practical for decision-makers because it sets certain parameters for parents in the decision-making process. His moral criterion is not a wooden formula that parents can apply to any situation and come to a concrete decision. Instead, his moral criterion illuminates a certain situation so that the facts of the situation are made clearer and the decision-makers can see, as much as possible, the full content and context of the situation. The guidelines and norms that make-up McCormick's moral criterion serve to guide and assist parents and health care professionals, not to make decisions for them. They cannot assure moral certitude. Doubts and conflicts will always be part of the decision-making process. What McCormick's moral criterion does is to allow parents a certain range of choices, a certain margin of error, a certain space, so that within those parameters they can use prudence to come to a well-reasoned moral decision.[100] As long as the decisions reached are reasonable and do not deviate too far from the newborn's "best interests," normatively understood, these decisions should be respected. McCormick believes, and most parents and health care professionals would agree, that his moral criterion, being reasonable and grounded in a time honored tradition, can assist Christian decision-makers on a practical level in making treatment decisions for handicapped newborns.

This author would agree with McCormick's assessment that his moral criterion is practical for Christian decision-makers. Rooted in right reason informed by faith, McCormick's moral criterion keeps Christian decision-makers focused on the "best interests" of the handicapped newborn. The Christian story provides a framework that illuminates the situation for Christian decision-makers. It clarifies what it means to be truly human, thus assisting Christian decision-makers to remain focused on the "best interests" of the newborn. McCormick's quality-of-life criterion sets limits and helps to guide Christian decision-makers in their use of right reason in deciding whether certain medical treatments will promote the "best interests" of the handicapped newborn. McCormick's moral criterion is practical because it sets up a structure with certain parameters in which Christian decision-makers have the flexibility to use their prudence in making well-reasoned decisions.

To determine if certain medical treatments are beneficial for a handicapped newborn, that is, will they promote the well-being of the newborn, McCormick proposes his category of "best interests" normatively understood. As previously stated, this is a patient-centered,

---

[100] McCormick and Paris, "Saving Defective Infants," *How Brave A New World?*, 360.

teleological assessment of what is considered to be in the "best interests" of the handicapped newborn and those involved in the decision-making process. McCormick's "best interests" category is a composite category that involves quality-of-life considerations, benefit-burden considerations, and the use of proportionate reason as a tool for establishing what is promotive or destructive for the good of the person "integrally and adequately considered." His understanding of "best interests" is grounded in his "revised" natural law position and in the Judaeo-Christian tradition.[101] McCormick assumes that most people are reasonable, and because they are reasonable that they will choose what is in the "best interests" of the handicapped newborn. He believes this is a safe and protective guideline. McCormick argues that most people want to act reasonably within parameters that are objective in character, even though they do not always do so.[102] In the event that decision-makers fail to act reasonably, McCormick proposes several internal and external safeguards that can be used to protect the newborn's "best interests."[103]

In this author's judgment McCormick's moral criterion is beneficial in determining treatment decisions for the handicapped newborn, because it is reasonable and it is grounded in a tradition that keeps the focus of the decision on what will promote the "best interests," normatively understood, of the newborn. Being reasonable people, this author would agree with McCormick's assumption that most people do want to act reasonably within parameters that are objective in character. His moral criterion sets those objective parameters and after applying it to the five diagnostic treatment categories of handicapped newborns, McCormick has shown them to be reasonable. His category of "best interests" normatively understood allows parents and health care professionals a certain discretion in their decision-making, but at the same time, there are built-in safeguards to protect the newborn against irresponsible decision-making.

McCormick argues that his moral criterion is appropriate for decision-makers because it considers not only the relevant medical facts and the pertinent circumstances of the situation, but also familial and social factors, such as, religious, cultural, emotional, and financial factors. Parents in consultation with health care professionals can best determine what the handicapped newborn ought to want and protect his or her "best interests" by using McCormick's quality-of-life moral criterion. As reasonable people, parents are most knowledgeable about the family situation into which the newborn is born. This includes

---

[101] This refers to McCormick's claim that his quality-of-life criterion has its foundation in the traditional ordinary/extraordinary means distinction that was later clarified by Pius XII. For a more detailed analysis, see Pius XII, "The Prolongation of Life," 1,031-1,032.

[102] McCormick, "The Rights Of The Voiceless," *How Brave A New World?*, 104-105.

[103] The internal safeguards would be the guidelines and norms McCormick proposes in his quality-of-life criterion. These are objective criteria that can be used by parents and health care professionals in discerning treatment decisions. The external safeguards, proposed by McCormick, are in the form of checks and balances that serve and protect the "best interests" of the newborn against the possibility of irresponsible decision-makers. These checks and balances are both individual and societal. Parents are the primary decision-makers; but for McCormick, health care professionals should always be consulted because they have the medical expertise, can best explain the diagnosis and prognosis based on similar cases, and they have the ability to compare newborns with the same anomalies and know the effectiveness of various treatments. In this capacity, health care professionals serve as a resource for parents and an advocate for the handicapped newborn. McCormick also advocates societal intervention should it be suspected that parents in consultation with health care professionals are not acting in a morally responsible manner. These safeguards include both Neonatal Infant Review Committees and the court system.

knowing the financial, emotional, and social factors. Parents can also weigh and balance the religious and cultural values that inform their decision-making. Health care professionals have the specialized medical knowledge and clinical expertise that can assist parents in the decision-making process. They also have a level of objectivity that parents may lack because of the overwhelming emotional stress of the situation. Together, parents and health care professionals are able to determine what are the appropriate needs of this newborn, to assess these needs, and to determine whether medical treatment is in the "best interests" of the newborn "integrally and adequately considered."

In this author's judgment McCormick's moral criterion is appropriate for Christian decision-makers because it emphasizes "the reasonable" from within a Christian context. It stresses the need for decision-makers to examine the medical facts, the circumstances of the situation, foreseeable consequences, social and familial factors, and other pertinent data before deciding on an appropriate course of action. McCormick's moral criterion also stresses that these facts are to be considered always within the context of the Christian story, so that the "best interests" of the handicapped newborn are always promoted and protected. Treatment decisions for handicapped newborns are value judgments that must be based on the appropriate needs of the newborn. These value judgments can possibly become distorted by self-interested perspectives and technological considerations. Christian decision-makers who use McCormick's moral criterion are not immune from making mistakes. We are a finite and sinful people. What is being said is that because the content of this moral criterion is reasonable, and because these decisions are made within the context of the Christian story, less chance exists that such treatment decisions will be pushed to the extremes. McCormick's moral criterion is appropriate for Christian decision-makers because it protects the "best interests" of the handicapped newborns by promoting value judgments that are grounded in reason and informed by the Christian story.

In conclusion, McCormick's quality-of-life criterion, as applied to never-competent patients, is based on a normative understanding of the "best interests" of the patient. This criterion has been concretized by his fundamental guidelines of relational potential associated with the newborn's condition and the benefit-burden calculus. However, these are only guidelines; they do not determine decisions. The quality-of-life criterion sets parameters and from within these parameters the appropriate decision-makers must use their reason to decide what is in the "best interests" of the handicapped newborn.

McCormick understands that these guidelines are open to the possibility of being misinterpreted. However, the potential for abuse does not mean they should be discarded. McCormick is attempting to examine new medical situations from within the value-perceptions and commitments of the Catholic tradition. The guidelines and norms he proposes for his quality-of-life criterion are an attempt to help in the decision-making process in regard to never-competent patients.

Parents and health care professionals have been searching for a normative moral criterion that will address the numerous treatment categories of handicapped newborns from an objective standpoint. At the same time, this criterion ought to incorporate individual differences and personal value judgments. This author believes McCormick's quality-of-life criterion gives parents and health care professionals an objective moral criterion for discerning treatment decisions, which is both reasonable and grounded in a tradition that promotes the "best interests," normatively understood, of handicapped newborns. As medicine and medical technology continue to advance parents and health care professionals will continue to be called upon to draw lines regrading treatments for handicapped newborns. In this author's judgment the future of infants born with congenital anomalies will be more humane, because McCormick's quality-of-life criterion will result in more effective courses of action in the medical treatment of these children.

Chapter 4

MENTAL HEALTH PARITY

C. Stephen Redhead

ABSTRACT

Private health insurers often impose more limitations on their coverage of mental illnesses compared to other medical conditions. In 1996, Congress enacted the Mental Health Parity Act (MHPA), which requires group health plans that choose to provide mental health benefits to adopt the same annual and lifetime dollar limits on their coverage of mental and physical illnesses. The MHPA which sunset on September 30, 2001, has been reauthorized through December 31, 2003. House conferences rejected a Senate amendment (S. 543) to the FY2002 Labor-HHS-Education appropriations bill, which would have renewed and expanded the MHPA by requiring plans to provide full parity (i.e., equality) in their mental health coverage. Twenty-three states have enacted parity laws, bur they do not apply to self-insured group plans. Health insurers oppose parity laws because of concerns that they drive up costs. Recent studies suggest that managed behavioral health care organizations can implement parity without significant premium cost increases.

INTRODUCTION

Private health insurers have often provided less coverage for the treatment of mental illnesses than for the treatment of other illnesses. For example, plans have imposed lower annual or lifetime dollar limits on mental health coverage, limited treatment of mental illnesses by covering fewer hospital days and outpatient office visits, and increased cost-sharing for mental health care by raising deductibles and copayments. There are several reasons why the health insurance market restricts mental health coverage. First, the restrictions reflect insurers' concerns about the high costs associated with long-term, intensive psychotherapy and extended hospital stays. Treatment of acute physical illness and surgery often require shorter and more predictable stays and costs. Second, insurers argue that the moral hazard problem is more pronounced in mental health care than it is in general medicine care. Moral hazard refers to the tendency for patients to demand more services as the price they pay for those services falls. While health insurance by its nature creates incentives for overuse by insulating patients from the total costs of care, studies show that the demand response to reduced cost-sharing in mental health care is approximately twice as large as that observed in general medical care.[1] The result has been for insurers to impose higher cost-sharing for mental health care. Finally, health plans restrict mental health coverage to protect themselves from adverse selection. That is, a plan with relatively generous mental health benefits is likely to attract patients with mental illnesses, who require extensive treatment and drive up costs.

Advocates for the mentally ill have long fought for legislation mandating full parity in health insurance coverage of mental and physical illnesses. Under full parity, a plan must impose the same treatment limitations and financial requirements on its mental health coverage as it does on its medical and surgical coverage. Treatment limitations include limitations on the number of visits or days of coverage, or other limits on the duration and scope of treatment. Financial requirements include deductibles, coinsurance copayments, and other cost-sharing requirements, as well as annual and lifetime limits on the total amount of coverage.

Mental health advocates argue that there is no longer any scientific justification for discrimination in mental health coverage, which they believe only reinforces the stigma that many in society attach to mental illness. Their efforts to combat discrimination received a boost with the release of the 1999 Surgeon General's Report on Mental Health.[2] The report reviewed the extensive scientific literature on mental health and concluded that mental illnesses are biologically based disorders just like many other medical conditions. It also found that the efficacy of mental health treatments is well documented, and a range of effective treatments exists for most mental disorders. Mental health experts point out that parity laws can help limit the consequences of adverse selection insofar as they reduce the differences in mental health coverage among plans. According to the National Institute of Mental Health, untreated mental illness cost the nation $79 billion in lost productivity in 1990, the most recent year for which estimates are available.

Health insurers are opposed to parity laws because of concerns that they will drive up costs. But advocacy groups have refuted those claims, pointing to recent studies that show that full parity can be implemented without significant cost increases within the context of comprehensively managed care (see discussion below). A majority of insured Americans now receive their mental health care from managed care companies that specialize in behavioral health (i.e., mental health, substance abuse). Health plans typically subcontract, or carve out, to managed behavioral health care organizations (MBHOs) the management of the mental health component of their benefit package.

---

[1] R.G. Frank and T.G. McGuire, "Economics and Mental Health," in *Handbook of Health Economics*, eds. A.J. Culyer and J.P. Newhouse (Amsterdam: Elsevier, 2000), 893-954.

[2] The Surgeon General's mental health report is available at [http://www.surgeongeneral.gov].

MENTAL HEALTH PARITY ACT OF 1996

In 1996, Congress passed the Mental Health Parity Act (MHPA), which amended the Employee Retirement Income Security Act (ERISA) and the Public Health Service Act to establish new federal standards for mental health coverage offered by group health plans, most of which are employment based.[3] Identical provisions were later added to the Internal Revenue Code by the Taxpayer Relief Act of 1997.[4] The MHPA prohibits group plans from imposing annual and lifetime dollar limits on mental health coverage that are more restrictive than those imposed on medical and surgical coverage. However, the law includes several important limitations. Group plans that chose not to provide mental health benefits are not required to add them, and employers with 50 or fewer employees are exempt from the law. In addition, plans that experience an increase in claims costs of at least 1% as a result of MHPA compliance can apply for an exemption. It is important to note that the MHPA does not require full parity. Group plans may still impose more restrictive treatment limitations or cost-sharing requirements on their mental health coverage compared to their medical and surgical coverage.

The MHPA applies to most group health plans, including fully insured and self-insured plans,[5] but not to the individual (non-group) health insurance market.[6] It also applies to the Federal Employees Health Benefits Program and to some state and local government health plans.[7] Under provisions included in the 1997 Balanced Budget Act (P.L. 105-33), Medicaid managed care plans and State Children's Health Insurance Programs also have to comply with the requirements of the MHPA.[8] The law does not apply to Medicare.

In 1999, the General Accounting Office (GAO) surveyed 863 employers in 26 states without state parity laws.[9] The GAO found that although 86% of the employers reported compliance with the MHPA, a majority of these plans (87%) restricted their mental health coverage in other ways. For example, about two-thirds of MHPA-compliant plans covered fewer outpatient visits and hospital days for mental health treatment than for other medical treatment. Surveys by the Labor Department and the Centers for Medicare & Medicaid Services found similar results.

Many plans that had to increase annual and lifetime dollar limits to comply with the MHPA reportedly introduced other more restrictive mental health design features to mitigate the financial impact of the law's more generous dollar limits. Despite concerns about the MHPA's effect on claims costs, only 3% of employers surveyed by GAO reported that their

---

3 P.L. 104-204, Title VII, codified at 29 U.S.C. 1185a and 42 U.S.C. 300gg-5.

4 P.L. 105-34, Section 1531(a)(4), codified at 26 U.S.C. 9812.

5 Employers provide group coverage to their employees either by purchasing a group policy from an insurance company (fully insured coverage) or by funding their own health plan and assuming the financial risk (self-insured coverage).

6 By amending all three federal statutes (i.e., ERISA, the Public Health Service Act (PHSA) and the Internal Revenue Code (IRC), the MHPA applies to a broad range of entities. The ERISA and IRC provisions apply to employers and others who sponsor group plans (both full insured and self-insured), while the PHSA provisions apply to state-licensed health insurance companies.

7 Self-insured state and local government health plans may elect exemptions from the MHPA.

8 42 U.S.C. 1396u-2(b)(8); 42 U.S.C. 1397cc(f)(2).

9 U.S. General Accounting Office, *Mental Health Parity Act: Despite New Federal Standards, Mental Health Benefits Remain Limited*, GAO/HEHS-00-95, May 10, 2000.

costs had increased, and less than 1% of surveyed employers dropped their mental health coverage altogether following the law's enactment. It is difficult to gauge the impact of the MHPA's increased dollar limits, however, because many plans took steps to counter increases in claims costs by restricting mental health coverage in other ways. Nonetheless, the MHPA appears to have had an important influence on the evolution of state mental health policy and managed behavioral care, towards greater coverage, since its enactment in 1996.

The MHPA sunset on September 30, 2001. Title VI of the FY2002 Labor-HHS-Education appropriations bill (H.R. 3061, P.L. 107-116) reauthorized the MHPA through December 31, 2002. Section 610 of the Job Creation and Worker Assistance Act of 2002 (H.R. 3090, P.L. 107-147) further amended the MHPA provisions in the IRC (but not ERISA or the PHSA) by extending the authorization 1 additional year to December 31, 2003.

Mental Health Equitable Treatment Act of 2001

The Mental Health Equitable Treatment Act (S. 543) would amend and expand the MHPA to require employer-sponsored group plans to impose the same treatment limitations and financial requirements on their mental health coverage as they do on their medical and surgical coverage, if they choose to offer mental health coverage. On August 1, 2001, the Senate Health, Education, Labor, and Pensions (HELP) Committee approved a substitute version of S. 543 (S.Rept. 107-61), which retained most of the major components of the original bill, including the full parity requirement. S. 543 would cover all medically necessary treatment of psychiatric conditions listed in the *Diagnostic and Statistical Manual of Mental Disorders*, Fourth Edition (DSM-IV).[10] The bill would exempt small employers with 50 or fewer employees. In an effort to address the concerns of health plans, the bill also includes language aimed at ensuring that employers and health plans can manage benefits and make certain that mental health treatment services are medically necessary, clinically appropriate, and part of an authorized treatment plan.

On October 30, 2001, the Senate added S. 543 as an amendment to the FY2002 Labor-HHS-Education appropriations bill (H.R. 3061). The House version of the Labor-HHS-Education appropriations bill did not include any parity language. During conference on H.R. 3061, House conferees rejected the Senate amendment on a strict party-line vote. However, the conferees included language in the conference report (H.Rept. 107-350) "strongly urging the committees of jurisdiction in the House and Senate to convene early hearings and undertake swift consideration of legislation to extend and improve mental health parity protections during the second session of the 107th Congress."

[10] The DSM, produced by the American Psychiatric Association, is a comprehensive system of diagnosis for psychiatric conditions. The fourth and current edition was published in 1995.

FEDERAL EMPLOYEES HEALTH BENEFITS PROGRAM

At the White House Conference on mental health in June 1999, President Clinton directed the federal Office of Personnel Management (OPM) to implement full parity for both mental health and substance abuse benefits in health plans offered under the Federal Employees Health Benefits Program (FEHBP) beginning in 2001. Covered services include medically necessary treatment for all categories of mental illness listed in the DMS-IV. According to the OPM, parity implementation resulted in an average premium increase of 1.64% for fee-for-service plans and 0.3% for HMOs. FEHBP health plans are providing mental health coverage in a variety of ways. Some plans are using the services of managed behavioral health care organizations, while others are managing their own provider networks. Under FEHBP, mental health parity is required only for services provided on an "in-network" basis. In-network generally refers to a contracted group of providers established by a managed health care organization and/or an insurance carrier. OPM and the Department of Health and Human Services are conducting a 3-year evaluation of the FEHBP parity initiative.[11]

STATE MENTAL HEALTH PARITY LAWS[12]

States began to address the inequities in mental health coverage in the 1970s. More than a dozen states enacted laws requiring health plans operating within the state to offer a specific set of mental health benefits. While these mandated-benefit laws increased coverage, they had important limitations. They seldom provided catastrophic coverage against the financial risk of severe mental illness and they did not apply to self-insured employers, which are exempt from state regulation under ERISA.

In 1991, Texas and North Carolina became the first states to enact mental health parity legislation. The laws required health insurers that covered state government employees to provide mental health coverage at full parity with their coverage of other medical conditions. Prior to MHPA's enactment, five more states passed laws that required state-regulated group plans to provide full-parity mental health coverage. Since 1996, an additional 16 states have enacted similar legislation, bringing to 23 the total number of states that now mandate mental health coverage with full parity.[13] These laws vary in their scope. In 13 states, the parity laws apply to group and individual plans, whereas in six states the laws apply only to group plans. In the remaining four states, the parity laws apply only to state employee plans. The state parity laws also vary in the types of mental illnesses covered. Although some state laws apply to all the illnesses listed in the DSM-IV, a majority of the laws require parity coverage only for specified "serious" or "biologically based" mental illness (e.g., schizophrenia, depression, bipolar disorder). Finally, about half of the state parity laws exempt small employers.

---

[11] Additional information on FEHBP's implementation of mental health parity may be found on the OPM's Website at [http://www.opm.gov/insure/health/index.htm].

[12] Information on state mental health parity laws is based on data compiled by the National Conference of State Legislatures' Health Policy Tracking Service [http://www.ncsl.org].

[13] The 23 states that mandate full mental health parity are: AR, CA, CO, CT, DE, HI, IN, ME, MD, MA, MN, MT, NH, NJ, NM, NC, OK, RI, SC, SD, TX, VT, VA.

As previously noted, self-insured group plans are exempt from state laws under ERISA. In 2000, the Department of Labor estimated that 43% of the nearly 130 million Americans enrolled in private employer-sponsored group health plans were covered by self-insured plans.

Impact of Managed Behavioral Health Care Organizations

Cost of Parity

Recent studies show that MBHOs have been successful in controlling the costs associated with mental health parity, which has helped build support for parity legislation among federal and state legislators. In 1996, estimates of the cost of implementing full parity ranged as high as 11% of the total health care premium. But in its June 2000 report to Congress, the National Advisory Mental Health Council (NAMHC) concluded that full mental health parity would raise premium costs by 1.4% adding that this figure may overestimate the true cost of parity because the forecasting models did not reflect the most recent changes in managed care. Magellan Health Services, the nation's largest MBHC covering nearly 70 million individuals, reported that it had yet to see a premium cost increase of more than 1% as a result of implementing state mental health parity requirements.

At a recent Robert Wood Johnson Foundation conference on the costs of mental health parity, actuaries, economists, and government officials discussed the assumptions and methods used in calculating parity costs estimates. The conference participants concluded that (1) baseline spending on mental health (i.e., the share of the total health insurance premium spent on mental health services without parity) has decreased as a result of changing medical practice; (2) demand response to lowered cost-sharing has been less than predicted; and (3) managed care has had greater impact in reducing costs than parity in increasing costs.

Quality of Care

While managed behavioral health care may help control the costs of full parity, there is concern among some advocacy and provider groups about the impact of MBHOs on patient care. The American Psychiatric Association and the American Medical Association (AMA) have criticized carve-outs as discriminatory because they separate behavioral health care from "mainstream" health care rather than integrating the two, thus reinforcing the notion that behavioral health is somehow different from other medical conditions. The AMA has also expressed concern that part of the reduction in mental health care costs has come from lower payments to providers, the result of selective contracting and market power.

Some mental health advocates worry that carve-outs may not provide patients with all the medically necessary care. While they support the efforts of MBHOs to trim costs by reducing inefficient treatment patterns, they are concerned about management decisions that may result in across-the-board reductions in treatment without regard to clinical circumstances. Even under federal and state parity laws, MBHOs still retain wide latitude to manage coverage and control access to mental health care in order to achieve premium goals. In contrast to using a primary care physician as the gatekeeper to more specialized care, which is a model used by many managed care organizations for most medical services, MBHOs employ a large range of techniques to manage mental health care (e.g., concurrent utilization review by clinical care managers, guideline implementation) and use a different mix of providers and services. The MBHOs maintain that by lowering costs and offering parity-level benefits, patients have greater access to treatment at an earlier point in the development of the illness. Others contend that the managed care tools employed by MBHOs widen the gap between a plan's nominal benefits (i.e., coverage defined by parity laws) and its effective benefits (i.e., care actually received by patients) and may have important policy implications.

Chapter 5

PATIENT PROTECTION AND MANAGED CARE

Jean P. Hearne and Hinda Ripps Chaikind

ABSTRACT

Most Americans have health insurance plans that provide services through some kind of managed care arrangement. While financial incentives under fee-for-service insurance can lead to wasteful and possibly harmful excess services, incentives under managed care plans could lead to underutilization of necessary services. Congress is responding to this concern by proposing to regulate, at the federal level, various aspects of managed care and other types of health insurance. During the 106th Congress, the House and Senate passed comprehensive patient protection bills but were unable to reconcile the differences and send a bill to the President. (H.R. 2990 passed on October 7th, 1999 and S. 1344, passed on July 15, 1999.) The 107th Congress is revisiting the patients rights debate. The Senate and the House have each passed a bill (S. 1052 and H.R. 2563, respectively) that would establish federal standards mirroring various state laws as well as recommendations in the 1997 Consumer Bill of rights as developed by former President Clinton's Advisory Commission on Consumer Rights and Quality in HealthCare. This document provides background information on the issues surrounding patient protection and reviews the major differences between the Senate-passed and House-passed bills.

Traditionally, the regulation of health insurance largely has been left to the states. They have passed numerous managed care and patient protection laws. However, the federal Employee Retirement Income Security Act of 1974 (ERISA) preempts the application of such laws for about 56 million persons enrolled in "self-insured" group health plans through private employers. These are plans in which the employer takes some or all of the risk of paying for covered items and services. For enrollees of self-insured plans, federal law applies, but few protections currently exist in the federal statutes. As a result, there is a patchwork of federal and state regulation leading many to seek federal standards that would apply broadly to all health plan enrollees, regardless of who sponsors their health plan or whether they self-insure.

Both of the bills under consideration would apply federal patient protections to all insured Americans. The most significant differences between these bills are in the provisions expanding patients' legal remedies against their health plan providers when medical care is unjustly denied and the denial results in harm. Other differences include provisions applying the protections to federal health programs, prohibiting discrimination on the basis of genetic information, and encouraging health insurance coverage expansions.

The health insurance industry and many employer groups are strongly opposed to increased federal regulation of managed health care. They argue that it is unnecessary because the market is responding to consumer concerns, and that more regulation will raise health care costs, increasing the number of uninsured Americans. On the other hand, supporters of increased federal regulation, including many providers and consumer advocacy groups, believe that such regulation is needed to restrain market excesses that could jeopardize health care quality and access and that such regulation would result in only small additional costs.

Most Recent Developments

Congress has not appointed a conference committee to negotiate between House and Senate-passed versions of patient protection bills. It is unlikely that patient protections will be raised before the August recess. The President and the Senate Leadership, however, have suggested that continued negotiations on patient protection is a priority for the 107th Congress and occasional press reports suggest that informal discussions about this issue continue to take place.

Background and Analysis

Managed care generally refers to a payment system or delivery arrangement in which a health plan attempts to control or coordinate the use of health services by its enrollees in order to control spending and promote health. Like fee-for-service insurers, managed care organizations (MCOs) accept financial responsibility for a set of benefits in return for a premium paid by or on behalf of each enrollee. Unlike fee-for-service insurers, many MCOs directly provide or arrange for health care services, through affiliated physicians, hospitals and other providers, instead of simply paying bills.

MCOs try to control hospital admissions, diagnostic tests, or specialty referrals, either through programs to review the use of services or by giving participating physicians a financial stake in the cost of the services they order. They may also select low-cost providers of services or negotiate discounted rates from providers.

At one time, the only type of arrangement that offered managed care was a health maintenance organization (HMO). Today, managed care is provided by an array of entities, such as preferred provider organizations (PPOs) and provider sponsored organizations (PSOs), many of which offer more open-ended access to providers than do traditional HMOs. Like traditional HMOs, these arrangements provide covered services through provider networks. Enrollees are given financial incentives to use services within the plan's provider network but still receive some coverage even if they decide to obtain care from outside providers.

Almost 93% of insured employees were covered by some form of managed care in 2001: over 23% of covered employees were enrolled in HMOs, twice as many workers, 48%, were enrolled in PPO plans and 23% were in point-of-service plans. Point of service plans are defined as being similar to HMOs but they allow patients to use non-network providers at a higher cost than for network providers. Since the early 1990s, insured workers' enrollment in traditional fee-for-service plans dropped from about 50% to only 7%, reflecting the addition of managed care features to many of the former fee-for-service plans. The broad shift to managed care has been driven, largely, by cost concerns. Among all size employers in 2001, average fee-for-service premiums were almost 20% higher than HMO premiums and about between 4% and 7% higher than PPO premiums, according to the *Employer Health Benefits 2001, Annual Survey by the Kaiser Family Foundation and Health Research and Educational Trust.*

REGULATION OF MANAGED HEALTH CARE

Employers' benefits plans, which often include health insurance (or health benefits through managed care), are regulated by the federal government under the Employee Retirement Income Security Act (ERISA). Such "ERISA plans" are subject to standards for reporting and disclosure, fiduciary conduct, enforcement of rights, and protections against discrimination whether the employer purchases health insurance for employees or self-insures by accepting some or all of the risk for the cost of services. Consequently, managed care entities that provide benefits under an employer benefit plan must include those ERISA protections in their products. (Employer benefit plans sponsored by governmental employers and churches are not subject to ERISA.)

States, too, regulate many health insurance products. States have traditionally had regulatory authority over the business of insurance and most have exercised that authority in areas where ERISA standards are largely absent or viewed to be inadequate. For example, reporting and disclosure rules under ERISA may not be particularly timely, procedures for claims denial leave great room for variation among plans, and court remedies available under ERISA do not allow for money damages. As a result, many states have stepped in to establish stronger protections for health plan beneficiaries. Since many managed care products are considered insurance, managed care entities must include those protections in the products they sell.

States, on the other hand, are not permitted under ERISA to regulate employers' benefit plans (this is known as the ERISA preemption clause, discussed in greater detail below). ERISA frees employer benefit plans from state regulations but many employers offer benefit plans that include health insurance products. In this case the employer purchases health insurance from a traditional insurer (or MCO) and the insurer bears the risk of covering the cost of the benefits. Despite ERISA's preemption on employer benefit plans, those insurance products have already met state requirements for insurance. Other employers offer "self-insured" health plans – where the employer bears some or all of the risk of paying for the plan's covered services. Such *self-insured* (or self-funded) plans are not generally considered insurance and therefore, care not subject to many of the states' insurance and patient protection laws.

This division of regulation between the states and the federal government is further complicated by the Health Insurance Portability and Accountability Act of 1996 (HIPAA, P.L. 104-191), as amended. Prior to HIPAA, the states regulated such aspects of health insurance and managed care is licensure, solvency, benefits, and rating. HIPAA, however, imposes *federal* requirements relating to portability of health insurance on state-regulated insurers and MCOs. It also applies such requirements to ERISA plans. (The term "portability" as used in HIPAA means, for example, the ability to change health plans without experiencing preexisting condition exclusions.)

Whether more federal regulation of health insurance is desirable or needed is hotly debated. HIPAA regulates only certain aspects of eligibility and coverage. It does not regulate broader aspects of health care delivery, such as choice of providers, grievance procedures, and quality assurance. States have been passing managed care laws, but these do not apply to the enrollees in self-insured ERISA plans. This means that roughly 30% of a state's privately insured population is not covered by these laws. State laws also are widely variable, with some providing for comprehensive protections, and other providing for narrowly targeted measures.

It is partly because of this patchwork of regulation that some are seeking federal standards for managed health care that would apply to all enrollees, regardless of whether the plan is sponsored by an employer or by an MCO. Proponents of federal action are divided, however, over the scope of federal regulation, how it should interact with ERISA, and its relationship to state laws. Should standards govern the entire range of plan-provider and plan-enrollee relationships or should they be more targeted? Should standards apply to fee-for-service insurance as well as managed care? Should there be uniform national standards or should there by flexibility for state laws similar to or more protective or consumer and provider rights?

MCOs and employer groups tend to oppose federal regulation of managed care. They argue that a market unimpeded by federal interference is the most efficient way to ensure that health plans meet consumer demands for affordable, accessible, and high quality health care. In their view, government regulation is not only unnecessary because the market is already responding to consumer concerns but also would add significantly to the cost of health insurance. This, in turn, would lead to greater numbers of uninsured. Moreover, they assert that national standards are inflexible and would impeded cost-effective innovations in the design of health insurance coverage.

The Role of ERISA

One concern during the patient protection debate is whether to apply such standards only to self-insured plans or to all group health plans and health insurance issuers ("health insurance issuers" is defined in HIPAA to include insurance companies, insurance services, or insurance organizations including HMOs licensed to engage in the business of insurance). As mentioned above, ERISA already imposes minimum standards for plans sponsored by private-sector employers, including fiduciary standards, reporting and disclosure requirements, nondiscrimination, and grievance procedures. It also requires such plans to comply with federal portability, maternity stay, coverage for reconstructive surgery following mastectomy (discussed below), and mental health requirements as a result of HIPAA, P.L. 104-204, and P.L. 105-277.

The ERISA preemption clause impedes states from implementing laws that "relate to" employer benefit plans. In practice, this frees self-insured plans from state laws regulating insurance because they are not considered to be insurance. This preemption provision was designed to ensure uniform national requirements for multi-state employer plans, and protects self-insured health plans from potentially costly state regulation, such as state mandated benefit laws, risk pool assessments, premium taxes, and consumer protection managed care laws. Continuation of ERISA preemption is viewed as critical by the self-insured, employer community. Other stakeholders, in contrast, such as governors, state insurance regulators, and consumer groups, see ERISA as a major impediment to state insurance reform. In their view, it is largely because of ERISA's regulatory limitations and its preemption of state insurance law that Congress needs to act.

THE BILLS

The two patient protection bills under consideration are S. 1052: the "*Bipartisan Patient Protection Act*", passed by the Senate on June 29th, 2001, and H.R. 2365, the "*Bipartisan Patient Protection Act*", passed by the House on August 2nd, 2001. S. 1052 was introduced in the Senate by Senators McCain, Edwards and Kennedy on June 14th, 2001. H.R. 2563, was introduced on July 19, and incorporated many of the amendments included in the Senate-passed bill, with several major exceptions: 1) H.R. 2563 includes only a sense of the Congress, rather than a requirement, that these protections would apply to federal health programs; and 2) H.R. 2563 does not include provisions expanding the current law prohibitions on discrimination based on genetic information, and 3) H.R. 2563 includes tax provisions not found in S. 1052.[1] H.R. 2563 was further modified before passage to include 2 new major amendments. The 2 major amendments resulted in other differences, the most increasing health insurance coverage options (Association Health Plans and Medical Savings Accounts), and defining the ability of states to apply substantially equivalent state laws in lieu of the federal laws.

MAJOR ISSUES

Scope of Application

One important distinction among the patient protection bills considered during the 107th Congress is in their scope of application. The question here is whether the federal protections should apply to all Americans, only to those who are covered under employer-based plans, or only to those with employer-based coverage who do not have access to similar protections from their states. The reach of the proposed protections is the subject of the first of the

[1] For a discussion of the tax provision, see CRS Issue Brief IB98037, *Tax Benefits for Health Insurance: Current Legislation*, by Bob Lyke and Christopher Sroka.

President Bush's principles: that federal protections should apply to all health plan enrollees while giving deference to existing state protections. Both of the bills under consideration in the 107th Congress would apply their standards to all (insured) Americans, but each also include provisions allowing state laws to apply under certain circumstances to those plans that are subject to state laws. Both bills allow for the substitution of state laws, if it meets criteria for substantial compliance to federal standards with two exceptions. The first exception is that the House-passed bill does not allow state laws defining internal and external appeals processes to apply in lieu of the federal laws. The second exception is related to state laws limiting damages in health care-related lawsuits. S. 1052 would allow a state to determine non-economic damage amounts in state court, while H.R. 2563 allows states to apply their own damage limits, but only up to the federally established maximum amounts.

The bills would apply to individually purchased plans as well as employer-sponsored plans, and to state and local government-sponsored plans. S. 1052 was amended before passage so that its provisions, including the expanded right to sue, would apply to all federally sponsored health plans including the Federal Employees Health Benefits Program, Medicare, Medicaid, the State Child Health Insurance Program, Veterans, Department of Defense and all other federal programs providing health care or coverage. H.R. 2563 does not specifically apply its provisions to federal government-sponsored plans, but since the Federal Employee Health Benefit (FEHB) program plans are offered by insurers and HMOs which are subject to the group plan provisions, FEHB plans would be expected to comply with patient protection legislation, if passed. Other federally sponsored health plans or programs, such as Medicare and Medicaid, would not be covered by the provisions of H.R. 2563, although this bill includes a provision expressing the sense of the Congress that the President should issue an Executive Order requiring Federal officials take feasible steps to apply patients rights to federal health programs.

Both bills include provisions that exempt fee-for-service plans from many of the protections in the bill, including a requirement for a consumer choice option, choice of health care professional, access to emergency care, specialists, OB/GYN and pediatric care, and continuity of care. S. 1052 does not apply its exemption to federal health plans and programs. Fee-for-service plans are defined in the bills as those that reimburse providers on a fee-for-service basis without placing them at financial risk, do not vary providers' reimbursement based on contract terms or use of health care services, allow access to any provider legally authorized to provide covered services (and are willing to accept the payment terms) and do not require prior authorization.

Access and Choice of Providers

S. 1052 and H.R. 2563 include a number of identical provisions ensuring that health plan enrollees have access to certain types of services and providers without such barriers as prior authorization and increased copayments. The provisions in common include:

- *Access to Emergency Services.* Some MCOs require prior authorization for emergency department services. Without it, consumers who go directly to the emergency room and for whom the plan later determines that emergency care was not medically necessary, may be responsible for the entire bill. The bills addressed this issue by establishing a "prudent layperson" standard for plans that cover emergency services. This standard would require plans that cover emergency care to cover such care for the treatment of any condition for which a prudent layperson would reasonably believe puts them at serious risk of injury or death. The bills also prohibit plans or issuers from charging patients more for using a non-network provider than would have been charged if the services were provided in-network. The bills include a provision requiring that emergency ambulance services be subject to the same type of standard.

- *Access to Physicians Specializing in Ob/Gyn and Pediatric Care and other Specialty Services.* Some MCOs restrict access to specialty care and specialists by requiring referrals from primary care or "gatekeeper" physicians. Although gatekeeping has enabled plans to reduce costs, its use has led to consumer complaints about difficulties in gaining access to medical services. The bills passed in the 107th Congress include provisions 1) requiring plans that cover obstetrical and gynecological care to allow enrollees to visit physician and non-physician specialists without first receiving a referral and prohibiting prior authorization for the OB/GYN services that they order, 2) requiring that pediatricians be considered as primary care providers for plans that require such a designation, and 3) requiring plans that cover the services of specialists to ensure enrollees have timely access to those specialists.

- *Continuity of Care.* A patient undergoing a course of treatment in the care of a health care provider whose contract with an MCO is terminated would be at risk of losing access to their established providers. The bills would require plans to cover some continued care with terminated providers for certain plan enrollees undergoing a course of treatment during a transition period of at least 90 days.

- *Point-of-Service Option.* Point-of-service options allow enrollees of closed-network plans to have access to non-participating providers, though typically at a higher cost and on a fee-for-service basis. By 1996, over 80% of HMOs reported having a POS option of some kind. The bills would require group health plans that have closed panels to provide point-of-service options. S. 1052 and H.R. 2563 do not require point-of-service coverage for those individuals given a choice of non-network coverage through another plan or issuer in the group market.

- *Information Disclosure.* Economists maintain that access to information and the ability to choose among competing options are the hallmarks of an efficiently functioning market. They reason that informed consumers and purchasers can help maximize value if cost and quality data are readily available and understandable. Although the health care system in total may diverge in significant ways from a free market model, many observers nevertheless believe that the disclosure of useful health care information is an important goal. Each of the bills requires extensive information to be provided to individuals at time of enrollment and annually thereafter.

- *Medical Communications.* The phrase "gag rules" refers to clauses in provider contracts that prohibit or limit provider-patient communications about: 1) medical conditions, care, and treatment; and 2) compensation arrangements that produce financial incentives to under-provide care. Although some recent studies suggest that gag clauses are not prevalent in today's contracts, other observers point to some of the more subtle ways plans may discourage certain forms of medical communications between health care professionals and patients. The bills include prohibitions on such contract clauses.

- *Access to Prescription Drugs and Clinical Trials.* The current bills include provisions requiring plans that limit coverage of drugs to those on a list, sometimes referred to as a formulary, to develop those formularies with physicians and pharmacists and to allow exceptions from the formulary when a non-listed drug is medially necessary and appropriate. S. 1052 and H.R. 2563 would limit additional cost-sharing for non-formulary drugs. The bills also include provisions requiring plans to cover routine patient costs incurred through participation in an approved clinical trial.

- *Discrimination Protection for Providers.* Both bills include a provision that would prohibit discrimination with respect to participation or indemnification against any provider who is acting in accordance with license or certification under state law.

One significant set of protections included in the Senate bill are provisions that expand upon the current law prohibition on discriminating against individuals based on genetic information. The Senate bill would prohibit plans or issuers, in both group and individual markets, from: 1) establishing rules for eligibility (including continued eligibility) for any individual based on genetic information of that individual or their dependent, 2) denying eligibility or adjusting premium or contribution rates on the basis of predictive genetic information for an individual or their family member, and 3) requesting or requiring that an individual or their family members provide predictive genetic information. It would also require plans to provide notice of confidentiality safeguards when requesting such information, to post or provide notice of confidentiality practices and to have safeguards in place with respect to predictive genetic information.

Grievance and Appeals Processes and Remedies

Most MCOs have internal procedures to address enrollee complaints about waiting times, unresponsive staff, and other quality of service issues. While such grievances may or may not be resolved to an enrollee's satisfaction, often they are not appealable. (Enrollees in state-regulated MCOs can complain to the state's department of insurance.)

In addition, many health plans have procedures to deal with complaints about reimbursement for, and coverage of, medical care. Under the traditional fee-for-service system where the insurer is separate from the health care provider, such complaints usually relate to a health plan issuer refusing to pay for care already received. In certain MCOs, on the other hand, where the entity managing care is also providing care, patients may be denied certain services or treatments in the first place – a practice which has led many to complain that they are not receiving sufficient medical care to retain or regain their health.

The House- and Senate-passed patient protection bills under consideration in the 107th Congress include provisions requiring and defining the internal review procedures for coverage denials. The timeframes for reviews are reflected in **Table 1**.

Table 1. Timeframes for Appeals: 107th Congress Patient Protection Proposals

	S. 1052 and H.R. 2563
Initial decision	ASAP – "As soon as possible" in accordance with the medical exigencies of the case, but no later than: *Routine*: 14 days after receiving information but no later than 28 days; *Expedited*: 72 hours; *Ongoing*: ASAP with sufficient time for appeal; *Previously provided services*: 30 days after receiving necessary information but not later than 60 days.
Internal review	ASAP – "As soon as possible" in accordance with the medical exigencies of the case, but no later than: *Routine*: 14 days after receiving information but no later than 28 days; *Expedited*: 72 hours after request; *Previously Provided Services*: 30 days after receiving necessary information, but no later than 60 days.
External review	ASAP: "As soon as possible" in accordance with the medical exigencies of the case, but no later than: *Routine*: 14 days after receiving necessary information (but no longer than 21 days after request); *Expedited*: 72 hours after request; *Ongoing*: 24 hours after request; *Previously Provided Services*: 30 days after receiving information (but no later than 60 days after request).

Internal Appeals Process

An enrollee in an ERISA plan has a right to reasonable opportunity for a full and fair review by the plan of a decision denying a claim. The Department of Labor has established procedures for such reviews (see 29 CFR Part 2560, 11/21/2000 for the final rule). Plans must conform with those requirements for all claims filed on or after January 1, 2002. Until the rules are in effect, there is little uniformity of internal appeals procedures. At present, if the internal review determination is in the enrollee's favor, then the plan provides the service and/or pays the claim. If it is not in the enrollee's favor, he or she may sue under ERISA for the benefit that has been denied (see below). As an intermediate step, some employers provide for an independent external review of the benefit denial (see below).

For an enrollee who is not in an ERISA plan (such as a managed care plan bought in the individual market or one that covers state and local governmental employees), the internal appeals process is different. State laws require that HMOs have a procedure in which they reconsider initial denials of payment or coverage. Upon being notified that an HMO has denied approval of a service or benefit, an enrollee (or an enrollee's provider) has a right to appeal a decision to an individual or panel within the HMO.

The 107th Congressional bills broadly allow for denied claims for benefits or coverage or dispute over cost-sharing amounts to proceed to internal review. The bills would require that internal review be conducted by an individual with appropriate expertise so long as that person was not involved in the initial determination, and also require that a physician with appropriate expertise conduct the review if the appeal is based on a denial of a claim for a lack of medical necessity, is experimental or investigation or requires evaluating medical facts. The only difference between the two bills on internal review is that S. 1052 would allow state internal review statutes that are determined to be substantially similar to those described in the bill, to apply in lieu of the federal provisions while H.R. 2563 would not.

External Appeals

Under current law, ERISA does not require plans and issuers to provide for external review of coverage determination, although some private employers voluntarily provide such a process. Enrollees in these plans, whether the plans are fully insured or not, can appeal adverse coverage decisions to an external appeals entity if one exists. On the other hand, enrollees in non-ERISA plans may have external appeal rights if they reside in states that have enacted laws requiring MCOs to provide for an external appeals process.

The debate on codifying a definition of "medical necessity" most often comes up with respect to establishing a standard of review for external appeals, although such a definition could also impact initial coverage decisions. Today, physicians and their patients sometimes complain that their treatment decisions and referrals are determined by the plan not to be "medically necessary". As a result, insurers refuse to pay for such services or MCOs refuse to provide the services. Some states have responded to such complaints by establishing a definition of medical necessity in state law – thereby legislating a standard for medical decision-making. Such a definition could provide enrollees who are appealing adverse coverage decisions with an objective standard to claim that a service is needed – a standard that is not set by the plan itself. Some advocates, including providers, argue for a standard of care for medical necessity that is the "generally accepted standard of practice." Opponents believe that a federal definition of medical necessity will be overly bureaucratic and will result in defensive and costly medical practices. Others propose that a federal definition of medical necessity is unnecessary if strong, valid, and scientific standards for external reviewers are defined and if those standards make clear that the review cannot be limited by insurers' contract clauses that define medical necessity in a restrictive way.

The external review provisions have evolved significantly since the 106th Congress where there were major differences between the bills especially with respect to the characteristics of the external review entities, standards for review (including the consideration of plans' medical necessity definitions), whether the decisions of the reviewers are binding, and whether other types of dispute resolution are allowed. Today the bills are mostly alike in those areas, with a few remaining differences. H.R. 2563 would not allow the external review laws to apply in lieu of the federal provisions, and further specifies that the external review panel 1) would consist of 3 individuals, and 2) in a case involving a physician, all three reviewers would be physicians.

The two bills are the same with respect to the types of adverse coverage decisions that may enter into external review. They would require a system for the external review for benefits denied because they are determined by the plan to not be medically necessary, are investigational or experimental, or involve medical judgment. The bills would also allow insurers to require payment of a refundable filing fee of no more than $25. They would allow plans to condition the external review on he completion of an internal review except when internal review decisions do not meet specified time lines, and to waive the internal review process allowing claims to proceed directly to external review.

The bills include selection criteria for external reviewers designed to ensure adequate expertise of panel members, independence from the plan issuer, as well as fairness. Both bills would also require the "applicable authority" to implement procedures to assure that the process of selecting the external review entity will not create incentives to bias the decisions of the entity. In addition, they would prohibit participants, beneficiaries, enrollees or the plan or issuer from determining or influencing the selection of the external review entity.

The bills would require the reviewing entities to screen the claim to determine if it meets the criteria to proceed to external review and require reviews to be consistent with standards developed by the appropriate Secretary. Reviewers would be directed to take into account whether the plan or issuer's decision is in accordance with the medical needs of the patient; the medical condition and personal medical information of the patient; the opinion o f treating physician or health care professionals; the plan's definition of medical necessity and experimental coverage, although the reviewers would not be bound by such definitions; and the decisions of internal reviewers. Other information, such as valid scientific and clinical evidence, treatment guidelines, and community standards of care may also be considered. The bills would require a de novo determination. The decision of the external reviewer would be considered to be binding.

S. 1052 and H.R. 2563 would authorize civil penalties of up to $1,000 a day if the determination of the external reviewers was not followed and additional penalties for cases in which the relevant Secretary determines that there is a pattern or practice of repeated refusals to authorize benefits following external review. This penalty could not exceed the less of 25% of the value of benefits not provided or $500,000. In addition, both bills would allow the Secretary to assess a civil penalty against any plan of up to $10,000 for the plan's failure to comply with deadlines, to be paid to the participant or beneficiary if the determination of the external reviewers is not followed.

Remedies and Access to Courts. **ERISA *Plans***

Under ERISA, enrollees in employer-sponsored plans can only sue an ERISA plan for benefits due under the plan. State law causes of action, which include consequential and punitive damages, are not available and ERISA does not provide for such damages. This is the case whether the employer-sponsored health benefits are insured or self-insured. It is also an exception to the usual interpretation of ERISA preemption – that is, that ERISA overrides state laws regulating employer benefit plans but not those regulating the business of insurance. This unusual interpretation results from a 1987 Supreme Court decision (Pilot Life Insurance Co. vs. Dedeaux, 481 U.S. 41).

It is less clear whether or not enrollees in ERISA plans can sue for negligence, wrongful death, or medical malpractice. Some courts have found that MCOs or other entities that contract with and ERISA plan can be held liable for the quality of the medical care, including substandard care and negligent or faulty delivery of services. In this case, an enrollee would be able to sue under state law. If, however, an enrollee sues the ERISA plan itself for malpractice, wrongful death, or negligence, the court could dismiss the suit because no such cause of action exists under ERISA and any state laws relating to the plan could be preempted.

Further complicating the question of liability is that for many self-insured employer plans, the line between the administrative functions of the plan and the medical decisions of the plan can be blurred. The courts have been clear that state laws that relate to administrative functions of ERISA plans are preempted. On the other hand, the courts have spoken equivocally on the question of where an administrative (i.e., quantitative) decision ends and a medical or qualitative decision begins. If, for example, a plan denies urgently needed medical care that a patient cannot afford to pay on his or her own, or promised coverage is delayed until it is too late to do any good, then is that a benefit decision or a medical decision? Because the federal circuit courts are divided on this issue, some legal experts predict the Supreme Court will take it up. Against this backdrop, however, are proposals to resolve the ERISA plan liability issue through legislation.

Non-ERISA Plans

If an enrollee in an individually purchased plan or other non-ERISA plan receives an adverse coverage determination at the external review stage, then he or she can attempt to sue the MCO in state court. Remedies vary by state. Typically, they include the cost of the denied service as well as consequential costs (such as lost wages) and non-economic costs (such as pain and suffering). An enrollee may also be able to sue for punitive damages.

State laws also vary as to whether they allow enrollees in non-ERISA plans to sue MCOs (as opposed to doctors or other providers) for medical malpractice. In many states, such suits never get to trial because the organization is protected by the anti-corporate practice of medicine laws. Simply stated, those laws hold that an MCO cannot make medical decisions because the HMO is not a health care professional. Since it cannot make medical decisions, it cannot be held responsible for medical malpractice. Many would like to see this shield against HMO liability removed. In their view, the organization should be legally responsible for withholding care or delivering poor quality care because it influences providers' actions through financial incentives or more direct controls over medial practice. In May 1997, Texas became the first state to explicitly override its corporate practice of medicine law with a new law that holds MCOs liable for medical decisions affecting a patient's health. This law was challenged in federal court by Aetna Health Plans, which argued that the law is preempted by ERISA because it improperly interferes with administration of employee benefits plans (see below). The court upheld the states' provisions subjecting MCOs to liability for such decisions.

Remedies and Access to Courts: The Bills

Provisions involving judicial remedies and access to courts have proved to be the most difficult to resolve during the debates in both of the chambers. While both the House- and Senate-passed bills allow some lawsuits to proceed at the state level and expand both the causes of action and the damages available at the federal level, the approaches approved by the House and Senate are significantly different. Compromise during conference negotiations will require addressing the two different approaches.

S. 1052 would allow state causes of action involving medically reviewable decisions and would expand federal law causes of action for denials of benefits that are not based on medical decisions. This approach is based on the traditional authority of ERISA over the administrative duties of the plan's fiduciary. S. 1052 would create a federal cause of action for personal injury or wrongful death but only when a state cause of actions if preempted by ERISA. It would also expand the remedies available under ERISA to include economic and non-economic damages in cases of personal injury or death but would not allow for exemplary or punitive damages. For state law claims, S. 1052 would not allow for punitive or exemplary damages when plans meet the requirements for the review and appeals process, with two exceptions: 1) when state law allows *only* for punitive or exemplary damages in cases of wrongful death, or 2) when the defendant can prove the plan's willful or wanton disregard for the rights or safety of others. Finally, S. 1052 would allow a civil assessment in any action of up to $5 million payable to the claimant if he can establish the bad faith and flagrant disregard on the part of the plan for the rights of its participants or beneficiaries.

H.R. 2563 would amend ERISA to create a federal cause of action if a designated decision maker fails to exercise ordinary care in making a determination for either an initial claim or for internal review, or fails to comply with the external review decision; if that failure is the proximate cause of personal injury or death. State courts would have concurrent jurisdiction over claims under this new federal cause of action, which means that state courts could hear those claims, the federal law would apply, but the state courts' procedural rules could be used to process those claims. The designated decision maker would be liable for economic and non-economic damages. Non-economic damages would be limited to $1.5 million and punitive damages of up to $1.5 million could only be awarded when benefits were not provided following an independent reviewer's determination that they should be provided. States may further limit those damages for federal law claims heard in state courts. Economic damages are uncapped.

Both bills include provisions intended to protect employers, by limiting federal or state causes of action against a group health plan, employer or plan sponsor unless such person or persons directly participated in the consideration of a claim for benefits and in doing so, failed to exercise ordinary care. The bills would shield employers from liability when those employers have "designated decision makers". Designated decision makers would assume all liability of the employer or plan sponsor. Finally, S. 1052 would prohibit any federal cause of action against a group health plan that is self-insured and self-administered by an employer or a multi-employer plan, for the performance of, or the failure to perform any non-medically reviewable duty under the plan.

Both bills generally require administrative processes (internal and external review) to be completed before a cause of action may be brought against any individual in connection with a denial of a claim for benefits. The bills allow, in federal causes of action, for a participant or beneficiary to seek injunctive relief before finishing internal and/or external review if he can demonstrate that completing the processes would result in irreparable harm. In state causes of action, S. 1052 and H.R. 2563 allows an exception to the exhaustion rule in cases where the external review entity fails to make a determination within the defined timelines. Finally, both bills would limit certain class action lawsuits and S. 1052 would limit attorneys' contingency fees.

MCOs, employers and the health insurance industry are strongly opposed to changes in the ERISA preemption enjoyed by private employer-sponsored plans. These and other critics argue that increasing access to such remedies as compensatory and punitive damages would significantly inflate health care costs. They assume that patients, attorneys and even providers would much more readily pursue state law causes of action against health plans and plan sponsors for medical negligence and malpractice. The result, critics predict, would be defensive medicine, higher liability insurance and thus premiums, and perhaps even reductions in covered benefits or a higher number of uninsured individuals. Conversely, many of those who support the modifications of ERISA consider the likely cost effects to be far more modest. To support this view, they cite the absence of runaway medical cost inflation in those sectors – non-ERISA employer sponsored plans and the individual insurance market – that do no now enjoy preemption from state causes of action. In June 1998, CBO estimated the cost of ending the ERISA preemption as 1.2% of the premiums of all employer sponsored plans. However, it should be noted that CBO cautioned that this estimate "depends on assumptions for which the supporting data are extremely limited or nonexistent." Recent CBO cost estimates for S.1052 conclude the liability provisions would increase premiums by .8 percent.

Association Health Plans and HealthMarts

The House bill creates a new legal entity called Association Health Plans (AHPs). AHPs are intended to increase incentives for employers to band together to purchase insurance coverage for their employees. The concept of employers grouping together to purchase insurance is not a new one. A number of different styles of employer-based health insurance purchasing groups exist today. There are both public purchasing groups and private purchasing groups; some that self-insure and others that bargain with carriers to offer a single or multiple insured products. There are a number of possible advantages for employers that purchase insurance through a well-designed group. By pooling their insurance risks together, the employers in the group may be able to increase their bargaining power with carriers and share administrative functions resulting in lower premium costs. Employees of those firms may be able to select from a larger number of plans than if their employers were to obtain insurance independently. Multiple employer welfare arrangements (MEWAs), a broad category of employer purchasing groups, have traditionally been established by trade or business associations to provide insurance to a particular group of employers. While the primary purpose, for those groups with below-average risk, is to buy lower-priced coverage reflecting their lower risk.

Advocates of purchasing groups look to them as a mechanism to extend coverage among the working uninsured by reducing the barriers that small employers currently fact in providing coverage for their employees. AHP proponents argue that state consumer protections, benefits mandates, and solvency standards raise the price of health insurance and the resulting inflated cost of insurance is a major barrier that prevents small employers from sponsoring health benefits. Under current law, large employers that self-insure their employees are exempt from such state laws while small employers are not. The advocates say that by exempting association-sponsored plans from state laws, the playing field will be made more level between small and large employers.

Opponents of the AHP provisions as they appear in the House bill, on the other hand, raise the concern that the provisions create increased opportunities for risk segmentation –

that AHPs will be able to offer plans to healthy groups at better prices leaving the more unhealthy people in the only market subject to states' laws. Opponents in the insurance industry as well as those representing consumers are concerned that the additional risk segmentation could actually increase the number of uninsured by undermining the traditional insurance industry wile substituting a market without the many protections that states have put into place over the last several decades. Some health policy analysts have staked out a middle ground arguing that association health plans are not likely to have as significant the impact on the number of uninsured, but raise fears that re-establishing association plans as entities exempt from state consumer protections will bring back the fraudulent health insurance schemes and insecure entities that have plagued association sponsored plans in the past.

The House-passed bill establishes AHPs as certified group health plans sponsored by associations. The primary differences between AHPs and existing MEWAs is that AHPs would not be subject to most state insurance laws including benefit mandates (except that they must comply with any federal or state laws that require coverage of specific diseases, maternal and newborn hospitalization, and mental health), solvency standards, and pricing rules. Those AHPs with at least one self-insured offering would be required to meet the bill's reserve requirements and provisions for solvency.

Other major requirements include the following:

- AHPs must offer at least one insured health coverage option unless the self-insured plan existed on the date of enactment of the Bipartisan Patient Protection Act, or it does not restrict membership to one or more trades but whose eligible participating employers represent a broad cross-section of trades and businesses or industries, or the plan covers eligible participating employees in one or more high risk trades that are listed in the bill.

- The association sponsoring the plan must have been in existence for at least 3 years and must be operated by a board of trustees with complete fiscal control and responsibility for all operations.

- Self-insured AHPs must meet reserve requirements and provisions for solvency, they must have at least 1,000 participants and beneficiaries, and have offered coverage on the date of enactment or represent a broad cross-section of trades, or represent one or more trades with average or above average health insurance risk.

- All employers who are members must be eligible to enroll, all geographically available coverage options must be made available upon request to eligible employers, and eligible individuals cannot be excluded because of health status.

- Premiums for any particular small employer are prohibited from being used on the health status or claims experience of its plan participants or on the type of business or industry in which the employer is engaged.

The bill also establishes an "Association Health Plan Fund" from which the Secretary of Labor (or applicable authority) could make (or authorize to the Secretary of Labor) payments to ensure continued benefits on behalf of AHPs in distress. The AHPF would be funded by annual payments made by AHPs. In addition, the Secretary of Labor would be required to report to Congress no later than January 1, 2006, on the effect of AHPs on reducing the number of uninsured individuals.

LEGISLATION

The following bills to establish comprehensive patient protections have been introduced during the 107th Congress.

S. 6 (Daschle)

Patients' Bill of Rights Act. Introduced January 22, 2001. Referred to Senate Committee on Health, Education, Labor, and Pensions.

S. 283 (McCain, Kennedy and Edwards)

Bipartisan Patient Protection Act of 2001. Introduced February 7, 2001. Referred to Senate Committee on Senate Health, Education, Labor, and Pensions.

H.R. 526 (Ganske)

Bipartisan Patient Protection Act of 2001. Introduced February 8, 2001. Referred to House Committee on Education and the Workforce and Energy and Commerce.

S. 872 (McCain, Kennedy and Edwards)

Bipartisan Patient Protection Act. Introduced May 14, 2001 and placed on Senate Legislative Calendar under General Orders on May 15, 2001.

S. 889 (First, Breaux and Jeffords)

Bipartisan Patient's Bill of Rights Act of 2001. Introduced May 15, 2001. Referred to Senate Committee on Health, Education, Labor, and Pensions.

H.R. 2563 (Ganske)

Bipartisan Patient Protection Act. Introduced July 19, 2001. Referred to House Committee on Education and the Workforce, Energy and Commerce, and Ways and Means Passed House August 2, 2001.

S. 1052 (McCain, Kennedy and Edwards)

Bipartisan Patient Protection Act. Introduced June 14, 2001. Referred to Senate Committee on Senate Health, Education, Labor, and Pensions. Passed Senate June 29, 2001.

H.R. 2314 (Fletcher)

Patients' Bill of Rights Act of 2001. Introduced on June 26, 2001.

Chapter 6

HEALTH CARE FRAUD: A BRIEF SUMMARY OF LAW AND FEDERAL ANTI-FRAUD ACTIVITIES

Kathleen S. Swendiman and Jennifer O'Sullivan

ABSTRACT

Heath care fraud and abuse commonly involve inappropriate billing for medical services and can encompass a variety of activities, such as overcharging, double billing, and charging for services not rendered. Estimates of health care fraud and abuse by the General Accounting Office and others range from 5-10% of total health expenditures under both public programs and private insurance plans.

In recent years, the Congress, the Administration, and others have become increasingly concerned about the nature and extent of health care fraud particularly in the Medicare and Medicaid program. The Department of Health and Human Services (HHS) and GAO have conducted a series of studies, audits, and related reviews which have both documented the pervasive nature of fraudulent and abusive actions in federal health care programs as well as outlining steps needed to combat these activities. Both the Office of the Inspector General (OIG) in HHS and the Department of Justice are devoting increasing resources to identifying and sanctioning program violators and have undertaken initiatives to combat fraud.

Congressional interest in combating fraud is not new. Since 1972, there have been a number of revisions to federal statutes which have been designed to strengthen the ability to identify and prosecute fraudulent providers. Most recently, the Congress significantly strengthened the federal role as part of the Health Insurance Portability and Accountability Act of 1996 (HIPAA) and the Balanced Budget Act of 1997 (BBA 1997). Federal penalties for fraudulent activities in health care include civil and criminal penalties as well as permissive and mandatory exclusions from federal health care programs. Medicare and Medicaid program-related anti-fraud provisions are generally found in Title XI of the Social Security Act. These provisions are reinforced by generic fraud provisions found elsewhere in federal statutes, including federal health care fraud criminal statutes in Title 18 of the United States Code.

The civil monetary penalties under the Medicare and Medicaid programs have recently been made applicable to similar violations in most other health care programs funded by the federal government. Federal criminal prosecutions for health care fraud and abuse include program-related felony and misdemeanor offenses, as well as the new federal health care crimes recently added to Title 18 of the United States Code which apply to violations in both public and private health care benefit programs. Mandatory and permissive exclusions of individuals and entities from participation in the Medicare and Medicaid programs may be imposed by the Secretary of HHS for a number of offenses and activities detrimental to these programs. In addition, under the recently added "three strikes and you're out" provision, a provider is excluded from federal health care programs for 10 years for a second fraud-related offense, and permanently excluded from federal health care programs for a third offense.

It is anticipated that Congress will continue to monitor the success of the Administration's anti-fraud activities including increased responsibilities authorized by HIPAA as well as implementation of the tightened sanctions provisions.

BACKGROUND

What is Fraud?

Fraud and abuse commonly involve improper billing practices by health care providers and consumers, although consumer based fraud is not as common according to prosecution data. Examples include double billing, charging for services not rendered, and unbundling (billing for a more complex service than was actually performed). These activities increase the amounts patients, employers and insurers pay for health care. Other activities are also considered fraudulent such as physicians or other health practitioners giving or receiving kickbacks for patient referrals or for prescribing certain items or services.[1]

Health care *fraud* has been described as an intentional attempt to wrongfully collect money relating to medical services, while *abuse* has been described as actions which are inconsistent with acceptable business and medical practices. Charges of abuse customarily lead to civil suits, while accusations of fraud can result in either civil or criminal action. Some have suggested that the health system's moves to managed care arrangements will reduce the incentives and opportunities to commit fraud that exist under a fee-for-service system. However, other observers have suggested that while the types of fraudulent activities may change, substantial opportunities for fraud will still exist.

[1] A related issue involves "physician self-referrals" where patients are referred to medical facilities in which the physician has financial interests, thereby allowing the physician to profit from the referral. See U.S. Library of Congress, Congressional Research Service. *Health Care: Physician Self-Referrals, "Stark I and II"*. CRS Report to Congress No. 97-5 EPW, December 6, 1996.

Extent of Fraud

Health care fraud is an expanding problem in the nation's health care system. In the past, fraud generally involved discrete acts on the part of single health care providers or consumers attempting to defraud the insurance industry. Over time, the schemes have become increasingly complex, frequently involving networks of people, sophisticated computer techniques and multiple geographic locations. The schemes generally involve multiple payers, including both private insurers and public programs such as Medicare and Medicaid.

It is difficult to determine the amount of money lost to fraud each year. A frequently cited estimate was made by the General Accounting Office (GAO); it estimated that as much as 10% of health care spending in the nation was the result of fraudulent activities.[2] A more conservative estimate of 5% was offered by the Federal Bureau of Investigation (FBI).[3] The National Health Care Anti-Fraud Association (NHCAA, an association of private health insurers and Federal/State law enforcement officials) suggested a range of 3-10%.[4]

A financial audit report issued by the Office of the Inspector General (OIG) of the Department of Health and Human Services (HHS) in July 1997, estimated that improper Medicare payments made in FY1996 totaled $23 billion or 14% of total Medicare benefit Payments (excluding payments to health maintenance organizations (HMOs)) made in that year. These improper payments ranged from inadvertent mistakes to outright fraud and abuse. The OIG could not quantify what portion of the error rate was attributable to fraud. Almost all of the errors uncovered during the audit fell into four major categories: (1) documentation, including both insufficient and no documentation (47% of errors); (2) lack of medical necessity (37% of errors); (3) incorrect coding (9% of errors); and (4) non-covered or unallowable services (5% of errors). The following provider types accounted for the majority of improper payments: inpatient hospital care, physicians, home health agencies, hospital outpatient care; skilled nursing facilities, and clinical laboratories.[5]

Regardless of the exact dollar figure attributable to health care fraud, it results in increased expenditures under federal and state health care programs and higher insurance premiums. It can also pose a risk to patients if medically necessary services are not provided or unneeded services are provided. While both public and private programs are affected by fraudulent activities, this chapter focuses primarily on federal programs, administered by HHS.[6]

---

[2] U.S. General Accounting Office. *Remedies Needed to Reduce Losses from Fraud and Abuse*. Janet Shikles, testimony before the Health Subcommittee, House Committee on Ways and Means, Mar. 8, 1993. Washington, 1993.

[3] U.S. Federal Bureau of Investigation. Freeh, Louis, testimony before Senate Special Committee on Aging, Mar. 21, 1995. Washington, 1995.

[4] National Health Care Anti-Fraud Association. Testimony of William J. Mahon before the Subcommittee on Human Resources and Intergovernmental Relations of the House Committee on Government Reform and Oversight, June 15, 1995.

[5] U.S. Dept. of Health and Human Services. Office of the Inspector General. Report on the Financial Statement Audit of the Health Care Financing Administration for Fiscal Year 1996. A-17-95-00096, July 1997. Washington, 1997.

[6] Fraud and abuse as they affect Department of Defense and Veterans Administration programs, and the Federal Employees Benefits Program are not discussed.

HISTORICAL OVERVIEW OF FEDERAL ANTI-FRAUD STATUTES

While the original Medicare and Medicaid statues, as enacted in 1965, did not contain program-specific fraud provisions, Congress did provide that the penalties for fraud which were contained in the Old Age, Survivors and Disability Program[7] were also applicable to the new Medicare and Medicaid programs. Then, in 1972, Congress added specific fraud provision to both programs.[8] Such provisions included misdemeanor penalties for false statements as well as penalties for kickbacks or bribes under either program. In 1976, Congress created the Office of Inspector General in the Department of Health, Education, and Welfare (now HHS), giving the Inspector General the authority "to conduct and supervise audits and investigations, relating to programs and operations of the Department to increase their economy and efficiency and to reduce the likelihood of fraud and abuse."[9]

In 1977, Congress passed the Medicare-Medicaid Anti-Fraud and Abuse Amendments, P.L. 95-142, strengthening the existing fraud and abuse penalties by upgrading them for misdemeanor offenses to felonies.[10] In addition, the Secretary was given authority to suspend providers convicted of program fraud from participation in Medicare or Medicaid. Disclosure of ownership and financial information requirements were added for providers and suppliers who received Medicare or Medicaid funds.

Thereafter, Congress has amended these basic fraud and abuse provisions numerous times, strengthening penalties, adding offenses, both civil and criminal, as new fraudulent schemes have been uncovered. For example, in the Omnibus Budget Reconciliation Act of 1981, P.L. 97-35, Congress authorized the Secretary to assess a civil monetary penalty of up to $2,000 for fraudulent claims under Medicaid and Medicare and to impose an assessment of twice the amount of the fraudulent claim, in lieu of damages. The Omnibus Budget Reconciliation Act of 1986[11] contained a number of additions and modifications to the fraud and abuse penalty provisions including clarifying the exclusion provisions and adding provisions concerning fraud hearings.

Extensive amendments were made to the fraud and abuse provisions by the Medicare and Medicaid Patient and Program Protection Act of 1987, P.L. 100-93. Included in the amendments were provisions to protect Medicare and Medicaid beneficiaries from unfit health practitioners, along with provisions re-codifying the anti-fraud provisions in the Social Security Act, and providing for additional exclusion provisions under the Medicare and Medicaid programs where an individual or entity has been convicted of a criminal offense related to neglect or abuse of patients. This 1987 statute also required states to have a system of reporting information with respect to formal proceedings concluded against a health care practitioner or entity by a state licensing authority. Congress also amended the fraud and abuse provisions in 1988,[12] 1989,[13] 1990,[14] and 1994,[15] further refining the criminal penalties,

[7] 42 U.S.C. §408 (1972).

[8] Public Law 92-603. These program-related fraud provisions were added to Title XI of the Social Security Act.

[9] S.Rept. 1324, 94th Cong., 2d Sess. 3-14 (1976); 42 U.S.C. §3521 (1977).

[10] Generally, misdemeanor offenses carry an imprisonment term of less than 1year while felony offenses prescribe an imprisonment term greater than 1 year. Both offenses may also provide for fines.

[11] Public Law 99-509.

[12] Public Law 100-360; Public Law 100-485.

[13] Public Law 101-234; Public Law 101-239.

civil monetary penalties and exclusion provisions applicable to the Medicare and Medicaid programs.

In 1996, significant new health care fraud and abuse provisions were added to both the existing program-related laws in the Social Security Act and to the Federal Criminal Code by Title II of the Health Insurance Portability and Accountability Act, (HIPAA, P.L. 104-191). The Medicare and Medicaid program-related fraud provisions were made applicable to other federal health care programs, such as Civilian Health and Medical Program of the Uniformed Services (CHAMPUS). Civil monetary penalties were increased from $2,000 to $10,000 for each item or service involved. New violations were added to the list of prohibited activities, such as for "upcoding," billing for unnecessary medical services and false certification of home health services.[16]

Significant new criminal provisions specifically involving health care fraud were added to the Federal Criminal Code provisions found in Title 18 of the United States Code. These include new federal health care fraud criminal offenses (applicable to violations in both public and private health care benefits programs), such as for false statements, theft of embezzlement, obstructing justice and money laundering. Upon conviction, a court may order forfeiture of property derived from a federal health care offense.

The amendments to HIPAA also established a number of new programs to combat fraud, including a fraud and abuse control program to coordinate federal, state and local law enforcement efforts against fraud in federal and private health care programs; a Medicare integrity program providing for contracts with private entities to carry out activities such as audits and reviews of provider payments; a beneficiary incentive program to encourage individuals to report fraudulent activities against the Medicare program; and, a national health care fraud and abuse data collection program containing reports of final adverse actions against health care providers, suppliers, and practitioners. The Act also required the Secretary to issue written advisory opinions regarding whether a proposed transaction would violate anti-kickback restrictions.

Most recently, Congress has amended the Medicare and Medicaid fraud and abuse provisions in Title IV of the Balanced Budget Act of 1997 (BBA 1997, P.L. 105-33), focusing on keeping fraudulent providers out of Medicare and increasing the penalties for those caught committing fraud and abuse. The amendments include a "three strikes and you're out" provision *permanently* excluding from federal health care programs persons convicted of three health care-related crimes. The Secretary of HHS is given authority to refuse to contract with providers or suppliers convicted of felonies for an offense which the Secretary determines "is detrimental to the best interests of the program or program beneficiaries."[17] A new civil monetary penalty is added for cases in which a person contracts with an excluded provider for the provision of health care services where the person knows or should know that the provider has been excluded from participation in a federal health care

[14] Public Law 101-508.

[15] Public Law 103-432.

[16] Section 231 of Public Law 104-191 also amended the level of intent associated with fraud violations punishable by civil monetary penalties. Under the new standard, similar to the False Claims Act, a person is subject to civil monetary penalties if the person "knowingly" presents a claim that the person "knows or should know" falls into one of the prohibited categories. Section 1128A(a) of the Social Security Act, 42 U.S.C. §1320a-7a(a).

[17] Section 4302 of Public Law 105-33.

program. Providers and suppliers are also required to provide full and complete information as to persons with an ownership or control interest in the supplier, and are required to post a $50,000 surety bond as a monetary guarantee of performance of statutory obligations. The Secretary is also directed to issue written advisory opinions concerning certain physician self-referral questions.

A detailed summary of current fraud and abuse penalty provisions is contained in the last section of this chapter.

IDENTIFICATION OF FRAUDULENT ACTIVITIES

Federal

Under current law, investigation and prosecution of fraud related to federal programs is the responsibility of the OIG within HHS, the FBI and the Department of Justice. The OIG investigates federal cases of fraud regarding Medicare, Medicaid, and the Maternal and Child Health Block Grant programs; it is authorized by the Secretary to sanction fraudulent providers by imposing exclusions and civil monetary penalties. The FBI can investigate both federal and private payer cases of fraud but cannot impose sanctions. Both the OIG and the FBI refer investigative findings to the Department of Justice, at which time officials determine whether to pursue the case. In the event the Department decides to prosecute, the accused person or persons may be brought up on criminal charges; damages may be sought through civil penalties; or exclusions from federal programs may be imposed.

State Medicaid Fraud Control Units

Federal funding is provided for 90% of the start-up costs and 75% of the operating costs of State Medicaid fraud control units. Forty-seven states have established these units which are usually part of the office of the state attorney general. They are responsible for the investigation, prosecution, or referral for prosecution, of fraudulent activities associated with state Medicaid programs. During FY1996, the OIG administered an estimated $74.8 million in grants to these entities.

SANCTIONS

Office of Inspector General, HHS

During the 6-month period October 1, 1996-March 31, 1997, the OIG imposed 1,353 sanctions in the form of exclusions or money penalties against individuals and entities engaged in fraud or abuse of Medicare and Medicaid. Over half of the exclusions were based on conviction of program related crimes, conviction of controlled substance manufacture or distribution, conviction related to patient abuse or loss of license to practice. During this period, the government imposed exclusions on 1,344 individuals and entities. It recouped

$937 million through both the civil money penalty provisions and the False Claims Act civil settlements relating to the Medicare and Medicaid programs.[18]

State Medicaid fraud control units reported 389 convictions and $16.5 million in fines, restitutions and overpayments collected for the period July 1, 1996-December 31, 1996.[19]

Department of Justice

The Department of Justice has significantly increased its health care fraud activities in recent years. In 1993, the Attorney General named health care fraud enforcement as one of the Department's top priorities. The FBI has seen a major increase in the investigative resources devoted to health care fraud and as a consequence the number of cases handled by federal prosecutors has also increased. The Department also provided for increased coordination among investigative and regulatory agencies.

Health care fraud investigations handled by the FBI increased from 657 in FY1993 to 2,200 in FY1996. Criminal prosecutions increased from 83 cases and 116 defendants in FY1992 to 246 cases and 450 defendants in FY1996. Convictions (including guilty pleas and guilty verdicts) rose from 90 defendants in FY1992 to 307 in FY1996. Civil health care fraud efforts also increased with civil investigations handled by the Department increasing from 270 in FY1992 to 2,488 in FY1996. Recoveries by the Department's Civil Division totaled $274 million for FY1995 and FY1996.

RECENT FEDERAL INITIATIVES

In recent years, considerable attention has been focused on allegations of health care fraud, particularly Medicare fraud. This attention has stemmed, in part, from a series of congressional hearings highlighting the pervasive nature of fraud, periodic reports in the media documenting egregious examples, and a series of reports from the OIG and the General Accounting Office (GAO) highlighting the need for improved mechanisms to combat fraud.

The sheer volume of Medicare claims (over 800 million annually) coupled with the program's administrative complexity makes it a target for fraudulent practices. In the past several years, federal agencies have intensified their efforts to identify, prosecute, and penalize providers and others involved in fraudulent activities. The agencies have targeted their efforts in those areas, such as home health care, where fraudulent practices appear to be the most widespread.

---

[18] U.S. Dept. of Health and Human Services. Office of Inspector General. Semi-Annual Report, Office of Inspector General. October 1, 1996-March 31, 1997. Washington, 1997. (Hereafter cited as HHS, Office of Inspector General, *Semi-Annual Report*)

[19] HHS, Office of Inspector General, *Semi-Annual Report*.

Operation Restore Trust

A major effort, launched by HHS in May 1995, is known as Operation Restore Trust (ORT). This 2-year pilot project is focusing on the five states (California, Florida, Illinois, New York, and Texas) which together account for 40% of Medicare and Medicaid beneficiaries. The project is targeting three areas the OIG has identified with systemic fraud – namely home health agencies, nursing homes, and durable medical equipment suppliers. ORT provides for coordination of enforcement activities by federal and state government representatives. The OIG assembled teams that included investigators from the OIG and state Medicaid fraud control units; auditors and evaluators from the OIG and the Health Care Financing Administration (HCFA); quality assurance specialists form state surveyors and durable medical equipment regional carriers; state long-term care ombudsmen through the Administration on Aging; and prosecutors from the Department of Justice and the State Attorney General. These teams conducted financial audits, criminal investigations and referrals to federal and state prosecutors, civil and administrative sanctions and monetary recovery actions, and surveys and inspections of nursing facilities.

The OIG reported that as of March 31, 1997, 74 criminal convictions, 58 civil actions and 54 current indictments were obtained under the ORT operation. In addition, 219 providers were excluded from Medicare and Medicaid. The OIG also identified a total of more than $167 million in fines, recoveries, settlements, and civil monetary penalties owed to the federal government.[20] Several other activities, including the establishment of a hotline, issuance of fraud alerts, and establishment of a voluntary disclosure program, were associated with ORT.

The 2-year demonstration project has ended. However, on May 20, 1997, HHS announced expansion of the ORT effort to several additional provider groups and services including partial hospitalization, psychiatric hospitals, and independent physiological laboratories. Twelve new states were added to the effort. They are: Arizona, Colorado, Georgia, Louisiana, Massachusetts, Missouri, New Jersey, Ohio, Pennsylvania, Tennessee, Virginia, and Washington.

Beneficiary Involvement

In June 1995, HHS established a toll-free hotline (1-800-HHS-TIPS) for beneficiaries and others to report suspected cases of health care fraud involving Medicare and Medicaid. As of March 31, 1997, the hotline received 13,794 complaints relating to HHS programs; resolving the complaints led to recoveries of $5.2 million in overpayments.

In June 1997, HHS awarded $2 million in grants to 12 advocacy groups to train seniors in fraud detection. Under the demonstration project, senior volunteers will be working in local areas to help seniors identify deceptive practices.

[20] HHS, Office of Inspector General, *Semi-Annual Report*.

Hospital Incentives

Physicians at Teaching Hospitals (PATH)

Medicare pays for the services of teaching physicians at teaching hospitals according to the type of service rendered. Physicians may bill under Part B only if they personally provide direct and identifiable services to Medicare patients or they are physically present when the services are furnished by residents and interns. Other services performed by teaching physicians, such as supervising interns and residents are considered part of their medical education function. Medicare pays under Part A for both the direct and indirect medical education costs associated with the training of residents and interns.

Under a nationwide PATH initiative, the OIG has undertaken a review of the compliance with Medicare rules governing reimbursement to physicians at teaching hospitals. While payment is being made under Part A for medical education activities, the OIG is concerned that physicians have also been billing for some services under Part B without having met the appropriate criteria. A number of hospitals indicated concern with the PATH initiative. They states that teaching hospitals had not been given clear and consistent guidelines on complying with Medicare regulations; further questions were raised as to whether the OIG was applying the policy retroactively in certain cases. The report of the House Appropriations Committee accompanying the HHS FY1998 appropriations bill reiterated these concerns.[21] The HHS indicated in July that it was discontinuing audits at those teaching hospitals which had not received clear instructions from carriers (i.e., Medicare claims processing entities) prior to December 1992.

Diagnosis Related Group 72-Hour Window Project

Medicare makes payments for inpatient hospital services under a prospective payment system (PPS). Under PPS, a fixed amount is paid on the basis of the patient's diagnosis. The PPS payment is intended to cover the costs of all services provided to the Medicare patient (except for physician's services which are paid for separately). The law prohibits separate payments for outpatient diagnostic services and other services related to an inpatient admission that are provided within 72 hours of such admission. The OIG found that many hospitals were submitting Part B claims for these services. As a result, in 1995, it initiated a national project that identified 4,600 hospitals that had submitted improper claims. These hospitals are being notified of the erroneous claims and their potential exposure under the Federal Civil False Claims Act. The hospitals will be given the opportunity to enter into a settlement with the federal government; such agreement must include compliance measures to prevent and detect erroneous billings. As of March 31, 1997, 804 hospitals had settled. The total anticipated recovery is $90-$110 million over the next 2 years.[22]

---

[21] U.S. Congress. House. Committee on Appropriations. Departments of Labor, Health and Human Services, and Education and Related Agencies Appropriations Bill, 1998. Report 105-205, 105th Cong., 1st Sess., July 25, 1997. Washington, GPO, 1997.

[22] HHS, Office of Inspector General. *Semi-Annual Report.*

Home Health Agencies

One of the major areas targeted for closer scrutiny is that of home health agencies. In July 1997, the OIG reported on the results of an ORT audit of home health services in four states (California, Illinois, New York, and Texas). The review found that 40% of services did not meet Medicare reimbursement requirements either because the services were not reasonable and necessary; they were provided to patients who were not homebound; or, they were for services that did not have valid physician orders or other supporting documentation.[23] A second OIG study found that 25% of home health providers in the five ORT states were problem providers who had abused or defrauded Medicare.[24] Both reports found that Medicare's controls over home health care were inadequate. Medicare's fiscal intermediaries (the entities that process home health claims) review only about 3% of claims because of limits on financial resources. In contrast, intermediaries reviewed 50% of home health claims in 1988.

Several provisions in the recently enacted Balanced Budget Act of 1997 (BBA 1997) are expected to address some of the problems; these include development of a prospective payment system for home health services and the requirement that home health agencies post $50,000 surety bonds before they are certified. HHS has also stepped up its efforts. On September 15, 1997, the Administration announced a temporary moratorium period, the agency will implement program safeguards included in the BBA and work on other key changes. New measures will include a requirement that home health agencies supply information about related businesses that they own. The Department also expects to propose regulations that will require agencies to re-enroll in Medicare every 3 years. As part of the re-enrollment process, agencies will have to submit an independent audit of their records and practices. The Department also plans to double the number of home health care audits.

Clinical Laboratories

The OIG, in conjunction with other law enforcement agencies is concluding a 3-year initiative which has targeted abusive billing practices in the country's largest independent clinical laboratories. Another interagency project, the Laboratory Unbundling Project, is a joint effort by the OIG and the Department of Justice to target fraud in hospital-based outpatient laboratories. The project, which began in hospitals in Ohio, was created to identify facilities which unbundled laboratory tests when using automated equipment, either by billing for each analysis separately, or billing for the automated test as well as several of the analyses separately. In effect, the facility receives a higher payment than for tests bundled into a single panel. Under the lab unbundling project, facilities are allowed to participate in a self-disclosure process (which allows disclosure of improper billing and which may prevent the imposition of more severe penalties). The project has recently been expanded to other states.

---

[23] U.S. Dept. of Health and Human Services. Office of Inspector General. Results of the Operation Restore Trust Audit of Medicare Home Health Services in California, Illinois, New York and Texas. Report A-04-96-02121, July 1997. Washington, 1997.

[24] U.S. Dept. of Health and Human Services. Office of Inspector General. Home Health: Problem Providers and Their Impact on Medicare. Report OEI-09096-00110, July 1997. Washington, 1997.

In a related development, the OIG released a model laboratory compliance plan in February 1997.[25] This plan describes the fundamentals of an effective program of provider compliance with rules in federal health care programs. The purpose is to help providers self-regulate, self-report and prevent health care fraud.

Implementation of Provisions in the HIPAA

As noted above, HIPAA included a number of provisions designed to strengthen federal anti-fraud and abuse efforts. HHS and the Department of Justice are in the process of implementing the new provisions. Some of these activities are noted below:

Health Care Fraud and Abuse Control Program

HIPAA provided for the establishment of a new Health Care Fraud and Abuse Control Program to be jointly administered by the Secretary of HHS and the Attorney General. The program was viewed as an extension and expansion of existing interagency and intergovernmental anti-fraud efforts including ORT and other anti-fraud working groups. The Secretary and Attorney general developed implementing guidelines and announced establishment of the program in January 1997. It is intended to promote the coordination of federal, state and local law enforcement; conduct investigations, audits, and evaluations relating to the delivery and payment for health care services; facilitate the enforcement of civil, criminal and administrative statutes, provide industry guidance (including advisory opinions, safe harbors, and special fraud alerts) relating to fraudulent practices; and establish a national data bank to receive and report final adverse actions against health care providers.

HIPAA provided that the Fraud and Abuse Control Program would be funded by recoveries from health care cases. These recoveries would be transferred to the Medicare Part A trust fund and subsequently be appropriated to a new Health Care Fraud and Abuse Control Account. A specified amount (between $60 and $70 million in FY1997 and between $80 and $90 million in FY1998) is earmarked for the OIG for Medicare and Medicaid work. An additional amount ($47 million in FY1997 and $56 million in FY1998) is to be appropriated from the general fund of the U.S. Treasury to the Account for transfer to the FBI for health care enforcement activities. This stable funding source provides increased resources for both the OIG and the FBI. The OIG plans to increase its staff by 20% in 1997.

Medicare Integrity Program

HIPAA also provided for the establishment of a new Medicare Integrity Program under which the Secretary enters into agreements with private entities to carry out certain activities including medical review, audits, and secondary payer reviews. A specified amount ($440 million in FY1997 and $490-$500 million in FY1998) is to be appropriated to the Health Care Fraud and Abuse Control Account from the Medicare Part A trust fund for this program. The Department is developing implementing regulations.

---

[25] Office of the Inspector General. Publication of the OIG Model Compliance Plan for Clinical Laboratories. Notice. *Federal Register*, v. 62, no. 41. March 3, 1997.

FEDERAL PENALTIES FOR FRAUD

Federal penalties for fraudulent activities in health care include civil and criminal penalties as well as permissive and mandatory exclusions from federal health care programs. Medicare and Medicaid program-related anti-fraud provisions are generally found in title XI of the Social Security Act, 42 U.S.C. §§1320a-7 *et seq.* These provisions are reinforced by generic fraud provisions found elsewhere in federal statues, including federal criminal statutes in title 18 of the United States Code, and civil statutes such as the Federal Civil False Claims Act, 31 U.S.C. §3729.[26] Many states have similar laws used to combat health care fraud and abuse.

Civil Monetary Penalties

Civil monetary penalties under Medicare and Medicaid are found generally in section 1128A of the Social Security Act, 42 U.S.C. §1320a-7a.[27] These provisions are also applicable to similar violations in other health care programs funded by the federal government, such as CHAMPUS. Civil penalties of up to $10,000 for *each* item or service involved, as well as additional assessments, may be imposed for false claims submitted to Medicare, Medicaid, or state health care programs receiving funds under the Maternal and Child Health Services Block Grant or the Social Services Block Grant. Civil monetary penalties may also be imposed for other fraudulent activities such as inflating charges for services, providing services when not a properly licensed physician, "upcoding," billing for medically unnecessary services, falsely certifying that an individual meets the requirements for home health services, and offering remuneration to individuals eligible for Medicare or Medicaid to influence such individuals to receive items or services from particular providers. In addition, civil penalties may be assessed against a health care provider who fails to comply with certain statutory obligations, including the provision of medically improper or unnecessary services, under section 1156 of the Social Security Act, 42 U.S.C. §1320c-5. Procedural provisions outlining the administrative process for the imposition of civil monetary penalties include notice and an opportunity for a hearing, representation by counsel and appeal rights following an adverse determination by the Secretary to federal circuit court.[28]

Other civil monetary penalty provisions may be found throughout the Medicare and Medicaid statutes. A number of these provisions apply (HMOs) and other Medicare and Medicaid managed care organizations which fail to provide medically necessary items or services to beneficiaries; or which impose premiums in excess of permitted amounts; or which expel or refuse to reenroll beneficiaries in violation of Medicare or Medicaid law; or

[26] Under this statute providers may be liable for three times the amount of damages sustained by the government as the result of a false claim and for civil penalties of between $5,000 and $10,000 for each false claim submitted. In addition, a private citizen can bring a "qui tam" action under this statute, and receive a percentage of the recovery, plus attorney's fees.

[27] Regulations implementing the civil monetary penalty authority are found at 42 C.F.R. § Pt. 1003.

[28] Section 1128A(c) of the Social Security Act, 42 U.S.C. §1320a-7a(c).

for other enumerated violations.[29] HMOs must also periodically survey their membership to determine their participants' degree of access to services and satisfaction with quality, and provide this information to HHS or face civil fines of up to $25,000 per violation and suspension of enrollments or plan payments under 42 U.S.C. §1395mm(i)(8).[30]

Criminal Penalties

Federal criminal prosecutions for health care fraud and abuse have been brought under as many as thirty different statutes.[31] Such prosecutions may be based upon the program-related provisions of section 1128B of the Social Security Act,[32] which apply to Medicare, Medicaid, or state health care programs receiving funds under the Maternal and Child Health Services Block Grant or the Social Services Block Grant. Program-related felony convictions, which usually apply to providers, may result in fines of up to $25,000 or imprisonment for up to 5 years or both. For persons other than providers, program-related convictions are generally misdemeanors.

Program-related criminal penalties include making false statements in matters relating to benefits or payments under federal health care programs, making claims for physicians services knowing that the individual who furnished the service was not licensed as a physician, and knowingly and willfully soliciting or receiving a kickback, bribe or rebate in return for referral of a patient for services paid for under a federal health care program.[33] There are explicit statutory exceptions to the general anti-kickback prohibitions,[34] and the HHS Inspector General has the authority to issue "safe harbor" regulations delineating business practices which could cause suspicion of fraud but which are in fact legitimate, provided they meet certain guidelines. If the guidelines are adhered to, the outlined practices are protected from federal civil penalties or criminal prosecution.[35]

Section 217 of HIPAA added a new crime to the list of prohibited activities under section 1128B of the Social Security Act, making it unlawful for a person to knowingly and willfully dispose of assets in order to become eligible for benefits under the Medicaid program, if disposing of the assets resulted in the imposition of a period of ineligibility.[36] More recently,

[29] Section 1876 of the Social Security Act, 42 U.S.C. §1395mm. This section provides for penalties of up to $25,000 per violation, with more severe penalties for violations involving misrepresentation of information to HHS. In addition, entities that overcharge beneficiaries can also be assessed an amount equal to twice the excess amount charged, with the excess amount deducted from the penalty and returned to the beneficiary. 42 U.S.C. §1395mm(i)(6)(B). Similar provisions apply to Medicaid HMOs under section 1903(m) of the Social Security Act, 42 U.S.C. §1396b(m)(5)(A),(B).

[30] The same procedural provisions as are applicable generally for civil monetary penalties under Section 1128A of the Social Security Act apply to HMOs under Section 1876 of that Act, 42 U.S.C. §1395mm(i)(6)(B)(iii).

[31] Pamela H. Bucy, "*Crimes by Health Care Providers*", 1995 UNIV ILL L REV 598, 591 (1996).

[32] 42 U.S.C. §1320a-7b.

[33] Section 1128B of the Social Security Act, 42 U.S.C. §1320a-7b(b).

[34] Section 1128B(b)(3) of the Social Security Act, 42 U.S.C. §1320a-7b(b)(3).

[35] There are also physician self-referral prohibitions, generally banning physician referrals to facilities in which they themselves have an ownership interest or from which they receive compensation. These are found in Section 1877 of the Social Security Act, 42 U.S.C. §1395nn. See Congressional Research Service, *Health Care: Physician Self-Referrals, "Stark I and II"*.

[36] 42 U.S.C. §1320a-7b(a)(6). This provision became effective January 1, 1997.

Congress has amended this section to make it a crime for a person, for a fee, to counsel or assist an individual to dispose of assets in order for the individual to become eligible for Medicaid, if disposing of assets results in the imposition of a period of ineligibility under that program.[37] This offense is a misdemeanor and carries with it a fine of not more than $10,000 or imprisonment for not more than 1 year, or both.

Federal criminal prosecutions may also be brought under the more general health care fraud provisions recently added to title 18 of the United States Code, or under the generic fraud provisions in title 18 such as mail fraud (18 U.S.C. §1341), false claims to government agencies (18 U.S.C. §287 and §1001) and conspiracy to defraud the federal government (18 U.S.C. §371). The new federal health care offenses generally apply to violations involving both public and private health care benefit programs. Upon conviction of a federal health care offense a court may order forfeiture of property derived from such an offense.

Exclusion Provisions

Section 1128 of the Social Security Act,[38] authorizes the Secretary to impose mandatory and permissive exclusions of individuals and entities from participation in the Medicare program, Medicaid program and programs receiving funds under the Maternal and Child Health Services Block Grant or the Social Services Block Grant.[39] Mandatory exclusions are authorized for convictions of criminal offenses related to the delivery of health care services under Medicare and state health care programs, as well as for convictions relating to patient abuse in connection with the delivery of health care services, and for convictions of felony offenses relating to health care fraud or controlled substances. Mandatory exclusions are for a minimum period of 5 years.

Permissive exclusions are authorized for a number of offenses relating to fraud, kickbacks, obstruction of an investigation, and controlled substances, and for activities relating to license revocations or suspensions, claims for excessive charges or unnecessary services, and the like. There is a minimum period of exclusion for permissive exclusions, ranging from 1 to 3 years, depending on the basis for the permissive exclusion.[40] In addition, the Secretary has the authority to bar certain felons from participation in federal health care programs. The Secretary may exclude individuals with ownership or control interest in a sanctioned entity and, under certain circumstances, may also exclude entities controlled by a family member of a sanctioned individual.

An individual who is excluded from program participation is entitled to reasonable notice and opportunity for a hearing by the Secretary, and to judicial review of the Secretary's final decision in federal district court.[41] If the HHS Inspector General excludes an individual or entity from Medicare program participation, state Medicaid agencies must also exclude that

---

[37] Section 4737 of H.R. 2015, as passed by Congress on July 31, 1997. This amendment was effective upon enactment.

[38] 42 U.S.C. §1320a-7.

[39] Regulations implementing the authority for Medicare exclusions are at 42 C.F.R. Pt. 1001, with the Medicaid exclusion regulations at 42 C.F.R. P. 1002.

[40] Section 1128(c) of the Social Security Act, 42 U.S.C. §1320a-7(f).

[41] Section 1128(f) of the Social Security Act, 42 U.S.C. §1320a-7(f).

individual or entity from participation in Medicaid for the same period of time, although a state may request that exclusion from state health programs be waived.[42] In addition, under the recently added "three strikes and you're out" provision, a provider is excluded from federal health care programs for 10 years for a second fraud-related offense, and permanently excluded from federal health care programs for a third offense.[43]

Advisory Opinions and Other Statutory Requirements

The Secretary is required to solicit proposals in the *Federal Register* for modifications to existing safe harbors and new safe harbors under the Medicaid Patient and Program Protection Act provisions.[44] These provisions specify certain business practices which are normally prohibited, but which are nevertheless protected, as safe harbors, from criminal prosecution or civil sanction under the anti-kickback provisions. The Secretary may modify existing safe harbors or establish new safe harbors, as appropriate. The Secretary is also directed to issue written advisory opinions regarding whether a proposed transaction would violate anti-kickback restrictions and whether certain physician self-referrals are prohibited under federal law.[45] The opinions are binding between the Secretary and the requesting party. Individuals may also request the Inspector General to issue special fraud alerts informing the public of practices which the Inspector General considers to be suspect or of particular concern under Medicare or State health care programs.[46] Special fraud alerts are published in the *Federal Register*.

The HIPAA contained a provision requiring the Secretary of HHS to establish a national health care fraud and abuse data collection program containing reports of final adverse actions against health care providers, suppliers, and practitioners.[47] Certain information is to be included in the report submitted by federal and state governmental agencies and health plans, including a description of the acts or omissions and injuries upon which the final adverse action was based. Information in the database may be disclosed to federal and state

---

[42] 42 U.S.C. §1320a-7(d).

[43] Section 4301 of H.R. 2015, as passed by Congress on July 31, 1997.

[44] Section 1128D(a) of the Social Security Act, 42 U.S.C. §1320a-7d(a).

[45] Section 1128D(b) of the Social Security Act, 42 U.S.C. §1320a-7d(b). On February 19, 1997, the OIG issued regulations which specify the specific procedures to be employed by the OIG, in conjunction with the Department of Justice, in issuing these opinions. To date, one opinion has been issued.

[46] Section 1128D(c) of the Social Security Act, 42 U.S.C. §1320a-7d(c).

[47] Section 221 of Public Law 104-191, Section 1128E of the Social Security Act, 42 U.S.C. §1320a-7e.

agencies and health plans under certain circumstances. At the same time, the Secretary is to include procedures to protect the privacy of the individuals receiving health care services. The Secretary also has the authority to impose a civil monetary penalty of $25,000 on health plans that fail to report adverse actions under this health care data collection program.[48]

[48] Section 4331 of Public Law 105-33.

Chapter 7

HEALTH CARE SPENDING: PAST TRENDS AND PROJECTIONS

Christopher J. Sroka

ABSTRACT

This chapter focuses on trends in personal health care spending, which includes spending on health care goods and services provided to individuals and excludes expenditures for administrative costs, research, and public health activities. Personal health care expenditures have grown considerably over the past 40 years. Between 1960 and 2000 (the most recent year available), personal health care spending increased from \$23.4 billion to \$1.1 trillion. It is estimated that personal health spending will exceed \$2.4 trillion in 2011. Data on health expenditures suggest four important trends. First, in recent years, health spending has grown at lower rates than in the past, but future growth rates are projected to increase. Second, health care spending as a percent of gross domestic product declined in the late 1990s, but is projected to grown significantly in the next ten years. Third, four types of health services consistently compose the bulk of health care expenditures: hospital care, physician and clinical services, nursing home and home health care, and prescription drugs. Spending on prescription drugs has grown since 1980 and is projected to continue growing during the next decade. Fourth, over the past 40 years, the primary financing of health care has shifted from out-of-pocket payments to payments by private insurance and the federal government.

GROWTH IN SPENDING

In 2000 (the most recent year available), over $1.3 trillion was spent on health care and health-related activities.[1] **Table 1** indicates how this amount was spent. Data on national health expenditures include spending on a broad range of health-related activities. A small portion of 2000 health expenditures (about $169 billion, or 13%) was spend on administrative costs, net cost of private health insurance,[2] government public health activities, research,[3] and construction. However, the vast majority of 2000 health expenditures were spent on personal health care. Personal health care includes goods and services provided to individuals to treat or prevent medical conditions. The remainder of this chapter will focus on personal health care expenditures.

Type of Expenditure	Amount in billions
Personal health care expenditures:	
Hospital care	$412.1
Physician and clinical services	$286.4
Other professional services	$39.0
Nursing home care	$92.2
Home health care	$32.4
Prescription drugs	$121.8
Other non-durable medical products	$31.2
Durable medical equipment	$18.5
Dental services	$60.0
Other Personal Health Care	$36.7
Total personal health care expenditures	**$1,130.4**
Government administration and net cost of private health insurance	$80.9
Government public health activities	$44.2
Research	$25.4
Construction	$18.6
Total national health expenditures	**$1,299.5**

Source: Health Care Financing Administration, Office of the Actuary.

Note: The "Home Health Care" category excludes funds spent under the Medicaid Home and Community Based Waiver program. Expenditures under this program are included in the "Other Personal Health Care" category.

Spending on personal health care continues to increase every year. Between 1960 and 2000, expenditures for persona health care grew from $23.4 billion to $1.1 trillion; in 2011,

---

[1] All dollar figures cited in this report were obtained from the Health Care Financing Administration (HCFA), Office of the Actuary. All percentages were calculated by Congressional Research Service (CRS) using data from HCFA.

[2] Net cost of private health insurance is equal to the difference between all premiums paid to insurance providers minus what insurance providers must pay for the provision of health care to its members.

[3] Research excludes amounts spent by pharmaceutical manufacturers, medical equipment suppliers, and other companies. Expenditures on research and development by such entities are implicitly included in the spending figures for other categories, e.g., prescription drugs and durable medical equipment.

personal health care spending is projected to exceed $2.4 trillion. **Figure 1** tracks past and projected growth rates of personal health care spending in nominal terms (i.e., not adjusted for inflation). Expenditures for personal health care grew at an average rate of about 10% per year from 1960 to 2000. In recent years, however, personal health care spending has increased at rates well below this 40-year average. Between 1992 and 2000, personal health expenditures grew at an average rate of about 5% per year due to increased enrollment in less costly managed care plans. Experts project that personal health care expenditures grew 9% in 2001 due to the one-time effects of the Medicare, Medicaid, and SCHIP Benefits Improvement and Protection Act (BIPA, P.L. 106-554).[4] The Act increased government payments for many services covered by the Medicare program. Because the provisions of the act are temporary, growth in personal health expenditures is projected to level off after 2002. Between 2002 and 2011, personal health care spending is projected to increase at an average rate of about 7% per year.

Figure 1. Growth in Nominal Personal Health Care Expenditures

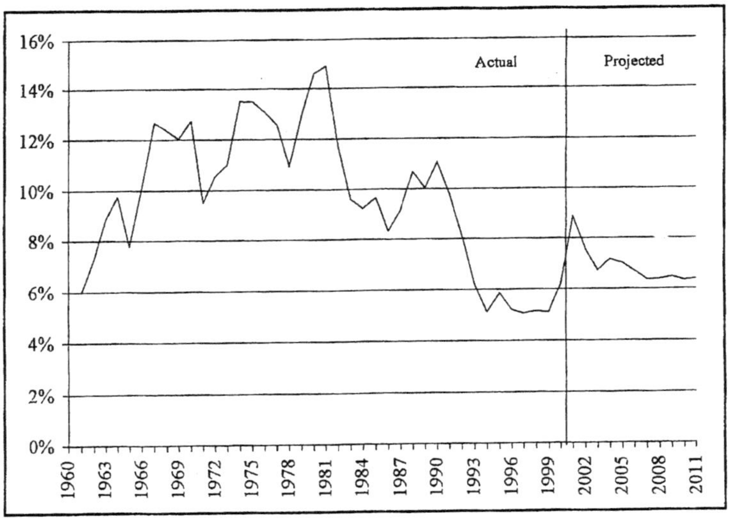

Source: CRS calculations using data from the Health Care Financing Administration, Office of the Actuary.

A combination of factors can cause nominal spending to increase: rising prices, population growth, increases in the quantity of medical services each person receives, advances in medical knowledge and technology, and other factors. Expenditures attributable to non-price factors are often referred to as "real" spending. Growth in real spending represents a quantitative and qualitative increase in the level of medical care that individuals are receiving and can indicate an improvement in the population's standard of living.[5]

[4] Heffler, Stephen, Sheila Smith, Greg Won, M. Kent Clemens, et al., *Health Spending Projections for 2001-2011: The Latest Outlook*. Health Affairs, March/April 2002.

[5] In general, higher consumption of goods and services (medical and non-medical alike) is usually viewed as improving the standard of living for an individual. However, some experts might argue that higher utilization is not always indicative of a higher standard of living. For example, an outbreak of a contagious disease would

Conversely, increases in health care expenditures attributable to higher prices represent only a pecuniary transfer from the payer to the providers and manufacturers of medical goods and services. Figure 2 depicts the share of nominal spending growth attributable to increases in medical care prices, increases in population, and increases in per capita real health expenditures (what some experts describe as the "intensity" of care). For much of the time period shown in Figure 2, prices played a larger role in nominal spending increases than population or non-price factors (e.g., improved medical technology or higher utilization). During the late 1990s, medical care prices, constrained by managed care, grew at lower rates than in any other year shown. Price growth is projected to increase during the next decade, though not to the high levels experience during the 1970s and 1980s.

Figure 2. Factors Influencing Growth in Nominal Personal Health Care Expenditures

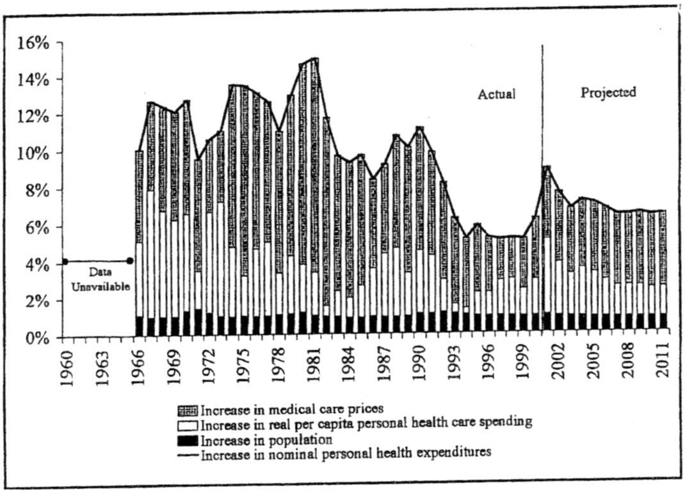

Source: CRS calculations using data from the U.S. Census Bureau and the Health Care Financing Administration, Office of the Actuary.

However, currently available price indexes may not accurately reflect changes in medical care prices. Ideally, a price index would measure only how much must be paid this year to receive the same level of care as that received in some base period, holding quality constant. But it is difficult to hold the quality of care constant over time considering the rate of medical advances. For example, heart surgeries today are of higher quality than those performed in the past, as measured by survival rates. Yet, price indices tend to treat both procedures as equal in quality. Thus, measures of increases in the price of heart surgeries capture both pure price increases as well of quality increases, which violates the basic principles of price indexes. By including quality effects in price measures, price indexes tend to overstate true increases in medical prices.[6]

increase the utilization of health services, yet no one would claim that those infected would have a higher standard of living.

[6] For more information, see Berndt, Ernst R., David M. Cutler, Richard G. Frank, Zvi Griliches, Joseph P. Newhouse, and Jack E. Triplett. "Price Indexes for Medical Care Goods and Services: An Overfiew of

HEALTH SPENDING AND GROSS DOMESTIC PRODUCT

Personal health expenditures as a percent of GDP have risen since 1960. This trend has two implications: (1) personal health care spending is growing faster than the overall economy, and (2) a larger share of the nation's economic resources is being devoted to providing medical goods and services to the population. **Figure 3** depicts past and projected personal health care spending as a percent of GDP. In 1960, personal health care expenditures were about 4% of GDP; in 2000, they were 11%. Much of this growth occurred between 1960 and 1991. During the mid-1990s, personal health expenditures as a percent of GEP remained relatively constant, indicating that these expenditures were growing at about the same rate as the overall economy. Since 1996, personal health expenditures as a percent of GDP declined, indicating that these expenditures grew at a slower rate than the overall economy. During the next decade, however, it is projected that personal health care spending will grow faster than the overall economy, accounting for 15% of GDP in 2011.

Figure 3. Personal Health Care Spending as a Percent of Gross Domestic Product (GDP)

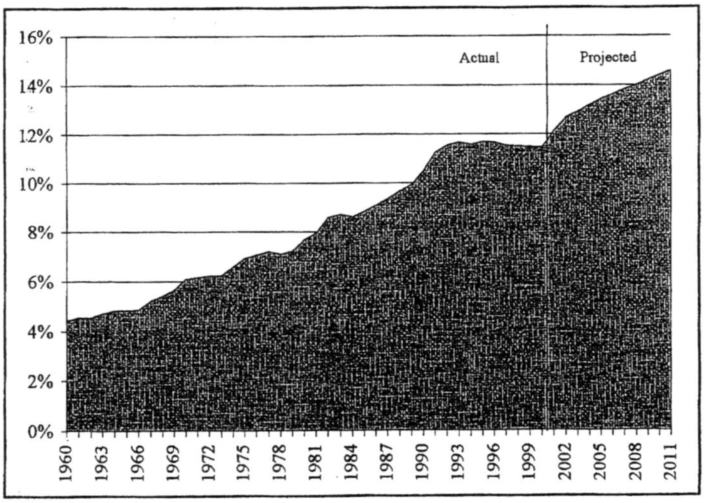

Source: CRS Calculations using the data from the Health Care Financing Administration, Office of the Actuary.

SPENDING ON SPECIFIC CATEGORIES OF HEALTH CARE

Of the total amount spent on personal health care, the largest categories of expenditures tend to be hospital care, physician and clinical services, nursing home and home health care, and prescription drugs. The contribution of these four categories to personal health spending has remained fairly constant, averaging 83% of total personal health care spending over the

Measurement Issues." Published in *Medical Care Output and Productivity*, edited by David M. Cutler and Ernst R. Brandt. (Chicago: The University of Chicago Press, 2001).

last four decades. However, the relative sizes of these categories have changed over time. **Figure 4** depicts past and projected spending on each of these categories as a percent of personal health care spending. Expenditures on hospital care, as a percent of personal health care spending. Expenditures on hospital care, as a percent of personal health spending, have decreased from 47% in 1980 to 36% in 2000. They are projected to decrease further in the future. This trend indicates that spending on hospital care is growing at a slower rate than spending on other categories of personal health care. Spending on prescription drugs as a percent of personal health care spending has increased from 6% in 1980 to 11% in 2000. It is projected to continue increasing through the next decade. Such a trend indicates that spending on prescription drugs is rising faster than other categories of personal health care. **Figure 4** probably underestimates the impact of prescription drugs on personal health care expenditures. Data on drug spending reflect prescription drugs obtained from retail pharmacies, but it excludes drugs provided from institutional pharmacies. Drugs dispensed to patients from a hospital or nursing home pharmacy are excluded from the prescription drug category. Instead, spending on drugs dispensed from institutional pharmacies is implicit in the amount spent for services at the respective institutions (e.g., hospital services or nursing home care).

Figure 4. Major Categories of Personal Health Care Spending as a Percent of Total Personal Health Expenditures

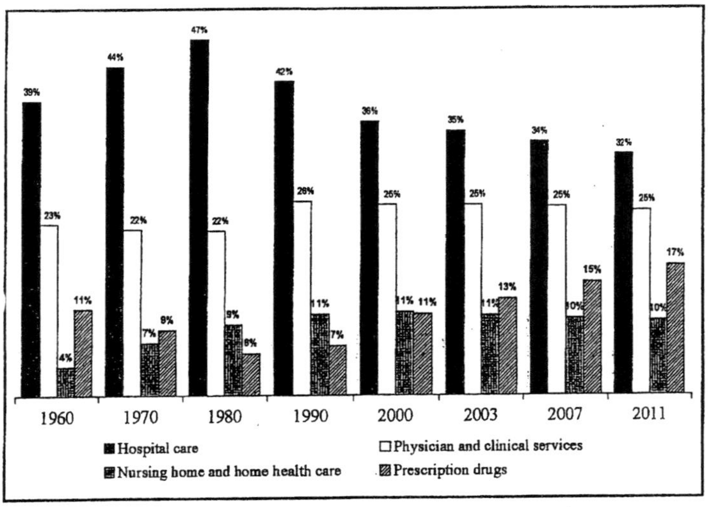

Source: CRS calculations using data from the Health Care Financing Administration, Office of the Actuary.

WHO PAYS FOR HEALTH CARE?

Direct payments for personal health care come from five general sources: consumer payments out-of-pocket, payments by private insurance companies, federal funds, state and local funds, and "other" private funds. Out-of-pocket payments include payments by those without health insurance. Out-of-pocket payments also include payments by the insured for deductibles, coinsurance, and costs not covered by insurance (excluding premiums). "Other" private funds consist mostly of philanthropic contributions to the health care system.

Ultimately, all health care spending is paid for by individuals through direct payments, cost-sharing, insurance premiums,[7] taxes. And charitable contributions. However, most of these payments are redistributed; what a person pays does not necessarily reflect how much health care that person receives. One who pays relatively high taxes might not have any of their health care financed by the government. Similarly, there are some people who pay health insurance premiums, yet use less care than the sum of the premiums paid. Only when individuals pay directly for the cost of treatment (either because they are uninsured or because they have not met their deductible) do personal expenditures directly reflect the amount of care received.

Figure 5 shows the percent of personal health care spending attributable to each source. In 1990, 55% of all personal health care was financed out-of-pocket, whereas private insurance paid for 21% and the federal government paid for 9%. In 2000, only 17% of personal health care was paid out-of-pocket while private insurance paid for 35% and the federal government paid for 33%. Much of the increase in the federal government's share of health spending occurred during the 1960s, when the Medicare and Medicaid programs were introduced. The increase in the federal government's share of payments during the 1990s is likely due to the ability of private insurance to reduce its share of expenditures through managed care. It is worth noting that during this period there was a dramatic increase in the quality and cost of health services.

Figure 5. Source of Payment for Personal Health Care as a Percent of Total Personal Health Expenditures

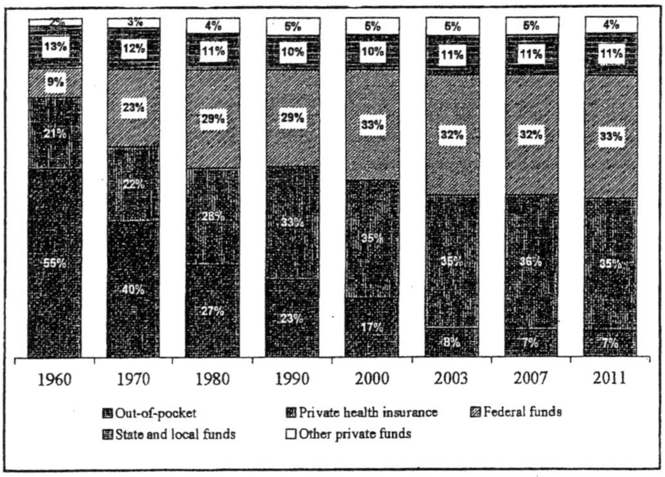

Source: CRS calculations using data from the Health Care Financing Administration, Office of the Actuary.

[7] Even if the employer is contributing all or a portion of the insurance premium, individual workers generally accept lower wages in exchange for this benefit. Thus, they pay for employer contributions to health care in the form of reduced wages that are lower than what they would otherwise be paid if the employer offered no health benefits.

Chapter 8

RURAL HEALTH CARE INITIATIVES IN CURRENT LAW

Celinda Franco

ABSTRACT

One-quarter of the U.S. population, about 65 million persons, reside in rural areas. Assuring access to health care services in rural areas has been an important component of national health care policy. Rural communities have unique characteristics and special needs that pose certain challenges to providing health care services. In general, rural populations have higher concentrations of elderly persons, higher levels of poverty, and higher unemployment. Health status indicators for rural populations also indicate that rural residents have higher rates of certain health problems than urban residents. Generally, rural populations have slightly higher infant mortality rates, significantly higher rates of deaths from accidents, and greater incidence of chronic illness and disability than urban residents.

Rural residents are slightly more likely than urban residents to be uninsured (in 1996, 16.3% in rural areas and 15.5% in urban areas). Rural residents are more often out of the mainstream of employment-based health insurance coverage because many are self-employed, seasonally employed, unemployed, or employed by small businesses that may not provide health insurance benefits. As a result, a higher proportion of rural residents do not have employer provided group health insurance. More rural residents purchase private, non-group health insurance policies (17.5% in rural areas compared to 11.8% in urban areas), that tend to be less comprehensive than group coverage. Some rural health experts raise the concern that, despite similar rates of uninsured in rural and urban areas, rural residents with privately purchased, non-group insurance coverage may be more likely to be purchasing less comprehensive insurance. A larger proportion of rural populations have incomes below the federal poverty line (16.2% compared to 13.4%).

Nearly half of all general hospitals in the United States are located in rural areas. Many of these hospitals face financial pressure as a result of a changing economic environment, and other factors. Since 1980, more than 300 rural community hospitals have closed. Many rural areas also continue to experience shortages of primary care physicians. Existing physician shortages are expected to become worse as many of these rural providers retire – almost 20% of physicians practicing in rural counties are over age 65.

Congressional concern over the special health care needs in rural areas over the years has prompted the creation of numerous programs designed to address some of the special needs of rural communities. Congress has created programs, demonstration programs, and studies aimed at ensuring continued rural access to health care. This chapter briefly describes federal programs designed to focus on the health care needs of rural residents. The descriptions of programs provided in this chapter include rural health initiatives specifically targeting rural health needs or predominantly service rural areas. It includes programs authorized under Medicare, Medicaid, the Public Health Service Act, the Department of Agriculture and the Appalachian Regional Development Act.

INTRODUCTION

One-quarter of the U.S. population resides in rural areas.[1] Assuring access to health care services in rural areas is an important component of national health care policy. Rural communities have unique characteristics and special needs that pose certain challenges to providing health care services. In general, rural populations have high concentrations of elderly persons and higher levels of poverty.

Health status indicators for rural populations indicate that rural residents have higher rates of certain health problems than urban residents. Rural populations are characterized as having lower mortality rates relative to urban areas, and injury-related mortality is significantly higher.[2] Rural populations also experience relatively higher rates of chronic disease and disability than urban populations.

According to the March 1997 Current Population Survey, rural residents are slightly more likely than urban residents to be uninsured (in 1996, 16.3% in rural areas and 15.5% in urban areas). Rural residents are more often out of the mainstream of employment-based health insurance coverage because many are self-employed, seasonally employed, unemployed, or employed by small businesses that may not provide health insurance benefits. As a result, a higher proportion of rural residents do not have employer provided group health insurance. More rural residents purchase private, non-group health insurance policies (17.5% in rural areas compared to 11.8% in urban areas), which tend to be less comprehensive than group coverage. Some rural health experts raise the concern that, despite similar rates of uninsured in rural and urban areas, rural residents with privately purchased, non-group insurance coverage may be more likely to be purchasing less comprehensive insurance. A larger proportion of rural populations have incomes below the federal poverty line (16.2% compared to 13.4%).

Nearly half of all general hospitals in the United Sates are located in rural areas. Many of these hospitals face financial pressure as a result of a changing economic environment, and

---

[1] The U.S. Census Bureau defines a rural area as places of 2,500 or fewer residents. However, rural areas are also generally defined as non-metropolitan counties.

[2] U.S. Congress. Office of Technology Assessment. Health Care in Rural America. OTA-H-434, September 1990. Washington, GPO, 1990. p. 6.

other factors. Since 1980, more than 300 rural community hospitals have closed. Many rural areas also continue to experience shortages of primary care physicians. Existing physician shortages are expected to soon become worse as many of these rural providers retire – almost 20% of physicians practicing in rural counties are over age 65. Furthermore, rural residents may also face additional barriers to obtaining health care as a result of geographic or physical barriers limiting access to providers, including the lack of public transportation in many rural areas.

Congressional concern over the special health care needs in rural areas over the years has prompted the creation of numerous programs designed to address some of the special needs of rural communities. Congress has created programs, demonstration programs, and studies aimed at ensuring continued rural access to health care. This chapter briefly describes federal programs designed to focus on the health care needs of rural residents. The descriptions of programs provided herein include all rural health initiatives specifically targeting rural health needs or predominantly service rural areas.

The organization of this chapter begins with provisions authorized under the Medicare and Medicaid programs that provide special payments to rural providers. The next section of the chapter includes programs authorized under the Public Health Service (PHS) Act which are designed to improve access to health care services by improving the supply and distribution of health professionals and health care facilities; provide for health care services block grants for low-income mothers and children; and provide for rural health policy and research development. The final section of the chapter briefly summarizes a program under the Department of Agriculture (DOA) which provides grants for projects using telecommunications technology to provide educational and medical benefits for rural residents, and a program authorized under the Appalachian Regional Development Act of 1965 providing grants that may be used for health care projects.

MEDICARE, MEDICAID, HEALTH CARE FINANCING PROGRAMS

Hospital Reimbursement

Medicare Prospective Payment System: Special Provisions for Rural Hospitals

Legislative Authority: Section 1886 of the Social Security Act sets forth Medicare reimbursement rules for inpatient hospital services.

Program Description. Under Medicare's prospective payment system (PPS), hospitals receive a fixed predetermined payment for each Medicare inpatient discharge. The payment amount varies according to the patient's diagnosis, the hospital's location (large urban areas or other area), the hospital area wage index, and other factors. The following special rules apply to rural hospitals.

Regional Referral Centers (RRCs). RRCs are relatively large rural hospitals that generally provide a broad array of services and treat patients from a wide geographic area. RRCs must have at least 275 beds or meet specific criteria that would indicate that the facility receives a high referral volume from other hospitals. Payments to RRCs were originally based on the rates for hospitals designated as **other urban** rather than the rural rates because the service mix of an RRC resembles that of an urban hospital. However, beginning in FY1995, the separate other urban and rural area payment rates were combined and RRCs are paid at the **other areas** hospital payment rate. The Omnibus Budget Reconciliation Act of 1993 (OBRA 93, P.L. 103-66) extended the classification through FY1994 for RRCs classified on September 30, 1992. Although RRCs lose some of the benefits of their classification status because of the equalization of the other urban and rural payment rates beginning in FY1995, RRCs continue to be entitled to higher disproportionate share adjustment payments and to preferential consideration before the Medicare Geographic Classification Review Board, described below. In FY1997, there were 130 RRCs estimated to receive $2.1 billion in Medicare PPS payments.

The BBA 97 provides that hospitals designated as RRCs since FY1991 are permanently classified as RRCs. The BBA 97 also prohibits the Medicare Geographic Classification Review Board (MGCRB) from rejecting a RRCs request for geographic reclassification on the basis of any comparison of its average hourly wage and the average hourly wage of hospitals in the area where the RRC is located.

Sole Community Hospitals (SCHs). SCHs are facilities located in geographically isolated areas and are determined to be the sole provider of inpatient, acute-care hospital services in a geographic area based on distance, travel time, severe weather conditions, and/or market share. SCH rates are based on a blend of the facility's own historic costs and costs for other rural hospitals. In FY1997, 754 hospitals were classified as SCHs. In FY1997, there were 648 SCHs estimated to receive $2.0 billion in Medicare payments.

Medicare-Dependent Hospitals (MDHs). MDHs are small rural hospitals that treat relatively high proportions of Medicare patients. To qualify as an MDH, a hospital must be located in a rural area; not be an SCH; have 100 or fewer beds; and have had at least 60% of hospital discharges or patient days during its base cost-reporting period (the hospital fiscal year beginning during federal FY1988) attributable to Medicare beneficiaries. MDHs are paid in the same way as SCHs. MDHs accounted for about 12% of rural Medicare discharges in 1991. OBRA 93 extended additional payments to MDHs through September 30, 1994, on a phase-down basis. As of September 1994, there were 393 hospitals classified as MDHs. Medicare payments for MDHs are not separated from other payments to rural hospitals and are not available.

The BBA 97 reinstated and extends the MDH classification beginning October 1, 1997 through October 1, 2001. As of September 1997, there were 366 MDHs.

Medicare Geographic Classification Review Board. The Omnibus Budget Reconciliation Act of 1990 (OBRA 90) established the Medicare Geographic Classification Board to evaluate hospitals' applications for reclassification to a different geographical area. The Board may reclassify a hospital for the purposes of determining its standardized amount, its wage index, or both. Urban and rural hospitals can apply if the hospital can prove that its geographic assignment is inappropriate because it competes for patients and employees with hospitals located in other areas. For FY1997, 477 hospitals were reclassified by the MGCRB.

Administering Agency: Health Care Financing Administration (HCFA), Department of Health and Human Services (DHHS).

Funding: Special payments to rural hospitals are made as regular Medicare payments and are not subject to annual appropriations.

Medicare Rural Hospital Flexibility Program

Legislative Authority: This program was created by the Balanced Budget Act of 1997 (BBA 97, P.L. 105-33) as a new limited service hospital program. The program grandfathers in the Montana Medical Assistance Facilities (MAFs) and the existing Essential Access Community Hospitals (EACHs) and Rural Primary Care Hospitals (RPCHs).

Program Description: Medicare Rural Hospital Flexibility Program is a new limited service hospital program that requires states to designate critical access hospitals (CAHs) and develop at least one rural health network. CAHs must be located more than a 35-mile drive from another hospital, have 24-hour emergency care, no more than 15 acute inpatient beds with a 96-hour length-of-stay limitation (with some exceptions) and may have swing beds. The program includes authorization of appropriations of $25 million for FY1998-FY2002 for grants to states for planning, network development and CAH designation activities.

Administering Agency: HCFA, DHHS.

Funding: No funds were appropriated for FY1998.

Rural Health Care Transition Grants

Legislative Authority: Authorized by the Omnibus Budget Reconciliation Act of 1987 (OBRA 87, P.L. 100-203) and extended through FY1991 by the Omnibus Budget Reconciliation Act of 1989 (OBRA 89, P.L. 101-239). The Social Security Act Amendments of 1994 (P.L. 103-432) extended the program's authority through FY1997.

Program Description: Rural health care transition grants of up to $50,000 per year are available to nonprofit acute care hospitals in rural areas with fewer than 100 beds. The grants can be used for improvement of outpatient or emergency services, recruitment of health professionals, or development of alternative delivery systems such as rural health networks. During FY1996, grants were made to 65 facilities in 40 states and Puerto Rico.

Administering Agency: ORD, HCFA, DHHS.

Funding: The FY1996 appropriation was $13.1 million. No funding was provided for FY1997 or FY1998.

Physician and Other Health Care Provider Reimbursement

Medicare Physician Reimbursement for Rural Physicians

Legislative Authority: Title XVIII of the Social Security Act, Section 1833(m) – originally enacted in OBRA 87 and amended by OBRA 89.

Program Description: Medicare requires that bonus payments be made to physicians who furnish covered services to Medicare beneficiaries in health professional shortage areas (HPSAs). This bonus payment is equal to 10% of amounts payable under the Medicare physician fee schedule.

Administering Agency: HCFA, DHHS.

Funding: Special payments to rural physicians are made as regular Medicare payments and are not subject to annual appropriations.

Medicare Reimbursement for Nurse Practitioners, Clinical Nurse Specialists and Physician Assistants (PAs)

Legislative Authority: Title XVIII of the Social Security Act, Section 1861(s)(2)(k) and 1842(b)(12) – originally enacted in the Omnibus Budget Reconciliation Act of 1986 (OBRA 86), amended by OBRA 87 and 89, and amended by BBA 97.

Program Description: Medicare pays for certain services provided by nurse practitioners, clinical nurse specialists and physician assistants practicing in rural or urban areas, provided under the supervision of a physician, but only if no facility or other provider charge is paid. (Prior to the enactment of BBA 97, the law specified that Medicare would reimburse for services provided by these non-physician practitioners only in certain settings.) Payment is limited to the lesser of the actual charge or 85% of the participating physician fee schedule amount.

Administering Agency: HCFA, DHHS.

Funding: Payments to nurse practitioners, clinical nurse specialists, and physicians assistants practicing in rural areas are made as regular Medicare payments and are not subject to annual appropriations.

Rural Health Clinics

Medicare and Medicaid – Rural Health Clinics

Legislative Authority: Title XVIII of the Social Security Act, Section 1861(aa), and Title XIX of the Social Security Act, as amended.

Program Description: Medicare and Medicaid make payments to rural health clinics. These are facilities that provide the following services: (1) physician services and services incident to a physician's service; (2) similar services furnished by a physician assistant, nurse practitioner, clinical psychologist, and clinical social worker and services incident to their services; and (3) part-time or intermittent nursing care and medical supplies (other than drugs and biologicals) furnished by a registered nurse or licensed practical nurse to a homebound patient in an area where there is a shortage of home health agencies. Rural health clinic services are paid by the programs when furnished to a patient at the clinic, at a hospital or other medical facility, or at the patient's place of residence. BBA 97 extends per visit payment limits, formerly only applicable to independent RHCs, to provider-based RHCs.

Administering Agency: HCFA, DHHS.

Funding: Medicare and Medicaid payments to rural health clinics are made as regular Medicare and Medicaid payments and are not subject to annual appropriations.

PUBLIC HEALTH SERVICE (PHS)

Health Professions Education and Training Programs

National Health Service Corps (NHSC)

Legislative Authority: PHS Act, Title III, Section 338A-I, as amended by P.L. 101-597.

Program Description: The NHSC provides scholarships for medical and other health professions students, and loan repayments of health professions education expenses for health professionals who agree to serve for a 2-year minimum period of obligated service in a federally designated HPSA in return for each year of scholarship assistance or loan repayment. Health professionals can include physicians, dentists, certified nurse midwives, certified nurse practitioners, and PAs as well as other health professionals that are determined to be needed by the program. The program also provides grants to states for operating a loan repayment program similar to the NHSC loan repayment program for the educational expenses of qualified health professionals willing to enter a period of obligated service in an underserved area of the state. The program is designed to improve the geographic misdistribution of health professionals in federally designated HPSAs.

Administering Agency: HRSA, PHS, DHHS.

Funding: The FY1997 appropriation was $115.9 million. The FY1998 appropriation was $115.4 million.

Area Health Education Centers (AHECs)

Legislative Authority: PHS Act, Section 746, as amended by P.L. 102-408.

Program Description: The AHEC program provides project grants to improve the supply, quality, utilization, and efficiency of health personnel in the health service delivery system and for the purpose of increasing the regionalization of educational responsibilities of health professional schools. The AHEC program establishes a network of health-related institutions to provide educational services to students, faculty, and practitioners, by linking the academic resources of the university health science center with local planning, educational and clinical resources in an area. The program assists health professions schools in the planning, development, and operation of an AHEC by requiring specific activities and relationships between the participating medical schools and the freestanding, community-based centers that provide training sites and resources for training activities. Eligible entities include accredited public or nonprofit schools of allopathic or osteopathic medicine, a consortium of such schools, or the parent institution on behalf of such schools. The participating institution is required to participate in the project funding by providing matching funds of at least 25% from nonfederal sources for each year of the project.

In addition, Section 746(f) of the PHS Act authorizes grants to schools of allopathic and osteopathic medicine for planning, developing, establishing, maintaining, and operating health education and training centers to improve the supply, distribution, quality, and effic9iency of personnel providing health services in the state of Florida or (in the United States) along the border between the United States and Mexico.

Administering Agency: HRSA, PHS, DHHS.

Funding: The FY1997 appropriation was $28.5 million. The FY1998 appropriation was $28.6 million.

Nursing Education Loan Repayment Agreements

Legislative Authority: PHS Act, Section 836(h), as amended by P.L. 100-607.

Program Description: This program provides grants to eligible health facilities located in areas experiencing a serious shortage of nurses to enter into agreements with registered nurses willing to work full-time for a 2-year minimum period of obligated service in exchange for the repayment of their nursing education loans. Eligible facilities include Indian Health Service health centers, Native Hawaiian health centers, nursing facilities, rural health clinics, or health facilities determined by the Secretary of DHHS to have a critical shortage of nurses.

Administering Agency: HRSA, PHS, DHHS.

Funding: The FY1997 appropriation was $2.2 million. The FY1998 appropriation was $2.2 million.

Interdisciplinary Training for Health Care in Rural Areas

Legislative Authority: PHS Act, Section 778, as amended by P.L. 102-408.

Program Description: This program provides grants to promote the recruitment and retention of health professionals in rural areas through interdisciplinary team training in rural health care settings. Grant funds are awarded to eligible applicants to carry out training projects using various methods, including student stipends, post-doctoral fellowships, faculty training, and the purchase or rental of transportation and telecommunication equipment where appropriate to the rural area.

Administering Agency: HRSA, PHS, DHHS.

Funding: The FY1997 appropriation was $4.2 million. The FY1998 appropriation was $4.2 million.

Primary Care Facilities and Services

Rural Health Outreach Grant Programs

Legislative Authority: Initiated by HRSA and the Office of Rural Health Policy (ORHP), the program was provided initially under P.L. 101-517, Departments of Labor, Health and Human Services, and Education FY1991 appropriation, under the general authority of the Secretary of DHHS provided in Section 301 of the PHS Act.

Program Description: This program provides grants to not-for-profit, public or private health care facilities located in rural areas to: enable services to be provided to rural underserved populations; enhance service capacity or expand service areas to increase access to health care services; facilitate integration and coordination of services in or among rural communities; and enhance linkages, integration and cooperation among the various entities eligible to receive grants. The program is designed to support projects demonstrating new and innovative models of outreach and health care services delivery in rural areas that lack basic health services.

Projects can include those designed to meet the needs of a wide range of rural population groups with special health care needs, including the poor, the elderly, the disabled, pregnant women, infants, adolescents, and rural minority populations. Applicants must apply in conjunction with two or more other entities as part of a consortium, in order to better integrate and coordinate the provision of health services in rural areas.

Administering Agency: ORHP, HRSA, DHHS.

Funding: The FY1997 appropriation was $27.8 million. The FY1998 appropriation was $32.6 million.

Consolidated Health Centers (CHCs)

Legislative Authority: PHS Act, Section 330 as amended, P.L. 104-299.

Program Description: This program provides project grants to support the development and operation of CHCs to provide access to comprehensive, high quality, case-managed, family-based primary health care services to populations at risk for numerous and complex medical problems living in rural and urban medically underserved areas, including uninsured children, women, migrant workers, homeless persons, public housing residents, and U.S./Mexico border residents. CHCs are required to provide primary health services which include the services of physicians, physicians' assistants and nurse clinicians; diagnostic laboratory and radiologic services; preventive health services; emergency medical services; transportation services; preventive dental services; and pharmaceutical services. CHCs may also provides supplemental services such as mental health services, health education, or other services appropriate to meet the health needs of the residents of their service area.

In FY1998, the CHC program has the total service capacity to treat 10.3 million persons through 700 public and non-profit community grantee organizations, 122 grantees at over 400 migrant farmworker sites, 123 grantees for homeless people in 48 states, 26 school-based sites, and 38 public housing sites.

Administering Agency: HRSA, PHS, DHHS.

Funding: The FY1997 appropriation was $802 million. The FY1998 appropriation was $826 million.

Maternal and Child Health Services Block Grant

Legislative Authority: Social Security Act, Title V, authorized by the Omnibus Budget Reconciliation Act of 1981 (OBRA 81, P.L. 97-35), as amended by OBRA 89, P.L. 101-239.

Program Description: This program provides grants to states as well as special project grants to other entities for the provision of health care services for low-income mothers and children who do not have access to adequate health care. States may also use funds for health-related activities that would enable states to maintain and strengthen their ability to promote, coordinate, and evaluate health care for mothers and children including planning, administration, education and evaluation. Beginning in FY1991, states are required to use at least 30% of their federal allotment for preventive and primary care services for children, and at least 30% for services for children with special health care needs.

During FY1998, over 17 million women, infants, children, adolescents, and children with special health care needs were provided services under the program.

Administering Agency: HRSA, PHS, DHHS.

Funding: The FY1997 appropriation was $681.1 million. The FY1998 appropriation was $683 million.

Rural Health Policy and Research

Agency for Health Care Policy and Research (AHCPR)

Legislative Authority: OBRA 89, P.L. 101-239.

Program Description: AHCPR focuses on the link between health research, evaluations of the effectiveness of health care interventions, and health policy. In its authorizing legislation, the agency is specifically required to pay particular attention to research, demonstration, and evaluation activities related to the delivery of health care services in rural areas.

In the area of rural health, AHCPR continues to support five rural centers, established in FY1993 (described below), that focus on regional issues related to the development of rural health policy for cost and quality of, and access to, health services particularly for disabled and minority populations. In addition, AHCPR provides support for up to five cooperative agreements for rural health service demonstrations to plan and initiate statewide or regional managed care system demonstration, incorporating certain features of primary care and clinical preventive services. The demonstrations projects are to be located in states with: limited public transportation or geographic features limiting transportation; significant health status problems; limited statewide managed care; high unemployment; and a high number of health professions shortage areas.

Administering Agency: DHHS.

Funding: The FY1997 appropriation was $143.6 million for all of AHCPR program activities. AHCPR estimates that in FY1997, $4.4 million was to be provided to fund rural health projects. The FY1998 appropriation was $146.4 million for all of AHCPR program activities. AHCPR estimated that in FY1998, $3.3 million will be provided to fund rural health projects.

Office of Rural Health Policy (ORHP)

Legislative Authority: OBRA 87, P.L. 100-203.

Program Description: ORHP advises the Secretary of DHHS on the effect of Medicare and Medicaid programs on access to health care by rural population; coordinates rural health research within DHHS, and administers grant programs supporting the Rural Health Research Centers (RHRCs) and Rural Telemedicine Grants (described below); provides staff support to the National Advisory Committee on Rural Health; articulates the views of rural constituencies within the federal establishment; and sponsors a national clearinghouse for the collection and dissemination of rural health information at the National Agricultural Library.

Administering Agency: HRSA, PHS, DHHS.

Funding: The ORHP does not receive a separate appropriation, but instead is funded out of the HRSA program management appropriation.

Office of Rural Mental Health Research:

Legislative Authority: Section 464T of the PHS Act as amended by Section 124 of the Alcohol, Drug Abuse, and Mental Health Administration (ADAMHA) Reorganization Act of 1992, P.L. 102-321.

Program Description: The Office of Rural Mental Health Research within the National Institute of Mental Health (NIMH) coordinates the research and information dissemination activities of DHHS related to mental health services for residents of rural areas. NIMH is conducting research on problems of limited access to mental health services in rural areas, including shortages of providers, poverty, geographic and transportation barriers, through rural research centers established for that purpose. Additional research centers focus on mental health service provision in rural areas and the behavior problems faced by youths in rural areas.

Administering Agency: National Institutes of Health, PHS, DHHS.

Funding: The FY1997 funding was $23.6 million. The FY1998 funding estimate was $24.3 million.

Grants to States for Operation of Offices of Rural Health

Legislative Authority: PHS Act, Section 338J, as amended by P.L. 101-597.

Program Description: This program provides states with a matching grant to support the establishment and ongoing operation of State Offices of Rural Health. Each state is required to: 1) establish an information clearinghouse; 2) coordinate state and federal rural health programs throughout the state; and 3) provide technical assistance to improve participation in state and federal programs. In addition, State Offices of Rural Health can conduct other activities to address unique state needs.

Administering Agency: ORHP, HRSA, PHS, DHHS.

Funding: The FY1997 appropriation was $3.0 million. The FY1998 appropriation was $3.0 million.

Rural Health Policy Development (RHPD)

Legislative Authority: Departments of Labor, Health and Human Services, and Education, and Related Agencies Appropriation Act of 1992, P.L. 102-170.

Program Description: RHPD provides grants to support the development and operation of an information base and policy analysis capacity on the full range of rural health issues, including reimbursement, recruitment and retention of health professionals, access to care, and alternative delivery systems. Grants may be made to public and private, nonprofit and for-profit entities that may include institutions for higher education, public or private health research organizations and foundations.

Administering Agency: ORHP, HRSA, PHS, DHHS.

Funding: The FY1997 funding estimate was $8.7 million. The FY1998 funding estimate was $11.7 million (includes appropriation for telemedicine grants, below).

Rural Telemedicine Grants

Legislative Authority: Departments of Labor, Health and Human Services, and Education, and Related Agencies Appropriations Act of 1994, P.L. 103-112.

Program Description: This program provides grants to demonstrate and collect information on the feasibility, costs, appropriateness, and acceptability (to practitioners and patients) of telemedicine for improving access to health care services for rural residents. Grants may be made to nonprofit public or private entities that can provide a wide range of medical specialty consultation services on a 24-hour basis to rural sites using telecommunication.

Program Jurisdiction: ORHP, HRSA, PHS, DHHS.

Funding: The FY1997 appropriation was $5.75 million. The FY1998 funding estimate was $15 million, including funding for a new project on telemedicine/telehealth.

DEPARTMENT OF AGRICULTURE (DOA)

Distant Learning and Medical Link Grants

Legislative Authority: Food, Agriculture, Conservation and Trade Act of 1990, title XXIII, P.L. 101-624.

Program Description: This program provides grants to organizations such as schools, libraries, hospitals, medical centers, or similar facilities to encourage and improve the use of telecommunications, computer networks, and related advanced technologies to provide education and medical benefits to people living in rural areas.

Program Jurisdiction: Rural Electrification Administration, DOA.

Funding: The FY1997 funding was $7.5 million. The FY1998 funding estimate was $20.9 million.

OTHER AGENCIES

Appalachian Health Programs

Legislative Authority: Appalachian Regional Development Act of 1965, Section 202 and 214, P.L. 89-4, as amended most recently by P.L. 102-104.

Program Description: This program provides project grants to assist in the reorganization of health care delivery, reduce infant mortality, and recruit needed health professionals in designated HPSAs in the Appalachia. Grants are limited to nonprofit institutions or units of government. Construction and operating grants are available only for publicly owned facilities or facilities owned by public or private nonprofit organizations and not themselves operated for profit. Upon determination that the state approved project is included within the Regional Appalachian Health Plan, DHHS is notified and is responsible for administering the grants and disbursing the funds.

Program Jurisdiction: Appalachian Regional Commission.

Funding: There is no specific appropriation for health programs. However, states may choose to fund rural health care as a part of their overall grant allocation.

Chapter 9

MANAGED HEALTH CARE: FEDERAL AND STATE REGULATION

Beth C. Fuchs

ABSTRACT

Numerous bills have been introduced in the 105th Congress to regulate managed health care. Some target specific aspects of the delivery of care, such as hospital length-of-stay for mastectomies. Others address a broad range of customer and provider concerns that have emerged as managed care has become more commonplace. State legislatures have been even more active on this issue with over 1,000 managed care bills introduced in 1996 alone. Key to understanding these federal and state proposals is the current regulatory environment in which managed care organizations (MCOs) function.

The regulation of managed care depends on who sponsors the plan and who bears the risk for paying for the insured services. Generally, the federal government regulates managed care and other health plans sponsored by private-sector employers. On the other hand, the states regulate the business of insurance, which includes the MCO (such as health maintenance organization (HMO)) that offers a managed care policy to an individual, employer, or other purchaser. If a private sector employer sponsors a plan that is not purchased from an MCO (i.e., the plan is self-insured), then the plan is regulated solely by the federal government. If that employer contracts with an MCO to provide managed care services to his or her employees, then the regulation of that plan depends on who bears the risk. If it is the MCO, the plan is regulated by the state; if the risk is borne to any degree by the employer, then the plan is subject to federal law only.

The tradition division of regulatory responsibilities between the federal government and the states resulted from provisions of several federal laws and subsequent decisions of federal courts. Most importantly, the Employee Retirement Income Security Act of 1974 (ERISA) preempted the states from regulating health plans of private sector employers but left to the states the regulation of the business of insurance. While the HMO Act of 1973 established certain federal standards for HMOs that elected to operate under federal law, almost all other regulatory authority over the business of health insurance remained with the states. This deferral to state regulation of insurers has been somewhat altered with the Health Insurance Portability and Accountability Act of 1996 (P.L. 104-191) to the extent that it applies certain federal *minimum* requirements to state-regulated insurers as well as to employer-sponsored plans, including managed care plans.

The regulation of managed care varies significantly across the 50 states. Many have HMO laws and regulations that are based on the National Association of Insurance Commissioner's (NAIC) HMO Model Act. Some have used the NAIC model as a floor and have adopted more stringent requirements on MCOs. Responding to the emergence of varying types of risk-bearing entities that provide both insurance and improvement, provider credentialing, network adequacy, grievance procedures, standards for utilization review, and will be issuing one on capital standards to ensure solvency. State laws may begin to incorporate these models as they respond to these and other issues arising from the growth of managed care.

OVERVIEW

Who regulates managed care plans and what requirements and standards must they meet in order to operate? This chapter explains the role of federal and state laws in regulating managed care, summarizes the relevant federal statues, and highlights major regulatory issues that are arising with respect to this growing sector of the health insurance marketplace. It also reviews the model laws developed by the National Association of Insurance Commissioners (NAIC) that often form the basis for state statutes. Last of all, it details some of the ways in which states have gone beyond NAIC model laws in regulating aspects of managed care, and provides a summary listing of selected managed care laws that have been enacted by the states.

The regulation of managed care is becoming an increasingly salient issue at all levels of government. In 1996 alone, state lawmakers introduced over 1,000 bills affecting managed care.[1] At the federal level, the 104th Congress responded to increasing consumer and provider concerns about access to and quality of managed care by passing a law to allow new mothers to remain in the hospital for at least 48 hours after a normal delivery.[2] Another bill, which would have prohibited the restriction of communications between providers and their patients, came close to enactment. In the first session of the 105th Congress, bills have been introduced regulating a wide range of managed care activities, including: the amount and scope of coverage for specific procedures, such as mastectomies; access to emergency care and specialist services; quality assurance; plan disclosure; due process standards for providers; and appeals and grievance procedures for enrollees.[3] The White House too has been active on

---

[1] Bodenheimer, Thomas. The HMO Backlash-Righteous or Reactionary? *New England Journal of Medicine*, v. 335, no. 21, November 21, 1996. p. 1601-1604.

[2] For more information, see: U.S. Library of Congress. Congressional Research Service. *Hospital Length-of-Stay for Obstetrical Care*. CRS Report 95-1114, by Sharon Kearney, updated November 1, 1996. Washington, 1996. (Hereafter cited as Kearney, *Hospital Length-of-Stay for Obstetrical Care*, 1996).

[3] The Balanced Budget Act of 1997 (P.L. 105-33) includes requirements on managed care plans that contract with Medicare and Medicaid. These requirements are summarized in: U.S. Library of Congress. Congressional Research Service. *Medicare Provisions in the Balanced Budget Act of 1997* (BBA-P.L. 105-33). CRS Report 97-802, by Jennifer O'Sullivan, et al., August 18, 1997. Washington, 1997. (Hereafter cited O'Sullivan, et al., *Medicare Provisions in the Balanced Budget Act of 1997* (BBA 97, P.L. 105-33), 1997); *Medicaid: FY1998*

this issue. The President's Advisory Commission on Consumer Protection and Quality in the Health Care Industry is expected to report in November 1997 on its recommendations for a consumer bill of rights that will, in part, by a response to concerns about managed care.

A key to understanding all of these managed care proposals is an understanding of the current regulatory environment in which managed care organizations (MCOs) function. Aiding such an understanding is the purpose of this chapter.

CONCEPTS AND TERMINOLOGY

Managed care is a term that generally means a system of payment or delivery arrangement where the health plan attempts to control or coordinate use of health services by its enrolled members in order to control spending and promote improved health. Like fee-for-service insurance, managed care arrangements accept financial responsibility for a defined set of health care benefits in return for a premium paid by or on behalf of each enrolled member. Unlike fee-for-service insurers, managed care arrangements directly provide or arrange for health care services, through affiliated physicians, hospitals and other providers, instead of simply paying bills. The enrollees covered by the managed care plan agree to obtain all covered services, except emergency and out-of-areas care[4], from or with the authorization of the managed care plan or its affiliated providers. The MCO may reduce unnecessary hospitalizations, diagnostic tests, or specialty referrals, either through programs to review the use of services or by giving participating physicians a financial stake in the cost of the services they order. It may also select low-cost providers of services or negotiate discounted rates from providers.

At one time, the only type of arrangement that offered managed care was a health maintenance organization (HMO). Today, managed care coverage is provided by an array of entities, such as preferred provider organizations (PPOs) and provider sponsored organizations (PSOs), many of which offer more open-ended coverage than do traditional HMOs. As in traditional HMOs, these arrangements provide covered services through provider networks. Enrollees are given financial incentives to use services within the plan's provider network, but still receive some coverage even if they decide to obtain care from outside providers.[5]

Managed care health insurance coverage, like fee-for-service coverage, is offered by several types of entities. An insurer, such as a commercial health insurance company or a Blue Cross/Blue Shield plan may offer managed care coverage to employers. It may also offer such coverage to individuals who purchase insurance directly (i.e., not as a member of a group such as an employer group). Similarly, an HMO, PPO, or other type of managed care arrangement may also offer managed care coverage to an employer. An employer may itself

Budget. CRS Issue Brief 97037, by Melvina Ford, et al., updated August 13, 1997. Washington, 1997. (Hereafter cited as Ford, *Medicaid: FY1998 Budget*, 1997).

[4] Many managed care plans require that enrollees obtain prior authorization from the plan for emergency care services that are not life-threatening and for any such services that are obtained from providers that are not part of the MCO's network, including those who are out of the MCO's service area.

[5] For additional background on managed care organizations, see: U.S. Library of Congress. Congressional Research Service. *Managed Health Care: A Primer*. CRS Report 97-913, by Jason Lee. Washington, 1997.

sponsor a health benefits program that includes one or more managed care options. It may therefore be considered the *sponsor or issuer* of the plan. Finally, a public program such as Medicare or Medicaid, may contract with MCOs to offer managed care to program beneficiaries.

To complicate matters, various forms of entities may serve as intermediaries between purchasers and insurers. Such entities help to facilitate the offering and marketing of managed care policies to employers (and sometimes individuals). Purchasing cooperative, for example, help to give purchasers (such as small employers) more buying clout in obtaining health benefits for their employees. Others, such as third party administrators (TPAs), may offer certain types of services to employers ranging from claims administration to *stop-loss insurance* for high cost claims or for overall claims in excess of some pre-established amount of money. **Figure 1** illustrates the many different types of entities that may issue managed care health insurance.

Insured Versus Self-Insured Plans

Self-insured Employer Plan – A plan in which the employer takes on some or all of the risk of paying for the plan's covered items and services. (Also known as self-funded or not-fully-insured plans.) Many self-insured plans assume risk for some amount of claims and then buy stop-loss coverage from a third party (such as a third party administrator) to cover losses over a preset amount or percentage of claims.

Insured Employer Plan – A plan purchased from an insuring entity, such as a commercial insurer, Blue Cross/Blue Shield, or a managed care organization. The employer pays the insurer a premium in exchange for the insurer assuming the risk of the plan's covered items and services.

Figure 1. Who Provides Managed Care Health Insurance?

Insurers/MCOs

(These entities offer/sell coverage to individuals, groups, or both)

- Commercial insurers
- Blue Cross/Blue Shield
- Managed Care Companies – HMOs, PPOs, PSOs.

Employers

(Employers can sponsor health plans that cover their employees and employees' dependents. These plans may be insured or self-insured.)

- Private-sector employers
- Governmental employers (nonfederal which include state and local governments and federal which includes the Federal Employees Health Benefits Program)
- Church sponsored plans
- Multiple Employer/Association Sponsors
- Multi-employer Plans

Public Insurance Sponsors

- Medicare
- Medicaid
- Department of Veterans Affairs
- Department of Defense

Insurance is a way to spread risk. The *risk* for paying for services covered under a managed care plan (and a fee-for-service plan too) can be handled in different ways. An employer, for example, can fully *self-insure* the services covered under its managed care plan. In so doing, it is assuming 100% of the risk of paying for the plan's covered services. No risk is transferred to an insurer. Alternatively, the employer can purchase a *fully-insured* plan from an insurer or managed care company, thereby transferring all of the risk of paying for covered services. In return for assuming the risk, the insurer gets a premium from the employer priced to cover the expected costs of services used by the employer plan's enrollees. Sometimes, however, risk is shared between an employer and another entity, such as an insurer, managed care company, or TPA. In this case, the plan is said to be *not-fully-insured* or *partially self-insured.*

THE DIVISION OF FEDERAL AND STATE RESPONSIBILITIES

The regulation of a managed care plan depends on who is its issuer. In general, the federal government regulates private sector employer health plans, including managed care plans that are sponsored by a private employer. The states regulate the business of insurance, which includes an HMO or other type of MCO that sells a health insurance policy to an individual, employer, or other purchaser. States also oversee plans sponsored by state and local governments. If a private sector employer sponsors a plan that is not purchased from a MCO (i.e., the plan is self-insured), then the plan is regulated solely by the federal government.[6] If a private sector employer contracts with a MCO to provide managed care services to the employer's employees, then the regulation of that plan will depend on who bears the risk.

Further complicating an understanding of this regulatory environment is the Health Insurance Portability and Accountability Act of 1996 (HIPAA, P.L. 104-191), as amended by P.L. 104-204.[7] Prior to its enactment, almost all regulatory authority over the business of health insurance had rested with the states. Once HIPAA's provisions are implemented; certain federal minimum requirements will apply to state-regulated insurers as well as employer-sponsored managed care plans. This marks the first time that the federal government will have extended its jurisdiction to health insurers.[8] While HIPAA generally allows states to impose on insurers requirements that provide for greater protections to consumers in lieu of federal minimum standards, certain federal standards relating to preexisting condition exclusions override state laws. Moreover, if a state fails to enforce at

[6] This discussion refers to single-employer plans only. The regulation of multiple employer entities, known under ERISA as multiple employer welfare arrangements (MEWAs), works differently. See: U.S. Library of Congress. Congressional Research Service. *Health Insurance: Reforming the Private Market.* CRS Report 95-877, by Beth C. Fuchs, updated January 23, 1997. Washington, 1997. (Hereafter cited as Fuchs, *Health Insurance: Reforming the Private Market*, 1997)

[7] P.L. 104-204 also includes new federal requirements relating to minimum hospital maternity stays and to mental health benefits.

[8] Arguably, the HMO Act of 1973 was the first major federal law affecting the business of insurance. However, the HMO Act only imposed requirements on HMOs that *elected* to become "federally qualified." Similarly, the federal government regulates the policies of private insurers who sell policies that supplement Medicare and of MCOs that contract with Medicare and Medicaid.

least the federal minimum standards, then the federal government is charged with enforcing the law in that state.

The traditional division of regulatory responsibilities between the federal government and the states resulted from provisions of several federal laws and subsequent decisions of federal courts. The following provides a basic overview of these laws, including the precedent-breaking HIPAA. The chapter then describes how states regulate MCOs, particularly HMOs. While this discussion is meant to be descriptive of the current regulatory environment, it also provides a foundation for a discussion of the major policy issues related to managed care facing the 105th Congress.

Major Federal Laws Affecting the Regulation of Managed Care

Numerous federal laws affect health benefits and health insurance. This section describes the key statutes, including the McCarran-Ferguson Act, ERISA, the HMO Act, and HIPAA. Other statutes, such as the health insurance continuation coverage requirement of the Consolidated Omnibus Budget Reconciliation Act (COBRA), impose requirements on certain health plans. These, however, are less directly relevant to issues of managed care and are thus not included.

McCarran-Ferguson Act of 1945 (P.L. 79-15)

This Act exempts the business of insurance from federal antitrust regulation to the extent that insurance is regulated by the states, and indicates that no federal law should be interpreted as overriding state insurance regulation unless it does so explicitly. The Act did not prevent the federal government from regulating insurance in the future; it merely affirmed that the government had so far abstained from doing so. HIPAA broke with the precedent established by the McCarran-Ferguson Act and established certain federal minimum requirements on the business of health insurance.

Employee Retirement Income Security Act of 1974 (ERISA, P.L. 93-406)

ERISA establishes federal uniform requirements for employee welfare benefit plans, including health plans. It was crafted in 1974 to leave the content and design of employer health plans to employers in negotiation with their workforce. ERISA does, however, establish certain regulations for health benefit plans. These relate to reporting and disclosure, fiduciary standards, claims review, and enforcement. It also provides participants in employee plans limited protection against discrimination. (See **Figure 2.**) Governmental plans and church plans are generally exempt from ERISA. Some plans are sponsored by entities, such as fraternal organizations, in which there is no employer-employee relationship involved. These too are not considered ERISA plans.[9]

---

[9] This discussion of ERISA relates to plans sponsored by individual employers (i.e., "single-employer" plans). Different rules apply to plans that are sponsored by two or more employers, such as multiple employer welfare arrangements. The regulation of these plans is not covered in this report. For more information, see: Fuchs, *Health Insurance: Reforming the Private Market*, 1997; Butler, Patricia and Karl Polzer. *Private-Sector Health Coverage: Variation in Consumer Protections under ERISA and State Law*. National Health Policy Forum, Washington, D.C., Special Report/June 1996. (Hereafter cited as Butler, et al., *Private-Sector Health Coverage*)

Figure 2. Major ERISA Requirements on Employer Group Health Plans

- *Fiduciary standards* – plan fiduciaries must act in the sole interest of plan participants in the management and disposition of employee benefits funds.
- *Reporting and disclosure requirements* – plans must disclose information about the plan to participants and beneficiaries.[10]
- *Nondiscrimination* – a person cannot "discharge, Fine, suspend, expel, discipline, or discriminate against a [plan] participant or beneficiary for exercising any right to which he is entitled under the provision of an employee benefit plan…"[11]
- *Claims review* – a plan must provide adequate notice in writing to any participant or beneficiary whose claim for benefits under the plan has been denied, setting forth the reasons for the denial, and afford a reasonable opportunity for a full and fair review by the appropriate named fiduciary of the decision denying the claim.
- *Continuation of coverage (COBRA)* - a plan with 20 more employees must offer participants and beneficiaries the option to continue group health coverage in the case of certain events (such as termination from the job or experiencing a change in family status) for 18 to 36 months, depending on the event.
- *Coverage of adopted children* – an employer group health plan that provides coverage for dependent children must treat children placed for adoption the same as natural children, even if the adoption does not become final under some time later.
- *Health Insurance Portability and Accountability Act (HIPAA)* – a plan must comply with the portability, access, and renewability requirements of the Act (as described below).

One of the most important provisions of ERISA (Section 514) preempts state laws affecting employee welfare benefit plans. While Section 514 confirms the states' continued authority to regulate insurance companies, the so-called "deemer" clause holds that no employee benefit plan or any trust established under a plan "shall be deemed to be an insurance company…" The courts have generally interpreted this language to mean that states cannot regulate employer-sponsored health plans. They may, however, regulate insurance that is sold to employers. As a result, if an employer fully or partially self-insures its own health plan, it is regulated solely by ERISA, and not state insurance laws. Federal regulation of employer plans includes those requirements discussed above.

As a consequence of ERISA's Section 514, employers that self-insure are exempt from state regulatory requirements such as taxes on insurance premiums, requirements that health plans include specific benefits or pay specific providers (known as state mandated benefit laws); solvency and funding standards; requirements to participate in the financing of state risk pools; and, of increasing prevalence, laws regulating various characteristics and actions of managed care plans. ERISA's preemption of state regulation has helped to increase the attractiveness of self-insurance to many employers, so that today, roughly 40% of all

[10] Plans used to be required to file summary plan descriptions and summaries of material modifications with the Department of Labor. However, under the Taxpayer Relief Act of 1997 (P.L. 105-34), sponsors of employee benefit plans are no longer required to file such information. Such documents have to be filed, however, at the request of the Department of Labor within 30 days of the request.

[11] Section 510 of ERISA.

employees are covered by self-insured plans. (Data on rates of self-insurance widely vary depending on the survey.)[12]

ERISA's exemption of employee health plans from state regulation means that a wide range of state health reforms face legal challenges by self-insured employers and unions if and when those laws are implemented.[13] The plaintiffs are likely to argue that they do not have to comply because they are exempt from state law under Section 514 of ERISA. Organizations representing state interests have argued that the threat of such court challenges discourages new state reform efforts and limits the effectiveness of existing state laws because such laws cannot be enforced on a sizeable portion of the insurance market, i.e., self-insured health plans. Opposing this view are groups representing larger employers, many of whom operate in two or more states, who argue that if they lose their preemption and become subject to state law, they will be financially and administratively burdened. Complying with 50 different state regulations would rive up their costs of operating a health plan and reduce their ability to implement innovative plan changes. Also in opposition are organizations representing self-insured firms and sellers of administrative services and stop-loss insurance to self-insured firms, arguing that ERISA preemption is necessary to ensure the continuation of their health plan arrangements.

The effect of ERISA's preemption clause on the regulation of MCOs is significant and complex. With the growth of managed care arrangements, the distinction between plans that are fully insured form those that are self-insured (i.e., to some extent risk bearing) has become less clear. An obvious case of a fully insured plan exists when an employer purchases for a premium a fee-for-service plan from an insurance company. Less obvious is the situation where an employer plan has contracted with an MCO to use its network of providers in order to offer plan participants an HMO option. Then the question becomes: who is bearing the risk? Is the employer paying the MCO a per enrollee premium which will not vary regardless of how much health care each participant uses? In this case, the MCO is at risk and the employer is buying a fully insured product that is clearly subject to state regulation. Alternatively, is the employer's plan operating as the risk-bearing entity and the MCO is simply contracting for a negotiated fee the use of its doctors, hospitals, and other providers?[14] In this instance, the MCO may or may not be subject to state regulation. State insurance regulators may wish to regulate the MCO if it were considered to be assuming any insurance

---

[12] The General Accounting Office has estimated that about 44 million Americans are in self-insured health plans that states cannot regulate. See: U.S. General Accounting Office. *Employer-Based Health Plans: Issues, Trends, and Challenges Posed by ERISA.* (GAO/HEHS-95-167), July 25, 1995. Washington, 1995. This number may actually be declining, partially as a result of employers' switching from fee-for-service plans to fully insured managed care plans. A 1996 study, using a different research methodology than GAO's, found that the number of Americans covered under self-insured plans that the states could not regulate was 35 million in 1995, a decrease from 38 million in 1993. Liston, Derek and Martha Priddy Patterson. *Analysis of the Number of Workers Covered by Self-Insured Health Plans Under ERISA of 1974-1993 and 1995.* Henry J. Kaiser Family Foundation, Menlo Park, CA, August 1996.

[13] For more information, see: U.S. Library of Congress. Congressional Research Service. *Health Benefit Plans: ERISA and the States.* CRS Report 93-747, by Joan Sokolovsky, August 11, 1993. Washington, 1993.

[14] About 65% of HMOs and PPOs were estimated to be offering employer self-insured products in 1996, including "network rental" options and third party administrative services, up from 53% in 1995. American Association of Health Plans. *1995 AAHP HMO/PPO Trends Report.* Washington, 1995.

risk. However, the state might be blocked from applying such regulation as a result of ERISA's preemption of state regulation of employer-sponsored plans.

In the same vein, an issue arises with respect to the question of whether a state law applies to the plan offered by a MCO. Does the law relate to an employee benefit plan? More specifically, does the law regulate the structure, content, method of administration, or plan requirements? Does it directly affect the participants of the plan? The federal courts have used the concept of relatedness as a major litmus test in determining, for example, whether a state health care provider tax could be assessed on participants of an employee health plan.[15] This "relatedness" test may be central to judicial challenges to state laws regulating managed care arrangements. For example, an employee health plan might argue that ERISA preempts a state provider network licensing law directed only at self-insured plans because the law is seeking to regulate activities related to the employee plan.[16] "Who shall regulate?" may become even more complicated with the emergence of increasingly complex risk-sharing arrangements, both between employers and MCOs, and MCOs and provider sponsored entities, such as physician-hospital organizations.

This rather intricate and confusing regulatory environment has led some to suggest that insurance regulation be federalized. In that way, one uniform set of laws would apply to health plans, regardless of whether such plans were insured or self-insured. Of course, a debate might then arise about the content of such a law. What requirements should the federal government impose on privately-sponsored health plans? The reverse view is also found. Some advocate that the states be given greater latitude to regulate the health plans sponsored by employers so that insuring entities are competing on the same "level playing field." There appears to be growing interest in the current Congress in legislation that applies federal minimum requirements to all health plans, regardless of whether they are purchased or self-insured, but that also gives states flexibility to apply their own laws if such laws are consistent with (or, in some bills, more restrictive than) the federal standard. (This approach is reflected in the HIPAA of 1996, discussed below.) Whether this approach results in more or less uniformity of insurance regulation remains to be seen.

McCarran-Ferguson and ERISA established the respective jurisdictional reach of the federal government and the states over health insuring entities. Other laws, such as the HMO Act of 1973, and the HIPAA of 1996, both affect "who regulates what" as well as the content of that regulation.

The HMO Act of 1973

The HMO Act of 1973 (P.L. 93-222) added a new title XIII to the Public Health Service (PHS) Act.[17] This title, as amended, is known as "the HMO Act." The HMO Act was enacted largely to encourage the growth of HMOs, thought by many to be a more cost-effective way to deliver health care than traditional, fee-for-service insurance. The Act originally provided federal funds to develop new HMOs and to help them through the start-up period. These

---

[15] *New York State Conference of Blue Cross and Blue Shield Plans, et al vs. Travelers Insurance Co.*, U.S. 93-1405, April 26, 1995.

[16] Butler, et al., *Private-Sector Health Coverage*, p. 57.

[17] This section is from: U.S. Library of Congress. Congressional Research Service. *Health Maintenance Organizations and Employer Group Health Plans*. CRS Report 91-261, by mark Merlis, March 19, 1991. Washington, 1991.

funds are no longer available. The Act also created certain financial and organizational standards. Certification of federal qualification was once the responsibility of the PHS. Currently, it is done by the Health Care Financing Administration, the agency of the Department of Health and Human Services (HHS) in charge of the Medicare and Medicaid programs.

It once was the case that the main reason for an HMO to obtain federal qualification was to take advantage of the HMO Act's "dual choice" requirement. Any employer with 25 or more employees that was subject to the Fair Labor Standards Act and that provided group health insurance benefits was required to offer an HMO option as an alternative to its existing health plan, if a federally qualified HMO was available in its areas and asked to be included. The employer had the right to choose among qualified HMOs if there were more than one in an area. The "dual choice" requirement was eliminated by the HMO amendments of 1988, effective 7 years after enactment, or October 24, 1995.[18]

As of the end of 1995, about 45% of all HMOs were federally qualified, although qualified HMOs accounted for 68% of total enrollment.[19] The process of seeking federal qualification is a voluntary one, and many HMOs operate only under state licensure because they choose not to meet some of the benefit and operating requirements of the HMO Act.

The HMO Act specifies that a federally qualified HMO is a public or private entity organized under the laws of any state that provides basic and supplemental health services to its members and meets certain financial and organizational requirements. These requirements include:[20]

- Each member has to be provided basic health services which are paid for on a periodic basis without regard to when the services are provided. The payment must be fixed without regard to the frequency, extent, or kind of health service (within the basic health services) actually furnished. These basic services may be supplemented by additional nominal copayments but such copayments cannot act as a barrier to care.[21]
- Basic health services include: physician services; inpatient and outpatient hospital services; medically necessary emergency services; short-term, outpatient mental health services; medical treatment and referral services for the abuse of or addiction

[18] The HMO Act of 1973 also required the employer to include the HMO option in the offering on terms no less favorable with respect to the employer's monetary contribution than the terms on which other alternatives (such as a fee-for-service plan) were included. The employer's contribution had to be equal, in dollar amount, to the largest contribution made by that employer, on behalf of a particular employee, to a non-HMO alternative included in the plan offering. This is known as the nondiscrimination requirement. While the dual choice provision was repealed by the HMO amendments of 1988, the nondiscrimination requirement was retained with modifications to enable employers greater flexibility in setting their contributions to HMOs that they offer voluntarily. HCFA issued a final rule implementing these changes on May 31, 1996. See *Federal Register*, May 31, 1996. p. 27282.

[19] Interstudy. *The Interstudy Competitive Edge. Part II: Industry Report*. St. Paul, 1996. Tables 3 and 5.

[20] Section 1301-1302 of Title XIII of the HMO Act. See also the regulations for federally qualified HMOs in *42 Code of Federal Regulations, Ch. IV*, Sections 417.1-417.169.

[21] This provision was amended by Section 193 of HIPAA (P.L. 104-191) to allow federally qualified HMOs to offer high deductible plans that could be sold in conjunction with tax-favored medical savings accounts (MSAs).

to alcohol and drugs; diagnostic laboratory and diagnostic and therapeutic radiologic services; home health services; and preventive health services.

- Basic health services have to be available and accessible with reasonable promptness and in a manner which assures continuity, and when medically necessary, be available and accessible 24 hours a day, 7 days a week. (Exceptions are provided for rural HMOs.)
- Each HMO must have a fiscally sound operation and adequate protection against the risk of insolvency which is satisfactory to the Secretary. It must also have administrative and managerial arrangements satisfactory to the Secretary. The HMO must assume full financial risk on a prospective basis for basic health services except that it may obtain insurance or make other arrangements to cover losses in excess of a specified level.
- The HMO must enroll persons who are broadly representative of the various age, social, and income groups within its service area. (Special provisions apply in the case of HMOs in medically underserved areas.) It cannot expel or refuse to re-enroll any member because of the individual's health status or need for health services.[22] It has to have meaningful procedures for hearing and resolving grievances between the HMO and the members of the organization. In addition, the HMO must have an ongoing qualify assurance program, and provide for the reporting of certain information.
- The HMO must generally use "community rating," that is, premium rates may not vary according to enrollees' need for health services.

Federally qualified HMOs are also subject to state insurance laws with exceptions. The HMO Act explicitly preempts "restrictive" state laws and practices, including those that: (1) require as a condition of doing business that a medical society approve of the furnishing of services by the entity; (2) require that physicians constitute all or a specified percentage of its governing body; (3) require that all physicians or a specific or percentage of physicians in a locale participate or be permitted to participate in the provision of services for the HMO; (4) require that the HMO meet state requirements for health insurers respecting initial capitalization and establishment of financial reserves against insolvency that would prevent it from doing business in the state; and (5) impose requirements which would prohibit the HMO from complying with requirements of the HMO Act.

The Health Insurance Portability and Accountability Act of 1996 (HIPAA, P.L. 104-191)

The HIPAA establishes federal minimal health insurance standards that apply to MCOs as well as indemnity insurers, plans sponsored by employers, and plans sponsored by unions, associations, and other entities. Most provisions take effect for plan years beginning after

[22] Under the Act, the HMO is prohibited from denying enrollment to a member of an employer group on the basis of health status. However, it can refuse an entire group or an individual applicant. This provision is superceded by HIPAA (P.L. 104-191), which generally prohibits an HMO from denying enrollment to a small employer group (2 to 50 employees), or any member of the group, on the basis of health status and related factors. It can reject new enrollees in the event of capacity limits.

June 30, 1997. HIPAA also establishes some minimal standards that apply to MCOs (and other insuring entities) operating in the individual insurance market.[23] These too are generally effective beginning July 1, 1997.[24] The standards are established under ERISA, the PHS Act, and the Internal Revenue Code (IRC). The following summarizes the basic requirements of the Act.

- *Limits on the use of preexisting condition restrictions.* Group health plans, and health insurance issuers[25] offering group health insurance coverage, are prohibited from imposing a preexisting condition exclusion that exceeds 12 months (18 months for late enrollment) for conditions diagnosed or treated within the previous 6 months prior to becoming insured. Preexisting conditions cannot include pregnancy and cannot apply to newborns and newly adopted children (including those newly placed for adoption). Such plans are required to credit periods of qualified previous coverage toward the fulfillment of a preexisting condition exclusion period when an individual moves from an individual or group source of health coverage to a source of group coverage. Plans and issuers have to provide a certification of the period of creditable coverage.
- *Guaranteed availability.* Group health plans, and health insurance issuers offering group coverage, cannot exclude from coverage or fail to renew coverage based on an individual's health status or on the health status of a dependent. (Health status is defined to include, with respect to an individual, medical condition, claims experience, receipt of health care, medical history, genetic information, evidence of insurability (including conditions arising out of acts of domestic violence, or disability.) A group health plan must provide for special enrollment periods for employees who experience a change in family composition, employment status, or employment status of a family member. The Act does not restrict the amount that an employer or issuer can charge for coverage or prevent the plan or issuer from establishing premium discounts or rebates or modifying applicable copayments or deductibles in return for adherence to programs of health promotion or prevention.
- *Requirements on issuers of group insurance (including HMOs and similar entities).* Each small group insurer or HMO is required to accept every small employer in the state that applies for such coverage. It must also accept for enrollment under such coverage every individual who applies for enrollment during the initial enrollment period in which the individual first becomes eligible for coverage under the group

[23] More information on the HIPAA is provided in: U.S. Library of Congress. Congressional Research Service. *The Health Insurance Portability and Accountability Act of 1996: Guidance on Frequently Asked Questions.* CRS Report 96-805, by Beth C. Fuchs, Bob Lyke, Richard Price, and Madeleine Smith, updated April 10, 1997. Washington, 1997.

[24] The provisions applying to the individual market may become effective later than July 1, 1997 in the case of states that, for example, that do not have a legislature that meets in 1997 or indicate that they intend to implement an alternative mechanism. Alternative mechanisms generally take effect January 1, 1998.

[25] The term "issuer" used below is defined under HIPAA as an insurance company, Blue Cross/Blue Shield company, or insurance organization (including an HMO which is licensed to engage in the business of insurance in a state and which is subject to state law which regulates insurance).

health plan. No exclusions can be placed on the coverage of an eligible individual based on health status or the health status of the dependent. Exceptions apply in the case of network plans that have limited capacity. (Many managed care plans are network plans.) The small group market is generally defined as employer groups with more than 2 and less than 51 employees. *All* health insurance sold in the group market must be guaranteed renewable, regardless of firm size, except for cause (e.g., fraud and nonpayment of premiums).

- *Enforcement.* Each state may require that health insurance issuers that issue, sell, renew, or offer health insurance in the state in the small or large group markets meet the above requirements. In the case of a determination by the Secretary of HHS that a state has failed to substantially enforce these requirements, the Secretary would generally enforce them. The group health insurance rules on private sector plans would be enforced through ERISA. Plans that fail to comply could be sued for relief and for recovery of any benefits due under the plan. They could also be subject to civil money penalties. Private group health plans would be subject to an excise tax of $100 per day violation under the IRC. Non-complying issuers (such as an HMO) would be subject to civil money penalties under the PHS Act. Individuals would also have a private right of action against such issuers under ERISA.

P.L. 104-204

Not long after HIPAA was enacted, it was amended to provide for federal standards related to maternity stays and coverage for mental health services.[26] Under the Act, group health plans and issuers of insurance plans in the group and individual markets will be prohibited from restricting benefits for any hospital length-of-stay for mothers and their newborns following a vaginal delivery to less than 48 hours and following a caesarean to less than 96 hours or from requiring that a provider obtain authority from the plan or the issuer for prescribing longer length-of-stays. Such prohibitions will be inapplicable in the case in which the decision to discharge the mother or her newborn prior to the 48/96 hour minimum requirements is made by an attending provider in consultation with the mother.[27] The provision applies for plan years beginning on or after January 1, 1998.

P.L. 104-204 also provides limited parity for mental health coverage under group health plans. It requires annual and aggregate lifetime limits for mental health coverage to be the same as for physical health coverage. Group health plans (or health insurance coverage offered in connection with group health plans) that cover mental health and medical/surgical conditions and have annual or aggregate dollar limits for medical/surgical conditions must establish either an inclusive limit for all benefits (e.g., $1 million lifetime limit for all benefits) or separate limits for mental health services that are no more restrictive than those for medical/surgical services (e.g., separate lifetime limits of $1 million for each type of benefit). The provisions do not apply to benefits for substance abuse or chemical dependency. Plans of employers with fewer than 50 employees are exempt from the requirement. The requirement also does not apply to any group health plan whose costs increase 1% or more

---

[26] These provisions were part of the fiscal year 1997 appropriations act for the Departments of Veterans Affairs and Housing and Urban Development.

[27] For more information, see: Kearney, *Hospital Length-of-Stay for Obstetrical Care*, 1996.

due to the application of the requirement.[28] This provision too applies to plan years beginning on or after January 1, 1998.

Other Federal Laws Affecting Managed Care Plans

MCOs that contract with Medicare, state Medicaid programs, and military health care programs must comply with requirements specific to those programs. For example, as of August of 1997, Medicare had 292 contracts across the United States with MCOs that have agreed to provide on a risk basis coverage for Medicare beneficiaries and comply with a set of Medicare rules. In return, the MCO receives a pre-established per capita payment called the adjusted average per capita payment or AAPCC. (As of September 1997, the capitation amount is calculated using a new methodology specified by the Balanced Budget Act of 1997 – BBA 97 – and is technically no longer the AAPCC.) Under Medicaid, many states contract with MCOs to provide services to their Medicaid beneficiaries in return for capitation payments. The regulation of managed care plans that contract with public programs is not addressed further in this document.[29]

State Regulation of Managed Care Plans

All 50 states regulate HMOs under self-contained state HMO enabling laws which address the insurance and delivery aspects of HMOs.[30] It is common for the state's department of insurance to oversee the insurer functions of the HMO and for its department of health to oversee the provider and quality assurance functions.[31] In some states, the agency administering Medicaid also is involved in MCO regulation.[32]

Other types of managed care arrangements may be regulated under separate state statutes. For example, as of 1996, about half of the states had statues or regulations authorizing and overseeing PPOs. Unlike HMOs, PPOs are provider networks developed to serve people insured through indemnity plans. They typically do not bear insurance risk; those that do are

---

[28] U.S. Library of Congress. Congressional Research Service. *Mental Health Parity Under P.L. 104-204*. CRS Report 96-827, by Jennifer A. Neisner, updated October 15, 1996. Washington, 1996. Note that P.L. 104-204 amended only the ERISA and PHS sections of HIPAA. The IRC provisions were amended to include the 48-hour stay and mental health parity provisions as part of the Taxpayer Relief Act of 1997 (P.L. 105-34).

[29] For Medicare managed care, see: U.S. Library of Congress. Congressional Research Service. *Medicare: The Restructuring Debate in the 104th Congress*. CRS Report 97-102, by Beth C. Fuchs, Bob Lyke, Jennifer O'Sullivan, and Richard Price, January 9, 1997. Washington, 1997; *Medicare Contracts With Managed Care Organizations*. General Distribution Memorandum, by Mark Merlis, March 27, 1995, RA 413B. Washington, 1995; O'Sullivan, et al., *Medicare Provisions in the Balanced Budget Act of 1997* (BBA 97, P.L. 105-33), 1997; Ford, *Medicaid: FY1998 Budget*, 1997.

[30] NAIC, table attached to NAIC HMO Model Act.

[31] Furrow, Barry R., et al. *Health Law*. St. Paul, MN, 1995. p. 525-532.

[32] Aspen Systems Corporation. *A Report to the Governor of State Regulation of Health Organizations*, prepared for the U.S. Department of Health and Human Services. Rockville, MD, 6th edition, 1996. Hereafter cited as Aspen Systems Corporation, *State Regulation of Health Maintenance Organizations*); Horvath, Jane and Kimberly Irvin Snow. *Emerging Challenges in State Regulation of Managed Care. Report on a Survey of Agency Regulation of Prepaid Managed Care Entities*. National Academy for State Health Policy, Portland, ME, August 1996. This report points out that in some states, there are overlapping responsibilities for MCO oversight of two or more state agencies. In some states, regulatory gaps exist in which no agency has responsibility. These are more likely with respect to quality assurance and monitoring than financial standards.

then regulated as HMOs.[33] A few states have developed laws to apply to physician-hospital organizations and PSOs. These are provider-owned and provider-operated entities that combine the financial intermediary role of an insurer with the health care delivery role of a provider organization. They differ mainly from HMOs to the extent that they are provider controlled.[34] Many HMOs are, in fact, owned and controlled by providers, thus making them, at least by some definitions, PSOs.

The Role of the NAIC

The NAIC is an association made up the chief regulatory officials from the 50 states, the District of Columbia, Puerto Rico and the territories. It develops model insurance laws and regulations that the states may elect to adopt, wholly or in part. The NAIC's Model HMO Act was designed to provide a flexible legal framework, enabling a wide variety of HMOs to operate; to provide a regulatory monitoring system to prevent or remedy abuse; and also to assist in the future development of this type of health care delivery system.[35] Twenty nine states have HMO laws which are based in part on the NAIC's Model HMO Act.[36]

The NAIC has an initiative called "the Consolidated Licensure for Entities Accepting Risk or CLEAR," which is aimed at consolidating the NAIC model statues for licensure of various health coverage products into one new model which would replace the existing model statues for HMOs and PPOs. This initiative is partly in response to the emergence of varying types of risk-bearing entities that provide both insurance and medical services. Indeed, new types of arrangement crop up regularly, adding to the alphabet soup of existing types of MCOs. Five health plan and accountability standards have been completed: (1) quality assessment and improvement; (2) provider credentialing; (3) network adequacy; (4) grievance procedures, and (5) standards for utilization review.[37] As of February 1997, no state had adopted these model acts bur the NAIC was expecting some to do so in the 1997 and 1998 state legislative sessions. The NAIC is in the process of finalizing risk-based capital standards for insuring entities that would base financial reserve requirements on the amount of risk assumed.[38] All of these model standards, those completed and those to come, are designed to be applicable to all plan "performing managed care functions, regardless of their structure or acronym."[39]

---

[33] Butler, et al., *Private-Sector Health Coverage*, p. 56.

[34] U.S. Library of Congress. Congressional Research Service. *Medicare Restructuring and Provider Sponsored Organizations (PSOs).* CRS Report 96-921, by Beth C. Fuchs, November 12, 1996. Washington, 1996.

[35] NAIC, Health Maintenance Organization Act, 1990.

[36] U.S. Congress. House. Ways and Means Committee. Subcommittee on Health. David Randall, Testimony of the National Association of Insurance Commissioners (Ex) Special Committee on Health Insurance. *Medicare HMO Regulation and Quality*. March 6, 1997. 105th Cong., 1st Sess. Washington, GPO, 1997. (Hereafter cited as House Ways and Means Committee, Testimony of David Randall, 1997)

[37] House Ways and Means Committee, Testimony of David Randall, 1997.

[38] National Association of Insurance Commissioners. The Risk-Bearing Entities Working Group of the State and Federal Health Insurance Legislative Policy (B) Task Force. *The Regulation of Risk-Bearing Entities*, September 1996 (Draft).

[39] House Ways and Means Committee, Testimony of David Randall, 1997.

State Actions

States also establish their own laws regulating MCOs that differ from those of the NAIC. In recent years, a large number of laws have been passed regulating various aspects of MCOs, ranging from their organizational structure to prohibiting certain types of financial incentives to providing standards for utilization review. Most recently, these laws have been enacted in response to consumer and provider concerns about access to and quality of MCO services (sometimes referred to as the managed care "backlash").

The following discussion summarizes state requirements on MCOs, drawing first from such requirements as spelled out in the NAIC's HMO Model Act, the model acts that emerged out of the CLEAR initiative, and from state laws that may illustrate or go beyond these model acts.[40] The section ends with a table providing information on selected types of managed care laws and the states that have adopted them (see **Table 1**).

Licensure/Certification/Organization

NAIC. The NAIC *HMO Model Act* establishes criteria fro licensing an organization as an HMO. An HMO is defined as an entity that undertakes to provide or arrange for the delivery of basic health care services to enrollees on a prepaid basis, except for enrollee responsibility for copayments and/or deductibles. The Act specifies that as a prerequisite to issuance of a certificate to operate, that the state entity responsible for health (such as public health department) determine whether the HMO applying for a license has satisfied quality assurance requirements.

The NAIC *HMO Model Act* does not regulate premium rates per se but does require that rates (or methodology for calculating the rates) be filed for approval by the state regulator, that rates be established in accordance with actuarial principles for various categories of enrollees, and that the premium applicable to an enrollee not be individually determined based on the person's health status. Rates should not be "excessive, inadequate, or unfairly discriminatory." It also provides that HMOs should be examined no less than once every 3 years for their overall operation and quality assurance program. Finally, it sets forth an enforcement process in which non-complying HMOs could have their licenses suspended or revoked. Monetary penalties could be used in addition to or instead of suspension or revocation.

State Laws. Some states require a consumer representative on the HMO board and for there to be a policymaking role for subscribers. Most states require that premium rates be approved. At least one state limits HMO licenses to non-profit organizations. Some states require that HMOs provide for annual open enrollment periods.[41]

Access to Services and Providers

NAIC. The NAIC *HMO Model Act* states under its provisions related to quality assurance that the plan maintains procedures to assure availability, accessibility, and continuity of care. The new NAIC *Network Adequacy Model Act*[42] establishes explicit standards for the creation

[40] For additional information on the managed care laws and regulations of the 50 states, see Health Policy Tracking Service. *Major Health Care Policies: 50 States Profiles, 1996*, 5th ed. Washington, January 1997.

[41] Aspen Systems Corporation, *State Regulation of Health Maintenance Organizations*, 1996, Chart 1.

[42] National Association of Insurance Commissioners. Model Regulation Service. *Managed Care Plan Network Adequacy Model Act*. October 1996.

and maintenance of provider networks which, in turn, are designed to ensure that services are available and accessible, and that enrollees benefit from continuity of care. For example, the carrier must maintain a network of providers that is sufficient in numbers and types of providers to assure that all services to covered persons are accessible without unreasonable delay. Emergency care must be accessible 24 hours a day, 7 days per week. Providers have to be within a "reasonable proximity" to covered persons. Carriers are required to file access plans with the state regulator. The *Network Adequacy Model Act* also specifies requirements to ensure that participating providers play by certain rules that protect covered persons from breaks in service in the event that the plan experiences financial shortfalls (see "Solvency" below).

The *Network Adequacy Model Act* also includes standards related to the selection of providers and the relationship between the carrier and the provider. Selection criteria for providers cannot be established in a manner that would allow a carrier to avoid high-risk populations (e.g., the MCO cannot exclude providers who specialize in treating high-risk patients (e.g., oncologists or physicians who specialize in treating patients infected with the human immunodeficiency virus (HIV)). Carriers could, however, exclude from its network providers who "fail to meet the other legitimate selection criteria of the carrier developed in compliance with this Act." Certain procedures designed to ensure due process would have to be followed before terminating a provider without cause.

The *Network Adequacy Model Act* also addresses several issues that have been much discussed in Congress and in state legislatures. One is the nature of communications between a managed care provider and his or her patient. A restriction on communications imposed by an MCO on providers is often referred to as a "*gag rule*" or (if part of a contract) "gag clause." The *Network Adequacy Model Act* includes an "anti-gag rule." It provides that a health carrier shall not prohibit a participating provider from discussing treatment options with a covered person or from advocating on behalf of covered persons.

State Laws. As shown in Table 1, 28 states (as of mid-1997) had enacted laws or issued regulations requiring plans to provide access to obstetricians/gynecologists, without referral from the enrollee's primary care physician. Twenty-eight states had enacted laws or regulations prohibiting the use of "gag rules."[43] Nine states had passed laws protecting physicians from termination from MCOs "without just cause."[44]

Quality Assurance

NAIC. The NAIC *HMO Model Act* requires an HMO to "establish procedures to assure that the health care services provided to enrollees are rendered under reasonable standards of quality of care consistent with prevailing professionally recognized standards of medical practice. Such procedures shall include mechanisms to assure availability, accessibility, and continuity of care."[45] The organization must have an ongoing internal quality assurance program which meets specific requirements, such as having a written statement of goals and objectives emphasizing improved health status; having a written quality assurance plan; ensuring the use of adequate patient record system; and making enrollee records available to

[43] *Health Policy Tracking Service*. Washington, September 1997. Unpublished tables.

[44] Families USA Foundation. The Text of Key State HMO Consumer Protection Provisions: The Best from the States. Part I. *Families USA Web*, March 1997. (Hereafter cited as Families USA Foundation, 1997)

the state public health entity to determine compliance. The *HMO Model Act* requires organizations to disclose specific information about the plan in its contracts for individual and group insurance policies, including eligibility requirements, benefits, emergency care benefits and services, cost-sharing requirements, limitations and exclusions, and enrollee grievance procedures. The organization is also required to file financial and other information at least annually and to provide enrollees notice of changes to the plan, and on how to obtain services.

The NAIC's new *Quality Assessment and Improvement Model Act* builds on these requirements. It establishes criteria for the quality assessment activities of all health carriers that offer managed care plans; for closed network plans it establishes additional criteria for quality improvement activities. It requires a carrier to include a summary of its quality assessment and improvement programs in its marketing materials and in the certificates of coverage issues to enrollees. Certain findings from the carrier's quality assessment and improvement programs would have to be made available to providers and enrollees, and enrollees would have to be given an opportunity to comment on the carrier's quality improvement process. The Act advises states that they may wish to consider accreditation by a nationally recognized accrediting entity as evidence of meeting some or all of the Act's requirements.[46] Another issue relates to the use of MCOs of financial incentive arrangements to encourage providers to hold down utilization of services. The *Network Adequacy Model Act* (described above) provides that a carrier cannot offer an inducement under the plan to a provider to provide less than medically necessary services to a covered person.

State Laws. Forty-two states require HMOs to develop and implement a quality assurance plan; about one-half of these states stipulate what HMOs must include in their plans. Consumer advocates have identified Minnesota, Maine, and New Jersey as having the "most carefully crafted quality assurance requirements."[47] As of August 1997, six states prohibit the use of physician financial incentive arrangements (California, Connecticut (relating only to utilization review companies), Maryland, Louisiana, Nevada, and Texas).[48] For example, the Maryland statute prohibits the use of withhold arrangements in which a health plan holds back from participating physicians a certain amount which is then only paid if referral services do not exceed some pre-established threshold.[49] Ten states require that the use of physician incentive arrangements be disclosed (Arkansas, Colorado, Georgia, Louisiana, Minnesota, Rhode Island, Tennessee, Vermont, Virginia, and Washington). In some cases (e.g., Colorado), the state law requires that the information be disclosed on request. In others (Louisiana), the disclosure of such arrangements must be made annually to every subscriber, enrollee, and participating provider.

---

[45] NAIC, Model HMO Act, Section 7, Quality Assurance Program.

[46] NAIC, Model Regulation Service. *Quality Assessment and Improvement Model Act*, July 1996.

[47] Families USA Foundation, 1997.

[48] Personal communication with American Association of Health Plans, September 1997.

[49] Families USA Foundation, 1997; also U.S. Library of Congress. Congressional Research Service. *Managed Health Care: The Use of Financial Incentives*. CRS Report 97-482, by Jason Lee and Beth C. Fuchs, April 21, 1997. Washington, 1997.

Protection Against Insolvency

NAIC. The NAIC *HMO Model Act* requires that before issuing any certificate of authority, that the state regulator require that the HMO have an initial net worth of $1.5 million and will thereafter maintain a net worth equal to the greater of:

(a) $1 million;
(b) 2% of annual premium revenues on the first $150 million of premiums and 1% of annual premium on the premium in excess of $150 million;
(c) an amount equal to 3 months uncovered health care expenditures; or
(d) an amount equal to the sum of 8% of annual health expenditures except those paid on a capitated basis or managed hospital payment basis and 4% of annual hospital expenditures paid on a managed hospital payment basis.

Under the *HMO Model Act*, each HMO has to deposit a specified amount (generally $300,000) with a trustee or other entity acceptable to the state regulator. This amount is intended to protect the HMO's enrollees and to assure continuation of services in the event that the organization runs into financial difficulties.

The *HMO Model Act* also requires that every contract between an HMO and a participating provider be in writing. The HMO must ensure that in the event that it fails to pay for services, the subscriber or enrollee is not liable to the provider for any amount owed by the HMO. This is known as a hold harmless provision. The Act further requires that each HMO have a plan for handling insolvency which allows for an enrollee's continuation of benefits for the duration of the contract period. If an HMO's uncovered expenditures[50] exceed 10% of total health expenditures, it is required under the model Act to deposit into a trust or approved account an amount equal to 120% of the HMO's outstanding liability for uncovered expenditures for enrollees in the state.

In addition, the *HMO Model Act* provides that in the event of an HMO insolvency, that other insurance carriers that participated in the enrollment process with the insolvent HMO be required by the state regulator to offer to the group's enrollees a 30-day enrollment period commencing on the date of insolvency. The carriers would have to offer the same coverage and premium rates that it had offered to enrollees of the group at its last regular enrollment period. If no such carrier existed, then the regulator would equitably allocate the insolvent HMO's enrollees to HMOs within the same service area. These HMOs would have to offer as similar coverage as possible but at rates consistent with the successor HMO's existing rating methodology. Successor HMOs could not deny benefits to an enrollee based on a preexisting medical condition.

Finally, the *HMO Model Act* provides that some states may want to adopt a mechanism to assess each HMO doing business in the state up to 2% of its premium to cover the claims for uncovered expenditures for enrollees of insolvent HMOs. This assessment could also be used to provide for the continuation of coverage for those enrollees not otherwise helped by the continuation measures described above.

---

[50] The NAIC Model HMO Act defines "uncovered expenditures: as the costs to the HMO for health care services that are the obligation of the HMO, for which an enrollee may also be liable in the event of an HMO's insolvency and for which no alternative arrangements have been made that are acceptable to the state regulator.

It should be noted that under the Federal HMO Act of 1973, a federally qualified HMO (and an HMO that has received federal financial assistance under Title XIII of the PHS Act) is exempt from state solvency and capitalization standards that would prevent it from operating in accordance with the HMO Act. In other words, if such a state law were inconsistent with federal law, the state law would be overridden or preempted. It appears that most state laws are, in fact, consistent with the solvency provisions of the HMO Act. In only a few states are the laws such that a question might arise. Such a state might, for example, apply to HMOs the reserve and capital requirements of indemnity insures instead of applying separate HMO requirements.[51]

As noted earlier, the NAIC is close to finishing work on a model act for regulating the capital needs of an insuring entity, officially called the *Health Organizations' Risk-Based Capital Formula*. This model standard, which is due to be voted on by the NAIC either late 1997 or early 1998, is designed to provide a uniform model act for capital requirements for all health care entities that take on risk, including HMOs, provider sponsored organizations (PSOs), and traditional indemnity insurers.

A major reason for developing the risk-based capital standard is that traditional capital/solvency requirements have not recognized some of the assets that may be held by the newer forms of MCOs. For example, a PSO that includes a hospital may have substantial assets in real property (so-called "bricks and mortar"). It may also have a substantial asset in its group of affiliated physicians and its other health care providers.

The formula being developed will set capital requirements specific to the risk borne by the insuring entity and will address five major risk elements:

- affiliated investment risk – the risk of ownership of affiliated entities to the managed care entity (if applicable);
- asset risk – the risk that existing assets will decline in value;
- underwriting (insurance) risk – the risk of errors in assumptions used in determining premium or capitation rates or deviations between assumptions and experience in payment of medical expense;
- credit risk – risk that parties with which the managed care organization (MCO) enters contractual arrangements will not fulfill their obligations, a risk common to all types of businesses; and
- general business risk – such as risk of overruns in administrative expenses, also common to all businesses.

These factors would then be assessed based upon the arrangements under which the health care is delivered and paid for. For example, if the financial risk for delivering the service were passed on to providers through contractual arrangements, then the entity would be permitted to have less capital.[52]

---

[51] Whether such a law is "potentially inconsistent with Section 1311(a)(1)(d) [of the HMO Act] has not been established." See: Aspen Systems Corporation, *State Regulation of Health Maintenance Organizations*, 1996.

[52] Bureau of National Affairs. Plan Regulation NAIC Approves Health Organization Risk-Based Capital Formula for Testing. *Managed Care Reporter*, v. 3, no. 25, June 18, 1997.

State Laws. About 14 states have adopted the NAIC reserve and capital requirements by law or regulation, although these states vary in the application of the requirement. Other states generally require HMOs to comply with specific reserve standards – higher or lower – that differ from those of the NAIC.[53]

Grievances

NAIC. The NAIC *HMO Model Act* requires that the HMO establish and maintain a grievance process that has been approved by the state insurance regulator. The HMO is required to maintain records regarding grievances which would be subject to examination by state regulators.

The NAIC *Health Carrier Grievance Procedures Model Act* contains more developed standards for internal grievance procedures to be used by carriers.[54] Carriers are required to file annually with the state regulator a certificate of compliance stating that the carrier had grievance procedures that fully comply with these standards. Grievance procedures have to be disclosed in materials provided to covered persons. Every carrier has to provide for an initial level of grievance review in which covered persons could seek to reverse the plan's decision, such as a decision not to cover or pay for a specific procedure. The covered person can appeal an adverse decision by initiating a second level of review. A majority of the individuals reviewing the grievance in this instance has to be health care professionals with appropriate expertise. In cases involving a denial of service, the reviewing health care professional generally cannot be a provider in the person's plan and cannot have a financial interest in the outcome of the review. (See "Utilization Review" below.) The time that can elapse at different stages of the grievance process is limited, especially in the case of expedited reviews involving decisions that could seriously jeopardize the life or health of a covered person or would jeopardize the covered person's ability to regain maximum function.

State Laws. All states require that HMOs have internal grievance procedures in which a plan member can appeal a benefit denial. At least 13 states provide specific direction on the nature of grievance procedures that should be used by HMOs. The remaining states require procedures for resolving grievances but "provide little direction" on what the grievance system should include.[55] Many states also regulate utilization review firms and require processes by which providers (e.g., hospitals and physicians) and plan members can appeal adverse decisions.[56] (See "Utilization Review below.) Members of HMOs who are *not* participants of ERISA plans may also be able to sue for damages under state law. Damages can include the cost of the service as well as consequential costs (such as lost wages) and non-economic costs (such as pain and suffering). They may also include punitive damages.[57]

Participants in health plans that are ERISA plans (private-sector, employee benefit plans) are *not* able to resolve grievances about claim denials through state remedies. This is the case regardless of whether the ERISA plan is insured or self-insured and is an exception to the more general interpretation of ERISA preemption that ERISA overrides state laws regulating

---

[53] Aspen Systems Corporation, *State Regulation of Health Maintenance Organizations*, 1996.

[54] National Association of Insurance Commissioners. Model Regulation Service. *Health Care Grievance Procedure Model Act*. October 1996.

[55] Families USA Foundation, 1997.

[56] Butler, et al., *Private-Sector Health Coverage*, p. 48.

[57] Ibid.

employer plans but not the plan that the employer buys from an insurer. Denial of access to state courts and remedies for ERISA participants was determined in *Pilot Life Insurance Co. vs. Dedeaux*, in which the U.S. Supreme Court held that ERISA preempted those state laws which permit insurance policyholders to sue insurance carriers for damages due to the bad faith denial of their claims.[58] It held that ERISA provides that participants and beneficiaries in ERISA plans may sue only in federal court. If successful, he or she is due recovery for the cost of the test, procedure, or other benefit denied.

Whereas indemnity health insurance plan disputes are usually over whether a claim should have been paid (the care having already been received), disputes emerging in managed care arrangements are more likely to be over services that may not have been provided or about a referral to a specialist that was not allowed. Such denials may be made on the basis that the service or referral in question was not medically necessary, or because the treatment was considered experimental. The federal courts seem to be moving in the direction of distinguishing between whether the dispute is over quantity or quality of services. In several cases decided over the past 2 years, the courts have said that ERISA gives employers substantial discretion to determine what benefits they should include under their health plan. However, issues of quality, such as failing to check on a doctor's background, or negligently delaying needed care, are not covered by ERISA.[59] Therefore, state remedies may be available.

Medical societies, trial lawyers, and consumer groups have been pressing for state legislation to hold MCOs responsible for negligence and poor quality of care that will survive ERISA preemption challenges. For example, such proposals would hold a health care organization liable for the harm (personal injury or death) it causes when it delays, denies, or fails to provide health care it is contractually or legally obligated to provide. In May 1997, Texas became the first state to enact a law that holds MCOs liable for medical decisions affecting a patient's health. A MCO whose doctor or other provider causes harm to a patient by failing to exercise "ordinary care" in making treatment decisions can be sued for malpractice. Plaintiffs have to exhaust the MCO's internal appeals and grievance procedures before filing suit. In June 1997, Aetna Health Plans of Texas sued in federal court in Houston to block the provision, arguing that it was preempted by ERISA because it improperly interferes with the administration of employee benefit plans.[60] Employers and MCOs, more generally, are concerned that the ERISA protections against liability will be eroded, thus exposing them to significant and costly litigation. However, the larger public policy question may be to what extent is an MCO merely administering a plan for an employer group health plan or is it influencing the medical treatment provided to the plan's members?

---

[58] *Pilot Life Insurance Co. vs. DeDeaux*, 481 U.S. 41 (1987).

[59] Bills in Five States Would Make HMOs Liable in Patient Lawsuits over Quality of Care. *State Health Watch*, March 1997. p. 1, 8.

[60] *Corporate Health Insurance Inc. vs. Texas Department of Insurance*, DC (Texas, No. H-97-2072), filed June 16, 1997. For additional information on this issue, see Coleman, David L. Crushing Your Health Plan's Legal Protection. *Business and Health*, August 1997. p. 40-46.

Utilization Review

NAIC. The NAIC *HMO Model Act* does not include any specific requirements relating to utilization review. Its new *Utilization Review Model Act*[61] requires health carriers that provide or perform utilization review to file certain information about utilization review with the state insurance regulator and satisfy other disclosure requirements. It would need to implement a written utilization review program that describes all review activities, including procedures to evaluate the clinical necessity, appropriateness, efficacy, or efficiency of health services and data sources and clinical review criteria used in decision-making. The carrier would be prohibited from using review decisions. Compensation is not allowed to be based on the quality or type of adverse determinations that reviewers render. In addition, the carrier would have to follow specific procedures in responding to requests from providers and patients for reconsiderations and appeals.

Perhaps one of the most important areas covered by the Utilization Review Model Act relates to emergency are services. Consumers have sometimes found that their managed care plan refuses to pay for services sought from a hospital emergency room because in the view of the plan reviewers, there was no actual medical emergency. The *Utilization Review Model Act* requires a carrier to cover emergency services necessary to screen and stabilize a covered person, without prior authorization from the plan if a "*prudent layperson*" acting reasonably would have believed that an emergency medical condition existed. Also, a covered person could obtain from a non-contracting provider within the carrier's service area those emergency services needed to screen and stabilize the person, without prior authorization, if a prudent layperson believed that using a contract provider would cause a delay worsening the emergency or if a provision of federal, state, or local law required the use of a specific provider.[62]

State Laws. Some states authorize judicial review of utilization review decisions.[63] Numerous states have acted to expand access to and provision of emergency services consistent with the NAIC *Utilization Review Model Act*. For example, some states prohibit plans from requiring authorization prior to the delivery of emergency services; some have adopted the prudent layperson standard; and some require payment for initial screening and stabilizing treatment in an emergency room. A few states go further. At least two states have provisions to ensure specialty and post-stabilization care in the emergency room.[64]

Additional State Laws

Numerous additional aspects of managed care are regulated under state law. These range from narrowly targeted laws, such as laws requiring that health plans pay for a minimum of 48 hours of inpatient hospital care following a mastectomy to those that incorporate a wider range of consumer protections and requirements relating to provider participation in a plan's network.

Table 1 provides in summary form information on which states have enacted certain managed care laws. The data for the table were provided by the *Health Policy Tracking*

---

[61] National Association of Insurance Commissioners. Model Regulation Service. *Utilization Review Model Act*. October 1996.

[62] Ibid.

[63] Furrow, Barry R., et al. *Health Law*. St. Paul, MN, West Publishing Co., 1995. p. 527.

[64] Families USA Foundation, Families USA Web (*www.epn.org/families/hmostate*).

Service of the National Conference of State Legislators.[65] A short description of the laws included in the table follows:

Hospital length of stay for mothers and newborns: This provision was a reaction to the perception that new mothers and their infants were being discharged prematurely from hospital after childbirth because insurers would pay for no more than a 24-hour stay. Most of the state laws allow an "attending provider" (varying in definition), in consultation with the mother, to determine what length of stay is most beneficial. However, if a longer stay is determined to be needed, the law requires insurers to pay for coverage for at least 48 hours of inpatient hospital care following a normal vaginal delivery and 96 hours following a Caesarean section. A federal law was enacted as part of P.L. 104-204 in 1996 which is similar.[66]

Hospital length of stay for mastectomies: This is a relatively new requirement on MCOs and other insurers similar to the provisions passed at the state and national level to mandate a minimum length of inpatient hospital stay for new mothers and their children. A typical state statute requires that insurers provide coverage for a defined minimum number of hours (ranging from 24 to 100) of hospital care following a mastectomy. It may also require that there be a minimum hospital stay after a lymph node dissection. Exceptions are provided in cases where a physician in consultation with a patient determines that a shorter length of stay is appropriate. Some statues require coverage of home care if a shorter length of stay is provided.

Any willing provider (AWP): A typical state requires a MCO to contract with any providers who are willing to meet the terms and conditions of the MCO's contract. Many state AWP laws apply only to pharmacies; a few apply only to other types of non-physician providers such as chiropractors and allied health professionals.

Freedom-of-choice: This provision states that an MCO or health insurer cannot limit an enrollee's choice of provider. The provision is often combined with any willing provider clause. Together, the provisions may specify that the MCO or health insurer cannot prohibit or limit an enrollee who is eligible for reimbursement for specific services from selecting a provider of his or her choice if the provider has agreed to the plan's terms and conditions. Some state laws apply to specific providers, such as pharmacists, chiropractors, or allied health professionals. One state, New Mexico, provides any person the right to exercise full freedom of choice in the selection of any licensed doctor of oriental medicine for treatment within his/her scope of practice.

Direct access to obstetricians and gynecologists: The provision gives women enrolled in managed care plans direct access to these specialists by either not requiring the woman to first get a referral from a primary care physician or by allowing a woman to designate an obstetrician or gynecologist as her primary care physician. These requirements target managed care plans that use primary care physicians as "gatekeepers" for access to the services of specialists.

Ban on gag clauses: The provision prohibits the use of gag clauses by MCOs in contracts with providers to restrict them from discussing treatment options with their patients. The

---

[65] *Health Policy Tracking Service*. National Conference of State Legislatures. Washington, D.C. Unpublished memoranda, 1997.

[66] Kearney, *Hospital Length-of-Stay for Obstetrical Care,* 1996.

states listed in **Table 1** have enacted laws that broadly prohibit a plan from refusing to contract, terminating a contract, or financially penalizing a provider for such communication. Some state laws are very specific about the content of the communication; others just refer to communication about treatment alternatives.

Comprehensive Consumer Protection Acts: Some states have enacted laws that are based on model laws developed by the American Medical Association or by consumer organizations. These concern a range of managed care issues, such as access, choice, benefits, quality, utilization review, procedural protections for physicians and the disclosure of plan information. The laws reflected in **Table 1** significantly vary in scope, from those that address only a few issues (e.g., disclosure of certain information, freedom of choice of providers, and a ban on gag clauses) to those that address the organization, delivery, and quality of the care provided by the MCO.

Table 1. Selected State Managed Care Legislative Strategies

State	Hospital length-of-stay after childbirth	Hospital length-of-stay for mastectomies	Any willing provider	Freedom-of-choice	Direct access to Ob/Gyn services	Ban on gag clauses	Comprehensive consumer rights/ protection acts
Total number of states	36 state (35 laws + 1 regulation)	13 states	24 states (23 laws + 1 regulation)	24 states	28 states (28 laws + 2 regulations)	39 states (37 laws + 2 regulations)	30 states (28 laws + 2 regulations)
Alabama	✓		Rx	Rx	✓		
Alaska	✓						
Arizona	✓					✓	✓
Arkansas	✓	✓		Rx, eye	✓	✓	✓
California					✓	✓	✓
Colorado					✓	✓	✓
Connecticut	✓	✓	Rx	Rx	✓	✓	✓
Delaware	Voluntary		Rx	Rx	✓	✓	
Florida	✓	✓	Rx/accountable health plans		✓	✓	✓
Georgia	✓			Rx	✓	✓	✓
Hawaii					✓		
Idaho	✓		Broad/Rx	Rx	✓	✓	✓
Illinois	✓	✓	Non-institutional providers	Preferred provider option	✓		
Indiana	✓		Broad/preferred provider organization		✓	✓	
Iowa	✓						Voluntary initiative
Kansas	✓		Rx			✓	✓
Kentucky	✓		Broad, chiropractors, psychologists, eye	Chiropractor			

State	Hospital length-of-stay after childbirth	Hospital length-of-stay for mastectomies	Any willing provider	Freedom-of-choice	Direct access to Ob/Gyn services	Ban on gag clauses	Comprehensive consumer rights/ protection acts
Total number of states	36 state (35 laws + 1 regulation)	13 states	24 states (23 laws + 1 regulation)	24 states	28 states (28 laws + 2 regulations)	39 states (37 laws + 2 regulations)	30 states (28 laws + 2 regulations)
Louisiana			Rx	Rx	✓	✓	✓
Maine	✓	✓			✓	✓	✓
Maryland	✓				✓	✓	✓
Massachusetts	✓				✓	✓	✓
Michigan						✓	
Minnesota	✓		Allies		✓	✓	✓
Mississippi			Rx	Rx	✓		✓
Missouri	✓				✓	✓	✓
Montana	✓	✓		Rx	✓	✓	✓
Nebraska					✓	✓	✓
Nevada				Allied		✓	✓
New Hampshire	✓		Rx			✓	✓
New Jersey	✓	✓	Rx	Rx	Regulation	✓	✓
New Mexico	✓ regulation	✓		Oriental medicine	Regulation	Regulation	Regulation
New York	✓	✓			✓	✓	✓
North Carolina	✓	✓	Rx	Rx	✓	Regulation	Regulation
North Dakota	✓		Rx	Rx		✓	
Ohio	✓						✓
Oklahoma	✓	✓	Rx	Osteopathy, podiatry, eye, dental, surgery		✓	✓
Oregon	✓				✓	✓	✓
Pennsylvania	✓					✓	
Rhode Island	✓	✓		Rx	✓	✓	✓

State	Hospital length-of-stay after childbirth	Hospital length-of-stay for mastectomies	Any willing provider	Freedom-of-choice	Direct access to Ob/Gyn services	Ban on gag clauses	Comprehensive consumer rights/ protection acts
Total number of states	36 state (35 laws + 1 regulation)	13 states	24 states (23 laws + 1 regulation)	24 states	28 states (28 laws + 2 regulations)	39 states (37 laws + 2 regulations)	30 states (28 laws + 2 regulations)
South Carolina	✓		Rx, allied	Rx			
South Dakota	✓		Rx	Rx			
Tennessee	✓					✓	
Texas	✓	✓	Regulation	Rx	✓	✓	✓
Utah				Broad	✓	✓	
Vermont						✓	✓
Virginia	✓		Broad	Rx	✓	✓	✓
Washington	✓			Opt-out	✓	✓	✓
West Virginia					✓		
Wisconsin			Rx, and other than HMOs and PPOs	Rx		✓	
Wyoming			Broad			✓	

Source: Health Policy Tracking Service. National Conferences of State Legislatures. Washington, D.C. Unpublished memoranda/tables, 1997.

Notes: Allied = allied health professionals (e.g., providers such as optometrists, podiatrists, and chiropractors)

Broad = broad array of health care providers (e.g., physicians, hospitals, pharmacies, chiropractors, etc.)

Eye = eye care

MD = physicians

Rx = pharmacies

OB = obstetricians/gynecologists

CONCLUSION

This chapter has sought to introduce the reader to the issues related to the current regulation of managed health care. Whether additional federal or state regulation is desirable or needed is likely to be an agenda item for the 105th Congress. As of October of 1997, a few congressional committees have announced plans to hold hearings and review pending managed care proposals.

In the event that Congress decides to tackle this issue, a first order question will be whether additional regulation is needed. Some may conclude that the market is better suited to weeding out MCOs that do not meet consumer demands for affordable, accessible, and high quality health care than is government regulation. Or, some may decide that the managed care industry's efforts to police itself will provide consumers and providers with sufficient protection.[67] For those who decide that regulation is necessary, opinions may be divided over whether the federal government or the states is the more appropriate focus for such regulation.

Should Congress decide to consider new federal regulations on managed care, it will be able to draw on the substantial experience of the states in regulating HMOs and to a lesser extent, other types of managed care arrangements. One of the major challenges, however, will be the regulatory treatment of managed care plans sponsored by employers. Many in Congress are reluctant to impose new requirements on employer plans, mindful of the concerns of business about the financial and administrative burdens that such requirements can entail. And perhaps most difficult will be resolving what to do when new federal law conflicts with existing state law. Should, for example, state laws be preempted thereby providing for uniform, national regulation? Or should state laws that are similar to or more protective of consumer and provider rights be allowed to apply? These and similar issues are likely to be hotly debated.

[67] In 1996, the American Association of Health Plans (AAHP), which is the national trade organization representing over 1,000 managed health care plans, initiated *Putting Patient First* "to improve communication with patients and physicians: to make clear that the AAHP and its member plans are listening to the concerns of patients and physicians and acting to meet their needs; and to demonstrate AAHP member plans' commitment to higher standards of accountability." In 1997, the membership of the AAHP voted to require health plans joining or renewing membership in the association to uphold the *Putting Patients First* initiative.

Chapter 10

HEALTH INSURANCE AND MEDICAL CARE: PHYSICIAN SERVICES UNDER MANAGED CARE

Patrick Purcell

ABSTRACT

Based on data from a 1995 national survey of physicians, this chapter compares the frequency of diagnostic services and therapeutic services during office visits to physicians who participated in health maintenance organizations (HMOs) and those who did not. It also describes the methods employed by managed care organizations (MCOs) to reduce unnecessary use of health care services, and summarizes the findings of previous research on the effect of managed care on health care utilization and outcomes. Results of the analysis of physician office visits in 1995 are then displayed in a series of tables that show the percentage of visits during which specific classes of services were performed by physicians who participated in each of four kinds of health insurance arrangements. Statistical analysis of the results indicates that while physician participation in an HMO had a significant positive effect of the proportion of visits during which these services were performed, the patient's health status had the largest impact among all variables studied on the likelihood of receiving a diagnostic or therapeutic service during an office visit.

SUMMARY

The financing and delivery of health care services in the U.S. have undergone significant changes in recent years. In response to rapidly rising health care costs, insurers, physicians, and employers have formed a variety of managed care organizations (MCOs) in an effort to achieve greater efficiency. Much has been written about the potential savings in national health expenditures that may be realized from the transition to managed care, but less is known about how this transition may affect the specific medical services that patients receive. Studies that focus on the *patient's* insurance would be likely to find differences in treatments between patients of comparable health status in prepaid and fee-for-service (FFS) plans only if physicians differentiated their treatment decisions based on the kind of health insurance by which the patient was covered. This chapter adds to the literature on medical services under managed care by analyzing data from a recent national survey of physicians. It compares the frequency with which several classes of medical services were performed during physician office visits classified according to the kind of insurance plans that the physician accepted.

This chapter makes several findings:

- In 1995, 84% of all office visits to primary care physicians by people under age 65 with employer-group or other private health insurance were made to physicians who participated in both managed and non-managed health insurance plans.
- Diagnostic and screening services were performed more frequently during visits both to pure FFS and pure HMO physician offices than during visits to physicians who accepted multiple kinds of insurance.
- Both male and female patients were more likely to receive diagnostic or screening services in a visit to an HMO-on physician office than during a visit to a physician office that participated in a PPO, but the difference from the overall average was greater for men than for women.
- Therapeutic and preventive services were performed more frequently during office visits to HMO-only physicians than during visits to physicians who accepted multiple kinds of insurance. For people who had no chronic medical conditions, the likelihood of receiving therapeutic or preventive services did not vary significantly according to the type of insurance accepted by the physician.
- Men were much more likely to receive therapeutic or preventive services in an HMO-only office setting than in physician offices that accepted other kinds of insurance. Women were equally likely to receive these services in HMO-only or fee-for-service-only office settings.

Managed care comes in many forms, but all managed care organizations (MCOs) share two basic goals. The most fundamental reasons for managing the delivery of health care are to *control costs* while providing *necessary and appropriate medical services*. The number and variety of MCOs reflect the multitude of approaches to achieving these objectives.[1] Although much has been written about the potential savings in national health expenditures that may be realized from the transition to managed care, less is known about how this transition may affect the specific medical services that patients receive. If medical care services differ between managed care and non-managed care or among the different kinds of MCOs, the reasons could be related to the physicians' treatment practices, characteristics of the patients being treated, or both. This information can be useful both to users of health care services and to policymakers who must decide priorities in selecting and managing the methods of financing and delivering health care for millions of beneficiaries in public programs such as Medicare and Medicaid.

This chapter uses data from a national survey of physicians to compare the frequency with which several kinds of medical services were performed during office visits in 1995 to

---

[1] For a description of the ways in which health care providers and insures have formed MCOs see CRS Report 97-913, *Managed Health Care: A Primer*, by Jason S. Lee.

physicians who participated in various kinds of MCOs and visits to physicians who did not participate in managed care. The results presented here are based on physician office visits by people under age 65 who were covered by employer-group or other private health insurance.[2] We have focused on privately insured, non-elderly patients because it is among this segment of the population that the transition to managed care has been occurring for the longest period of time, and because the analysis is not complicated by issues of eligibility, enrollment, financing and regulation that pertain specifically to the Medicare and Medicaid programs. Nevertheless, the experience of patients and physicians in the delivery of office-based medical care under privately-financed MCOs may hold important lessons that can be used to make the transition to managed care in the Medicare and Medicaid programs more efficient and equitable for all interested parties.

MANAGED HEALTH CARE USE AND COSTS

Arrangements for managing the financing and delivery of health care have become more common in recent years, in part because the cost of health care rose faster than the prices of most other goods and services from the 1960s through the mid-1990s. Managed care seeks to make the provision of health care services more efficient by using no more than the resources necessary to deliver care, while meeting the community's prevailing standards of quality. The challenge faced by any MCO, therefore, is one of controlling the *cost* of health care while maintaining the *quality* of care. MCOs attempt to control costs by eliminating unnecessary or inappropriate services. To do this they can:

- create a *financial relationship* with the health care provider that encourages efficient use of resources,[3]
- substitute *less expensive care* (for instance, office-based care) for more expensive care (such as inpatient hospital care), and
- *reduce the demand for health care services* by promoting good health practices among those who are enrolled in the managed care plan.

The Financial Relationship with the Health Care Provider

The two most common types of payment for medical care are "fee-for-service" (FFS) and prepayment, which is also called "capitation." As its name implies, in a FFS reimbursement arrangement the health care provider bills the patient for each individual service provided. If the patient is insured, the insurer will usually pay some or all of the bill, generally after the patient has paid the first few hundred dollars of medical bills incurred during the calendar year, which is called a *deductible amount*. Insurance that pays expenses as they are incurred for each office visit, hospital stay, or other episode of care is called *indemnity insurance*.

---

[2] Some of these individuals also may have been covered by Medicare or Medicaid, but the office visits included in this report all were covered by a private health insurance plan.

[3] See also CRS Report 97-482, *Managed Health Care: The Use of Financial Incentives* by Jason S. Lee and Beth C. Fuchs.

Some indemnity insurers have negotiated special low reimbursement rates with providers of health care. In exchange for these lower rates, the insurer designates the health care professional as a "preferred provider." Patients who visit an insurer's preferred providers are usually rewarded with a lower copayment (the share of the total bill that is the patient's responsibility) than if they visit providers who are not members of this network. Preferred provider organizations, or "PPOs," are considered to be MCOs because they are financial incentives to induce health care providers to deliver services efficiently. The financial incentives used by PPOs can include amounts added to or withheld from the FFS reimbursement paid to the provider. Inefficient providers may be dropped from the PPO, creating another incentive for the provider to eliminate unnecessary services.

Under the FFS method of reimbursing health care providers, each additional fest, procedure, or office visit increases the provider's revenue, creating a financial incentive for health care professionals to provide more services. This incentive exists even in a PPO, although it may be tempered by the possibility that the provider could be dropped from the PPO. Another type of MCO, the health maintenance organization, or HMO, reduces the financial incentive to provide additional care either by employing the physician directly on a salary basis or by "prepaying" the physician a fixed amount per month for each of the HMO's members in exchange for providing all (or most) or the health care services that they require. In the so-called "staff-model" HMO, the physicians are employed directly, and their medical practice patterns can be monitored and rewarded or sanctioned, just like the performance of an employee in any other kind of firm. In "group-model" HMOs and in another kind of HMO called an "independent practice association" (IPA), the HMO contracts with physician groups or independent physician practices to provide health care services to the HMO's members, usually in exchange for a monthly "capitation payment."[4] If the total cost of care provided to the members of the HMO is less than the sum of these capitation payments, the physician group keeps the difference as profit. If costs exceed the sum of the capitation payments, the physicians suffer a financial loss.[5]

Substituting Less Expensive Care for More Expensive Care

MCOs also are able to reduce costs by employing primary care physicians as "gatekeepers" to regulate patients' access to more expensive specialists, and by providing as much care as possible in physician offices, clinics, and hospital outpatient departments rather than in an inpatient hospital setting. Lower rates of hospitalization and shorter stays in hospitals associated with MCOs – specifically with HMOs – have been shown to be an important source of savings in MCOs compared with traditional indemnity insurers.[6]

---

[4] Even HMOs that pay most primary-care physicians on a capitation basis will often reimburse specialists FFS. Members of an HMO may sometimes see non-participating physicians who are reimbursed on a FFS basis if the HMO offers a "point-of-service" (POS) option.

[5] In 1996, 74% of HMO contracts with primary-care physicians provided for prepaid, capitated reimbursement, according to Hoechst-Marion-Roussel's *HMO-PPO Digest*.

[6] To date, reductions n health and care costs resulting from managed care have been attributed mainly to reductions in the number and length of inpatient hospital stays. See, for example, KPMG Peal Marwick. *The Impact of Managed Care on U.S. Markets*. Washington DC, 1996 and; Richardson, James C. Decline in Hospital Utilization

Reducing the Demand for Care

By promoting good health practices that emphasize early intervention and preventive medicine, such as immunizations, screening for specific conditions, and regular check-ups, MCOs may lower the total cost of health care by catching incipient illnesses when they can be treated with the greatest effectiveness and at the least expense. In such cases, more frequent use of health care services in the near-term may result in reduced need for medical services in the long-term.[7]

PREVIOUS RESEARCH ON AMBULATORY SERVICES UNDER MANAGED CARE

Access to Care

Numerous studies published in recent years have examined issues of access to care, intensity of service utilization, and quality of care in managed and non-managed health insurance plans. A review of the literature evaluating managed care plan performance between 1980 and 1993 found that, compared to indemnity insurance plans, HMOs had "the same or more physician office visits per enrollee, less use of expensive procedures and tests, greater use of preventive services, [and] mixed results on outcomes."[8] A more recent literature review by the same authors found that "there was no overall pattern to physician use or expenditure results" in 10 studies published between 1993 and 1997.[9] Another recent study found that as the average number of inpatient hospital days among patients in HMOs has been declining, the frequency of physician office visits has been rising.[10] Data from the 1994 Health Interview Survey show that the frequency at which people in HMOs visited physician offices did not differ substantively from the rate for people in traditional indemnity insurance plans. These data show that 15.0% of privately insured people under age 65 in HMOs had made at least one office visit in any given 2-week period in 1994, compared to 14.1% of people covered by indemnity insurance plans that paid providers on a FFS basis.[11]

One reason that the frequency of physician visits differs only slightly between people enrolled in HMOs and those with FFS insurance is that average health status, as measured by the percentage of people who have chronic health problems differs very little between these

and Cost Inflation Under Managed Care in California. *Journal of the American Medical Association*, v. 276, no. 13, October 2, 1996.

[7] Early diagnosis and treatment of illnesses may be desirable for their public health benefits, but they may not result in savings to national health expenditures. A person who detects a medical condition at age 70, for example, and has it treated successfully, possibly preventing premature death, may eventually suffer another illness or series of illnesses requiring medical treatment and additional expenditures.

[8] Miller, R.H. and H.S. Luft. "Managed care Plan Performance Since 1980. *Journal of the American Medical Association*, v. 271, no. 19, May 18, 1994.

[9] Miller, R.H. and H.S. Luft. "Does Managed Care Lead to Better or Worse Quality of Care?" *Health Affairs*, v. 16, no. 5, September/October 1997.

[10] Wholey, D., at al. HMO Market Structure and Performance: 1985-1995. *Health Affairs*, v. 16, no. 6, November/December 1997.

[11] Although small, this difference is statistically significant at the 95% confidence level, based on a two-tailed t-test.

two groups. In the 1994 National Health Interview Survey, 37% of people enrolled in indemnity insurance plans and 37% of those in HMOs reported that they had a medical condition of any kind. Among those covered by indemnity plans, 30.7% reported one or more *chronic* medical conditions, versus 29.9% of those in HMOs.[12] The frequency of office visits was similar between the HMO and FFS enrollees even among those who reported having a medical condition.[13] Of the people who reported having an acute or chronic medical condition, 34.8% of HMO enrollees had seen a doctor in a given 2-week period, compared with 33.2% of those enrolled in indemnity insurance plans.[14]

Health Outcomes

Studies of outcomes between managed and non-managed health care plans also have found mixed results. Clement and others (1994) found that Medicare beneficiaries in HMOs who reported either joint pain or chest pain were less likely to have seen a specialist for care, to have a follow-up recommended, or to have their progress monitored. Less improvement in symptoms was found among the HMO enrollees in one of four outcomes studied. In a 4-year study of chronically ill patients, Ware and others (1996) found that physical and mental health outcomes did not differ between FFS and HMO plans for the average patient, but they did for certain sub-groups of patients. Among elderly patients, declines in physical health were more common among those in HMOs than in FFS plans. Outcomes tended to be better in FFS plans among poor patients, but better outcomes were found in HMOs for non-poor patients. Yelin, Criswell, and Feigenbaum (1996) examined data on health outcomes over periods of up to 11 years for patients with rheumatoid arthritis in FFS insurance plans and prepaid group practices. They found that the "two groups did not differ on any outcome measure on either an annual or long-term basis."

---

[12] The extent, if any, to which HMOs experience favorable selection in terms of the health status of their enrollees remains in open question. Data from the 1994 National Health Interview Survey indicate little difference in the health status of people enrolled in HMOs compared to those in indemnity insurance plans. Taylor and colleagues (1995), reporting on an analysis of data from the 1987 National Medical Expenditure Survey, also found "very little evidence that individuals enrolled in HMOs were healthier than those in FFS plans." Likewise, Fama and colleagues (1995) found little observable difference in the health status of people in HMOs and those in other insurance plans. Hellinger (1995) however, in a review of the literature on the subject reported that a majority of studies found that HMOs and other plans with closed provider networks experienced favorable selection bias among their enrollees when compared to people enrolled in non-HMO plans.

[13] Among people who reported no medical conditions, 3.6% of those who were enrolled in an HMO saw a physician in a 2-week period, compared with 3.0% of those covered by indemnity insurance, not a statistically significant difference.

[14] Although the differences in chronic conditions and 2-week office visits are not large enough to suggest dramatic behavioral differences either by patients or physicians in HMOs compared to indemnity plans, both are statistically significant at the 95% confidence level based on a two-tailed t-test.

DATA AND METHODS

Access to ambulatory medical care services often is measured in terms of the frequency of contacts with a physician or other health care professional. Another measure of access is the likelihood that a physician office visit will result in a specific service being provided. If the likelihood that a specific service will be performed during an office visit appears to differ according to the kinds of insurance accepted by the physician, we would like to know the extent to which this variation reflects differences in the patients being treated, the physicians' practice patterns (including the influence of managed care), or a combination of these factors. This chapter uses data from a nationally representative survey of physicians to examine the frequency with which particular classes of medical services were performed during office visits to physicians who participated in different kinds of insurance arrangements. The chapter focuses on two broad classifications of services identified in the National Ambulatory Medical Care Survey: *diagnostic and screening services* and *therapeutic and preventive services*.

For this chapter, the author analyzed the frequency with which specific services were performed during physician office visits *according to the kind of health insurance plans accepted by the physician*. Most prior studies have looked at the kind of insurance that covered the individual patient; however, in 1995 more than four-fifths of all office visits to primary care physicians by privately insured individuals under age 65 were made to physicians who saw some patients in managed health plans *and* some with non-managed insurance. Studies that focus on the kind of insurance that covered the patient would be likely to find differences in treatments or outcomes between patients in prepaid and FFS plans only if a significant proportion of physicians differentiated their treatment decisions based on the kind of health insurance by which the patient was covered. This hypothesis is not generally supported by empirical findings.[15] The methodology employed for this analysis permitted us to see whether the frequency of services differed between physicians who accepted only prepaid insurance such as HMOs or *only* FFS insurance. This classification scheme also allowed us to see whether the frequency with which certain categories of medical services were performed differed between physicians in pure-HMO or pure-FFS practices and physicians who see patients in both prepaid and FFS plans.

The analysis presented here focuses on office visits to physicians who are *primary-care providers* because it is these physician offices in which managed care principles have been most widely adopted. Likewise, in some of the tables that follow, the sample has been restricted to office visits made by patients who were reported by the physician to have no chronic medical conditions. This restriction can help to make clear whether a difference in the frequency with which specific services were provided was the result of differences in physician practice patterns between managed care and non-managed care; differences in the

[15] Fore example, many physicians are unaware even whether patient is covered by private insurance or by a publicly financed program such as Medicaid. Research into state compliance with the early, periodic, screening, diagnosis and testing (EPSDT) requirements for children covered by Medicaid indicates that most physicians performing a physical exam or well-child checkup are unaware of the child's source of health insurance coverage. (Elicia Herz, Ph.D., MEDSTAT Group, Washington DC, personal communication with author.)

proportion of people enrolled in each kind of plan who were in poor health; or a combination of these two factors.

Data on health care services provided during visits to office-based physicians were collected as part of the 1995 National Ambulatory Medical Care Survey (NAMCS) conducted by the National Center for Health Statistics, a division of the U.S. Department of Health and Human Services. All non-federally employed office-based physicians who were primarily engaged in patient-care activities were eligible to be included in the Ambulatory Medical Care Survey with the exception of physicians who specialties were anesthesiology, pathology, or radiology. Contacts with patients by telephone, outside the physician's office, in hospital settings (inpatient or outpatient), in institutional settings such as nursing homes, or office visits for administrative purposes (such as paying bills, filing out insurance forms, or dropping off a specimen) were not included in the survey. Of the 2,587 physicians contacted in 1995, 73% participated in the survey.

The 1995 survey data consist of 36,875 patient record forms collected from 1,883 physicians who participated in the NAMCS. Each record represents one visit by a patient to an office-based physician, and each has been assigned a patient visit weight, which when aggregated across all visits, represent the estimated total of 697 million physician office visits in the U.S. in 1995. In this chapter analysis is limited to physician visits by people under age 65 with employer-group or other private health insurance. This sub-sample comprised 27,067 patient record forms (73.4% of the total), and represented 254.5 million physician office visits.

Of the 254.5 million office visits by people under age 65 with employer-group or other private health insurance, 168.3 million visits (66.1%) were made to primary-care physicians, including general and family practitioners, internists, pediatricians, and obstetricians/gynecologists. Just 10% of these visits were made to physicians who accepted only insurance that reimbursed the physician on a FFS basis and who did not participate in either a PPO or HMO. Only 6% of these office visits were made to physicians who only saw patients who were enrolled in an HMO. Thus, relatively small proportions of physician office visits in 1995 were made to physicians who had *no* patients in managed care or to physicians who saw *only* patients who were enrolled in the most strictly managed form of managed care. The vast majority of physician office visits in 1995 – 84% of the total – were made to physicians who treated some patients who were enrolled in a managed care plan, and some who were not.

Patient records on the NAMCS include both the expected source of insurance and the expected source of payment. The categories for expected source of insurance are Blue Cross/Blue Shield, other private insurance, Medicare, Medicaid, worker's compensation, other insurance, and unknown. These are eight source-of-payment categories on the survey instrument:

- blank with no source of insurance reported,
- preferred provider option,
- insured FFS,
- HMO or other prepaid,
- self-pay,
- no charge,

- other source of payment, and
- type of payment was not specified but source of insurance was reported.

In this chapter, physician office visits have been grouped according to the source of payment reported on patient records during the week that each physician participated in the NAMCS. We used the unique physician identifiers to classify physicians into four groups, based on the kinds of insurance that covered patients seen by the physician. The four groups of physicians were:

- those who saw *only* patients whose insurance reimbursed the physician on a FFS basis with no PPO discounts,
- those who saw patients in both regular FFS plans and in PPO plans, but who saw no patients who were enrolled in an HMO,
- those who saw patients enrolled in HMOs, in PPOs, and in non-PPO plans,
- those who saw *only* patients who were enrolled in an HMO.[16]

This classification allows us to discern not only whether services differed between managed care and non-manage care, but also whether the frequency of services provided during visits to "mixed insurance" physician offices was more like the frequency seen in visits to HMO-only physician offices or like that which occurred during visits to physicians who accepted only pure FFS payments.

RESULTS: SERVICES PROVIDED DURING PHYSICIAN OFFICE VISITS

Physician Office Visits: Patient Demographic Characteristics (Table 1)

Patient demographic and health characteristics, geographic variations in physician practice patterns, and whether the physician has seen the patient before all may influence diagnostic and treatment procedures. These characteristics are arrayed in **Table 1** according to the proportion of office visits made by people in each category to physicians who accepted each of four kinds or combinations of health insurance plans.

Age

Children and young adults were less likely than adults 35 or older to have made an office visit to a physician who accepted only FFS insurance arrangements, and were more likely than people in other age groups to have visited a physician office that accepted both HMO and PPO insurance plans. People between the ages of 55 and 64 made up 18.1% of visits to physicians who accepted only FFS insurance arrangements, significantly higher than the

[16] The data collected on the Ambulatory Medical Care Survey do not differentiate between group/staff model HMOs and IPA-model HMOs, a distinction that could increase the explanatory power of these data with respect to differences *among* HMOs in the frequency with which specific services were provided during office visits. Nevertheless, because neither kind of HMO typically uses FFS reimbursement, the NAMCS data allow us to distinguish between kinds of insurance payment that respond to increases in the number of patient visits or volume of services and those that do not.

overall average of 10.0%; however, they also comprised a higher-than-average share of visits to physicians who treated only patients enrolled in HMOs.

Sex

In 1995, 107 million out of 168 million office visits (63.5%) to primary care physicians by privately insured people under age 65 were made by female patients. Male and female patients had very similar probabilities of visiting a physician who treated only HMO patients, but males made up an above-average share of all visits to physicians who accepted only FFS insurance plans.

Race

Both while and non-white patients had similar likelihoods of visiting a primary care physician who saw only HMO enrollees, but non-white patients had an above-average probability of visiting a physician who accepted only FFS insurance reimbursement.

Health Status: Chronic Medical Conditions

Office visits to physicians who accepted only FFS reimbursement included a higher-than-average proportion of visits made by patients with chronic medical conditions, while visits to physician offices that accepted both FFS and PPO plans included a lower-than-average proportion of visits made by chronically ill patients.[17] Visits to FFS-only physician offices made up 10% of all visits by privately insured patients under age 65, but they comprised 14.8% of all visits made by patients with one or more chronic medical conditions. Visits to physician offices that participated in both FFS and PPO plans made up 16.1% of all visits by privately insured patients under age 65, but they comprised 14.2% of all visits made by patients with one or more chronic medical conditions.

Region

There were significant regional differences in the proportion of office visits that were made to physicians who participated in an HMO. In the West, 11.1% of all visits were made to physicians who treated *only* patients enrolled in an HMO, while in no other region were more than 4.2% of visits made by HMO-only physician offices. In both the Northeast and the West, more than 80% of all office visits were made to physicians who saw some HMO patients, usually along with PPO patients. In the Midwest and South, fewer than 70% of all office visits were made to primary care physicians who participated in at least one HMO.

Urban/Rural Location

In 1995, 78.7% of office visits in urban areas were made to physicians who treated at least some patients who were enrolled in an HMO. Only 7.1% of office visits to physicians in urban areas were to offices that accepted only FFS reimbursement. In contrast, just 48.1% of office visits in rural areas were made to physicians who treated at least some patients who were in an HMO. More than a quarter of all office visits in rural areas were made to physicians who accepted only insurance plans that reimbursed the provider on a FFS basis.

---

[17] In the National Ambulatory Care Survey, chronic conditions are defined to include arthritis, arteriosclerosis, chronic obstructive pulmonary disorder, renal disease, clinical depression, diabetes, human immunodeficiency virus/acquired immune deficiency syndrome (HIV/AIDS), hyperactivity, hypertension, and obesity.

New or Previously Established Physician-Patient Relationship

Among office visits to primary care physicians by privately insured people under age 65, 90.2% were made to a physician who had seen the patient before (151,818 out of 168,289). Office visits by patients that the physician had never seen before were most likely to have occurred in among physicians who participated in both HMO and PPO insurance plans. While two-thirds of all office visits by privately insured people under age 65 were made to physicians who saw patients in both HMO and PPO plans, visits to HMO and PPO offices comprised three-fourths of all visits in which the physician had not seen the patient before.

Table 1. Office Visits to Primary Care Physicians by Privately Insured People Under Age 65

		Percentage of visits that were to physicians who accepted:				
	Visits (000s)	FFS only	FFS and PPO	HMO and PPO	HMO only	Total
Patient demographics:						
Under age 18	59,144	***7.9%***	***18.4%***	***71.5%***	***2.3%***	*100%*
Ages 18 to 34	36,224	***8.4%***	***11.8%***	***72.6%***	*7.3%*	*100%*
Ages 35 to 54	53,413	*10.5%*	*16.4%*	***65.6%***	***7.4%***	*100%*
Ages 55 to 64	19,508	***18.1%***	*16.3%*	***56.8%***	***8.8%***	*100%*
Female	10.6,942	***8.8%***	*15.7%*	*69.8%*	*5.8%*	*100%*
Male	61,347	***12.1%***	*16.9%*	***65.4%***	*5.7%*	*100%*
White	147,423	*9.5%*	*16.9%*	*67.9%*	*5.7%*	*100%*
Black or other	20,865	***13.8%***	***10.2%***	*70.1%*	*6.0%*	*100%*
Has Chronic Condition(s)	36,434	***14.8%***	***14.2%***	*64.0%*	*7.0%*	*100%*
No Chronic Conditions	131,853	***8.7%***	*16.6%*	*69.3%*	*5.4%*	*100%*
Physician Location:						
Northeast	29,070	*10.9%*	***4.5%***	***81.5%***	***3.2%***	*100%*
Midwest	40,991	*10.3%*	***19.9%***	***65.6%***	*4.2%*	*100%*
South	52,684	*9.3%*	***25.6%***	***61.4%***	***3.8%***	*100%*
West	45,544	*10.1%*	***9.1%***	*69.8%*	***11.1%***	*100%*
Urban	141,671	***7.1%***	***14.2%***	***72.1%***	***6.6%***	*100%*
Rural	26,616	***25.5%***	***26.4%***	***46.9%***	*1.2%*	*100%*
Patient Seen Previously	151,818	*10.3%*	*16.7%*	***67.4%***	*5.6%*	*100%*
Not Seen Previously	16,470	***7.5%***	***10.7%***	***75.2%***	*6.6%*	*100%*
Total	168,289	*10.0%*	*16.1%*	*68.2%*	*5.7%*	*100%*

Source: CRS analysis of data from the 1996 NAMCS.

Note: Percentages that are significantly different from the column average at 95% or greater confidence are shown in boldface type.

Performance of Diagnostic or Screening Services (Table 2)

Diagnostic or screening services were performed during 74.3% of all office visits to primary care physicians in 1995, but the frequency varied according to the type of insurance accepted by the provider. (Diagnostic and screening services are defined in Appendix II). Visits to HMO-only physicians had the highest probability of a diagnostic or screening service, at 85% of visits. Office visits to FFS-only physicians had the second highest probability of a diagnostic or screening service (78%). Office visits to physician practices that accepted both FFS and PPO plans had lower-than-average rates of screening and diagnostic services. The pattern was similar among patients with no chronic conditions, except that among this group the proportion visits to FFS-only physicians during that diagnostic and screening services were performed was not statistically different from the average for all office visits by patients with a chronic condition.

Table 2. Diagnostic and Screening Services, Privately Insured Patients Under Age 65

Type of insurance accepted by physician	*Were diagnostic/screening services performed?* Visits (000s)	Yes	No	Total
FFS only	16,848	***77.9%***	***22.1%***	*100%*
FFS or PPO	27,075	***70.5%***	***29.5%***	*100%*
HMO or PPO	114,703	*73.8%*	*26.2%*	*100%*
HMO only	9,662	***84.8%***	***15.2%***	*100%*
Total	168,288	*74.3%*	*25.7%*	*100%*

Privately Insured Patients Under Age 65 Who Had No Chronic Medical Conditions

Type of insurance accepted by physician	*Were diagnostic/screening services performed?* Visits (000s)	Yes	No	Total
FFS only	11,459	*71.3%*	*28.7%*	*100%*
FFS or PPO	21,915	***65.3%***	***34.7%***	*100%*
HMO or PPO	91,365	*69.8%*	*30.2%*	*100%*
HMO only	7,115	***81.4%***	***18.6%***	*100%*
Total	131,854	*69.8%*	*30.2%*	*100%*

Source: CRS analysis of data from the 1995 NAMCS.

Note: Percentages that are significantly different from the column average at 95% or greater confidence are shown in boldface type.

Diagnostic and Screening Services: Differences by Sex (Table 3)

Overall, diagnostic or screening services were more likely to be performed during office visits made by female rather than male patients, (78% vs. 68%). Both female and male patients were most likely to have received diagnostic or screening services during a visit to an

HMO-only physician, but the difference was about twice as large for males (83% in pure-HMO offices vs. 67% in other offices) as for females (86% in pure-HMO offices vs. 77% in other offices). Male and female patients were equally likely to receive diagnostic or screening services in physician offices that accepted only traditional FFS insurance (78% in both sexes). Among female patients, the likelihood of receiving these services was significantly different from the overall average only for visits to pure-HMO physician offices. Among male patients, the likelihood of having a diagnostic or screening service performed was significantly higher than average in both pure-HMO and pure-FFS physician offices, and it was significantly below average in offices that accepted both FFS and PPO plans.

Table 3. Diagnostic and Screening Services by Sex of Patient

Female patients	*Were diagnostic/screening services performed?*			
Type of insurance accepted by physician	Visits (000s)	Yes	No	Total
FFS only	9,408	*77.6%*	*22.4%*	*100%*
FFS or PPO	16,738	*75.7%*	*24.3%*	*100%*
HMO or PPO	74,602	*77.8%*	*22.2%*	*100%*
HMO only	6,194	***85.6%***	***14.4%***	*100%*
Total	106,942	*77.9%*	*22.1%*	*100%*

Male patients	*Were diagnostic/screening services performed?*			
Type of insurance accepted by physician	Visits (000s)	Yes	No	Total
FFS only	7,440	***78.3%***	***21.7%***	*100%*
FFS or PPO	10,337	***62.0%***	***38.0%***	*100%*
HMO or PPO	,40,101	*66.3%*	*33.7%*	*100%*
HMO only	3,469	***83.3%***	***16.7%***	*100%*
Total	61,347	*68.0%*	*32.0%*	*100%*

Source: CRS analysis of data from the 1996 NAMCS.

Note: Percentages that are significantly different from the column average at 95% or greater confidence are shown in boldface type.

Performance of Therapeutic or Preventive Services (Table 4)

Only 36.5% of office visits to primary care physicians in 1995 included performance of at least one therapeutic or preventive services. (Therapeutic and preventive services are defined in Appendix II.) As was also the case with diagnostic and screening services, office visits to physicians who treated only patients enrolled in an HMO had the highest frequency of therapeutic and preventive services (43.4%), and visits to physicians who accepted both FFS and PPO insurance plans included performance of these services at a rate that was significantly below the overall overage.

One possible explanation for differences in the proportion of visits during which therapeutic or preventive services were administered would be differences in the health status of patients seen by physicians in each of the four insurance categories. The bottom panel of Table 4 shows office visits by people who were reported by the physician to have no chronic medical conditions. Among patients with no chronic medical conditions, the rate of therapeutic and preventive services did not differ significantly from the overall average for any of the four insurance classifications.

Table 4. Therapeutic and Preventive Services, Privately Insured Patients Under Age 65

Type of insurance accepted by physician	*Were therapeutic or preventive services performed?* Visits (000s)	Yes	No	Total
FFS only	16,848	*38.6%*	*61.4%*	*100%*
FFS or PPO	27,075	***32.2%***	***67.8%***	*100%*
HMO or PPO	114,703	*36.7%*	*63.3%*	*100%*
HMO only	9,662	***43.4%***	***56.6%***	*100%*
Total	168,288	*36.5%*	*63.5%*	*100%*
Privately Insured Patients Under Age 65 Who Had No Chronic Medical Conditions				
Type of insurance accepted by physician	*Were therapeutic or preventive services performed?* Visits (000s)	Yes	No	Total
FFS only	11,459	*30.2%*	*69.8%*	*100%*
FFS or PPO	21,915	*28.7%*	*71.3%*	*100%*
HMO or PPO	91,365	*32.2%*	*67.8%*	*100%*
HMO only	7,115	*35.7%*	*64.3%*	*100%*
Total	131,854	*31.6%*	*68.4%*	*100%*

Source: CRS analysis of data from the 1995 National Ambulatory Medical Care Survey.

Note: Percentages that are significantly different from the column average at 95% or greater confidence are shown in boldface type.

Therapeutic or Preventive Services: Differences by Sex (Table 5)

There was little difference in the proportion of office visits by male and female patients during which therapeutic or preventive services were performed. These services were performed during 37.5% of physician office visits by men and 36% of visits by women. Among female patients, therapeutic or preventive services were equally likely to be administered during a visit to an HMO-only or FFS-only physician practice (41%), while visits to physician offices that participated in both FFS and PPO plans included therapeutic and preventive services at a rate significantly lower than the overall average – (30.7% versus 36.0%). Among men, visits to HMO-only physicians had a higher-than-average frequency of therapeutic and preventive services (48%), while visits to all other physician offices included these services at rates near the overall average of 37.5%.

Table 5. Performance of Therapeutic or Preventive Services by Sex of Patient

Female patients Type of insurance accepted by physician	*Were therapeutic or preventive services performed?* Visits (000s)	Yes	No	Total
FFS only	9,408	*40.9%*	*59.1%*	*100%*
FFS or PPO	16,738	***30.7%***	***69.3%***	*100%*
HMO or PPO	74,602	*36.2%*	*63.8%*	*100%*
HMO only	6,194	*40.8%*	*59.2%*	*100%*
Total	106,942	*36.0%*	*64.0%*	*100%*

Male patients Type of insurance accepted by physician	*Were therapeutic or preventive services performed?* Visits (000s)	Yes	No	Total
FFS only	7,440	*35.7%*	*64.3%*	*100%*
FFS or PPO	10,337	*34.5%*	*65.5%*	*100%*
HMO or PPO	40,101	*37.7%*	*62.3%*	*100%*
HMO only	3,469	***47.9%***	***52.1%***	*100%*
Total	61,347	*37.5%*	*62.5%*	*100%*

Source: CRS analysis of data from the 1995 National Ambulatory Medical Care Survey.

Note: Percentages that are significantly different from the column average of 95% or greater confidence are shown in boldface type.

Multi-variate Analysis: Diagnostic and Screening Services

To evaluate the relationship of each the variables described in **Table 1** through **Table 5** to the probability that a physician office visit included a diagnostic/screening or therapeutic/preventive service, we processed the data through a regression model.[18] This form of analysis shows the relative impact of each specified characteristic of the patient or physician while all of the other factors are held constant.

Age, Sex, and Race

Other things being equal, the probability that a privately insured individual under age 65 had a diagnostic or screening service performed during a physician office visit increases by about 4.6% for each additional year of age, and a female patient was about 33% more likely to have a diagnostic or screening service performed during an office visit than was a male patient. (See the column labeled "Odds Ratio.") A patient's race (defined here as white or

[18] The results presented in this section are from a logistic regression model. We also processed the data through a probit model and found substantively the same results.

nonwhite) was unrelated to the likelihood that he or she had a diagnostic or screening service performed, once other patient and physician characteristics were taken into account.

Region and Urban/Rural Location

Both the region and urban or rural location of a physician office had a statistically significant relationship to the probability that a diagnostic or screening service was performed during a physician office visit. Relative to physician office visits in the Midwest, office visits in the Northeast, South, and west all had a greater likelihood of including a diagnostic or screening service, with the probability ranging from 33% higher in the South to 47% higher in the Northeast. Likewise, visits to physician offices in urban areas were about one-third more likely than those in rural areas to include a diagnostic or screening service, other factors being equal.

Health Status; New or Established Physician-Patient Relationship

Patients who had one or more chronic conditions according to the patient records maintained by the physician were much more likely to have undergone a diagnostic or screening service during an office visit than patients who had no chronic conditions. The rate at which these services were performed was almost 80% higher for a patient with a chronic condition when other characteristics were held constant. Having seen a patient during a previous visit was associated with a lower probability of receiving diagnostic or screening services. Patients who had been seen by a health care provider previously were about 26% less likely to have had a diagnostic or screening service performed than those who were being seen for the first time. Office visits also were more likely to include diagnostic and screening services if the provider was a physician rather than a nurse practitioner, registered nurse, or other provider; however, visits to these other providers accounted for only 4% of all office visits.

Insurance Plans Accepted by Physician

For the regression analysis, we used office visits to physicians who accepted only non-PPO FFS insurance plans as the reference group for estimating the probability of a diagnostic or screening service being performed during an office visit. Compared to the reference group, there was no significant difference in the likelihood of a diagnostic or screening service being performed during visits to physicians who accepted both FFS and PPO insurance plans. Visits to HMO-only and HMO/PPO physician offices, however, were both associated with higher rates of diagnostic and screening services, than office visits to pure-FFS offices, other things being equal. An office visit to a physician who participated in both PPO and HMO plans was about 20% more likely to include a diagnostic or screening service than a visit to a FFS-only office, while the likelihood of having these services performed during a visit to an HMO-only physician office was about 40% higher than in a pure-FFS office, other things being equal.

Table 6. Diagnostic and Screening Services, Privately Insured Patients Under Age 65: Logistic Regression Results

Response Variable: Were diagnostic or screening services performed?				
Analysis Variable	**Weighted Mean**	**Parameter Estimate**	**Standard Error**	**Odds Ratio**
Intercept		-2.3615***	0.2572	
Age	29.1	0.0449***	0.00202	1.046
Sex (1 = female)	0.6345	0.2843***	0.0670	1.329
Race (1 = white)	0.8778	-0.0551	0.1060	0.946
Northeast	0.1736	0.3835***	0.1043	1.467
South	0.3241	0.2874***	0.0866	1.333
West	0.2640	0.3262***	0.0931	1.386
Urban Area	0.8336	0.2876***	0.0916	1.333
Has Chronic Condition(s)	0.2189	0.5840***	0.1099	1.793
Patient Seen Previously	0.9035	-0.3066***	0.1146	0.736
Provider is an M.D.	0.9583	1.8145***	0.1499	6.138
Reg. FFS or PPO accepted	0.1569	0.1600	0.1265	1.174
HMO or PPO accepted	0.6645	0.1828*	0.1083	1.201
Only HMO accepted	0.0560	0.3341*	0.1921	1.397

Source: CRS analysis of data from the 1995 NAMCS.
n = 6,028 observations
* significant at >= .10
*** significant at >= .01

Multi-variate Analysis: Therapeutic and Preventive Services

Age, Sex, and Race

When the response variable of the regression model was changed to indicate whether therapeutic or preventive services were performed during an office visit, the relationship of the patient's age was significant, but negative. Each additional year of age reduced by about 1% the likelihood of a therapeutic or preventive service being performed during an office visit. The signs of the variables indicating the patient's sex (female = 1) and race (white = 1) also were negative, but neither of these variables was statistically significant.

Region and Urban/Rural Location

Relative to being located in the Midwest, an office visit in the Northeast was more likely to include a therapeutic or preventive service, and an office visit in the South was less likely to include these services. Physician office visits in the West had effectively the same likelihood of including therapeutic and preventive services as office visits in the Midwest. As was the case with diagnostic and screening services, therapeutic and preventive services were more likely to be administered during a physician office visit in an urban area than in a rural area, with the probability being about 23% greater in urban settings.

Health Status; New or Established Physician-Patient Relationship

The presence of one or more chronic medical conditions had a positive and statistically significant relationship to the probability that therapeutic and preventive services were performed during a physician office visit. Other things being equal, patients with chronic conditions were almost three times as likely to have these kinds of services performed as were patients with no chronic conditions. Office visits to a health care provider who had seen the patient previously were less likely to include therapeutic and preventive services than visits to a provider who had never before seen the patient. An office visit with an M.D. was much more likely to include therapeutic and preventive services than a visit with a primary-care provider who was not a physician.

Insurance Plans Accepted by the Physician

Relative to visits to physicians who accepted only regular fee-for-service (FFS) insurance plans, neither visits to providers that accepted both FFS and PPO or both HMO and PPO plans had a significantly different likelihood of including a therapeutic or preventive service, other things being equal. As was also the case with diagnostic and screening services, however, office visits to primary-care providers who accepted only HMO insurance plans were significantly more likely than visits to a pure-FFS provider to include a therapeutic or preventive service, once other factors were taken into account. Relative to an office visit to a provider who accepted only FFS insurance plans, a visit to an office that accepted only HMO plans was about 37% more likely to include delivery of therapeutic or preventive services.

Table 7. Therapeutic and Preventive Services, Privately Insured Patients Under Age 65: Logistic Regression Results

Response Variable: Were therapeutic or screening services performed?				
Analysis Variable	**Weighted Mean**	**Parameter Estimate**	**Standard Error**	**Odds Ratio**
Intercept		-1.1327***	0.2340	
Age	29.1	-0.00796***	0.00162	0.992
Sex (1 = female)	0.6345	-0.0417	0.0585	0.959
Race (1 = white)	0.8778	-0.1265	0.0850	0.881
Northeast	0.1736	0.2931***	0.0856	1.341
South	0.3241	-0.5034***	0.0768	0.605
West	0.2640	0.0588	0.0781	1.061
Urban Area	0.8336	0.2054**	0.0812	1.228
Has Chronic Condition(s)	0.2189	1.0960***	0.0738	2.992
Patient Seen Previously	0.9035	-0.1733*	0.0936	0.841
Provider is an M.D.	0.9583	0.6921***	0.1602	1.998
Reg. FFS or PPO accepted	0.1569	0.0866	0.1111	1.091
HMO or PPO accepted	0.6645	0.0598	0.0924	1.062
Only HMO accepted	0.0560	0.3176**	0.1444	1.374

Source: CRS analysis of data from the 1995 NAMCS.
n = 6,028 observations
* significant at >= .10
*** significant at >= .01

Discussion

The data reported in **Table 1** show that patients with particular demographic and health characteristics are more likely to have visited the offices of primary-care physicians that accept certain kinds of insurance and less likely to have visited physician office that accept other kinds of insurance. Pure FFS physician offices had a smaller-than-average percentage of visits by children and young adults and a greater than average percentage of visits by adults aged 55 to 64. Pure HMO physician practices also had a lower-than-average proportion of visits by children, but a greater-than-average proportion of visits by adults aged 35 to 64. Male patients, non-white patients, patients with one or more chronic medical conditions, and patients in rural areas each made up a greater-than-average proportion of visits to pure-FFS physician offices. Visits to pure FFS offices had a lower-than-average percentage of visits by patients whom the physician had never seen before, while offices that accepted both HMO and PPO plans had a disproportionately large share of visits by patients who were seeing a particular provider for the first time.

The data presented in **Table 2** and **Table 3** show consistently higher rates of diagnostic and screening services being performed in pure-HMO physician offices and that the relative difference from the average was much greater for men than for women. In contrast, while men also were more likely to have received a diagnostic or screening service in a visit to a FFS-only office and were less likely to have received these services in a mixed FFS/PPO office, no such differences were found for women. Overall, women were more likely than men to have received diagnostic or screening services during a typical office visit, but among all visits by women the likelihood of receiving diagnostic or screening services was significantly above average only during visits to pure-HMO physician offices. Patients with no chronic medical conditions were less likely to receive diagnostic or screening services than those who had a chronic condition. Patients without a chronic condition were most likely to receive diagnostic or screening services in an HMO-only office.

Table 4 and **Table 5** show a different pattern with respect to therapeutic and preventive services than **Tables 1** and **2** showed for diagnostic and screening services. Overall, the likelihood of receiving therapeutic or preventive services was similar for male patients and female patients. Visits to pure-HMO offices had a greater likelihood of including a therapeutic or screening service, while visits to mixed FFS and PPO offices had a lower-than-average likelihood of including these services. The higher rate in HMO offices was statistically significant only for men while the lower rate in FFS/PPO offices was significant only for female patients. Among patients with no chronic medical conditions, office visits to all four insurance categories of primary care providers had statistically similar probabilities of including a therapeutic or preventive service.

With respect to diagnostic and screening services, office visits to providers who accepted both HMO/PPO or pure HMO plans had a greater likelihood of including these services than did visits to physicians who accepted only FFS insurance plans, even when controlling for the patient's health status and demographic characteristics. In the case of therapeutic and preventive services, however, only visits to pure HMO offices had a significantly higher likelihood of receiving such a service than visits to pure FFS offices. For both diagnostic/screening services and therapeutic/preventive services, the presence of a chronic medical condition exerted a much stronger influence on the likelihood that a patient would receive either kind of service than did the types of insurance coverage accepted by the provider.

The finding that female patients were more likely than male patients to have received diagnostic or screening services regardless of the health care provider's insurance affiliation most likely reflects female patients' greater frequency of visits for exams and check-ups. More than 63% of all office visits in 1995 were made by female patients, and a subset of these visits – such as those for mammograms or pap smears – *always* involve a test or exam. The greater probability of receiving either diagnostic/screening services or therapeutic/preventive services in an HMO-only office compared to a physician office that accepts only FFS insurance plans could be the result of several characteristics of HMOs. Health maintenance organizations have historically emphasized preventive care as a way of promoting good health and potentially reducing health care expenses over the long term. HMOs also frequently screen patients with phone consultations before making an appointment for an office visit. If effective, this would result in a greater proportion of patients who ultimately see a physician in a pure HMO being in need of medical services compared with patients in purely FFS physician offices. Finally, an emphasis on primary care is among the fundamental principles of HMOs, and HMOs are staffed mainly by primary-care physicians. Consequently, it may be that some services performed in the offices of primary care physicians in HMOs are referred to specialists in FFS office settings.

Differences in the frequency with which diagnostic or therapeutic services are performed by any given group of physicians on any given group of patients do not necessarily mean that the rates at which these services are performed in one case or the other is inappropriate. However, while this analysis showed that a patient's health status has a much stronger relationship to the likelihood of receiving services during an office visit than does the provider's insurance affiliations, these too appear to influence the likelihood of some kinds of services administered. Differences in the rates at which diagnostic and therapeutic services are performed among male and female patients and among office visits to physicians who participate in HMOs or PPOs or do not participate in any kind of managed care naturally raise the question of *why* these differences occur.

Previous research ahs shown that patients enrolled in HMOs typically have a higher number of physician office visits and fewer inpatient admissions in a given period of time than non-HMO patients, but that they also have less access to specialists and use fewer complex tests and procedures. This analysis presents evidence that, even when controlling for the patient's health status, diagnostic and screening services are most likely to be provided during office visits to primary care physicians in HMO or HMO/PPO practices, and that therapeutic and preventive services are most likely to be performed during office visits to HMO-only physician practices.

APPENDIX I: STANDARD ERRORS OF ESTIMATES

Table A1. Standard Errors for Estimates Displayed in Table 1

Patient age, sex, race; physician location	Visits (000s)	*Standard error (+/-)*			
		FFS only	FFS or PPO	HMO or PPO	HMO only
Under age 18	**59,144**	*0.7%*	*1.0%*	*1.2%*	*0.4%*
Ages 18 to 34	**36,244**	*0.9%*	*1.1%*	*1.5%*	*0.9%*
Ages 35 to 54	**53,413**	*0.8%*	*1.0%*	*1.3%*	*0.7%*
Ages 55 to 64	**19,508**	*1.7%*	*1.7%*	*2.2%*	*1.3%*
Female	**106,942**	*0.5%*	*0.7%*	*0.9%*	*0.4%*
Male	**61,347**	*0.8%*	*0.9%*	*1.2%*	*0.6%*
White	**147,423**	*0.5%*	*0.6%*	*0.8%*	*0.4%*
Black or other	**20,865**	*1.5%*	*1.3%*	*2.0%*	*1.0%*
Has chronic condition(s)	**36,434**	*1.2%*	*1.1%*	*2.5%*	*0.8%*
No chronic conditions	**131,853**	*0.5%*	*0.6%*	*0.8%*	*0.4%*
Northeast	**29,070**	*1.1%*	*0.8%*	*1.7%*	*0.6%*
Midwest	**40,991**	*0.9%*	*1.2%*	*1.5%*	*0.6%*
South	**52,684**	*0.8%*	*1.2%*	*1.3%*	*0.5%*
West	**45,544**	*0.9%*	*0.8%*	*1.3%*	*0.9*
Urban	**141,671**	*0.4%*	*0.6%*	*0.7%*	*0.4%*
Rural	**26,616**	*1.7%*	*1.7%*	*1.9%*	*0.4%*
Physician					
Has seen patient before	**151,818**	*0.5%*	*0.6%*	*0.8%*	*0.4%*
Has not seen patient before	**16,470**	*1.3%*	*1.5%*	*2.1%*	*1.2%*
Total	**168,289**	*0.5%*	*0.6%*	*0.7%*	*0.4%*

Table A2. Standard Errors for Estimates Displayed in Table 2

Type of insurance accepted by physician	Total visits (000s)	*Were diagnostic services performed?* Yes/No *Standard error (+/-)*
FFS only	**16,848**	*2.0%*
HMO only	**9,662**	*2.3%*
FFS or PPO	**27,075**	*1.7%*
HMO or PPO	**114,703**	*0.8%*
Total	**168,288**	*0.7%*

People Who Had No Chronic Medical Conditions

Type of insurance accepted by physician	Total visits (000s)	*Were diagnostic services performed?* Yes/No *Standard error (+/-)*
FFS only	**11,459**	*2.6%*
HMO only	**7,115**	*2.9%*
FFS or PPO	**21,915**	*2.0%*
HMO or PPO	**91,365**	*1.0%*
Total	**131,854**	*0.8%*

Table A3. Standard Errors for Estimates Displayed in Table 3

Female Patients

Type of insurance accepted by physician	Total visits (000s)	*Were diagnostic or screening services performed?* Yes/No *Standard error (+/-)*
FFS only	**9,408**	*2.7%*
HMO only	**6,194**	*2.8%*
FFS or PPO	**16,738**	*2.1%*
HMO or PPO	**74,602**	*1.0%*
Total	**106,942**	*0.8%*

Male Patients

Type of insurance accepted by physician	Total visits (000s)	*Were diagnostic or screening services performed?* Yes/No *Standard error (+/-)*
FFS only	**7,440**	*3.0%*
HMO only	**3,469**	*4.0%*
FFS or PPO	**10,337**	*3.0%*
HMO or PPO	**40,101**	*1.5%*
Total	**61,347**	*1.2%*

Table A4. Standard Errors for Estimates Displayed in Table 4

All Privately Insured People Under Age 65 *Were therapeutic or preventive services performed?*		
Type of insurance accepted by physician	**Total visits (000s)**	**Yes/No** *Standard error (+/-)*
FFS only	**16,848**	*2.3%*
HMO only	**9,662**	*3.2%*
FFS or PPO	**27,075**	*1.8%*
HMO or PPO	**114,703**	*0.9%*
Total	**168,288**	*0.7%*

People with No Chronic Medical Conditions *Were therapeutic or preventive services performed?*		
Type of insurance accepted by physician	**Total visits (000s)**	**Yes/No** *Standard error (+/-)*
FFS only	**11,459**	*2.7%*
HMO only	**7,115**	*3.6%*
FFS or PPO	**21,195**	*1.9%*
HMO or PPO	**91,365**	*1.0%*
Total	**131,854**	*0.8%*

Table A5. Standard Errors for Estimates Displayed in Table 5

Female Patients *Were therapeutic or preventive services performed?*		
Type of insurance accepted by physician	**Total visits (000s)**	**Yes/No** *Standard error (+/-)*
FFS only	**9,408**	*3.2%*
HMO only	**6,194**	*3.9%*
FFS or PPO	**16,738**	*2.2%*
HMO or PPO	**74,602**	*1.1%*
Total	**106,942**	*0.9%*

Male Patients *Were therapeutic or preventive services performed?*		
Type of insurance accepted by physician	**Total visits (000s)**	**Yes/No** *Standard error (+/-)*
FFS only	**7,440**	*3.5%*
HMO only	**3,469**	*5.3%*
FFS or PPO	**10,337**	*2.9%*
HMO or PPO	**40,101**	*1.5%*
Total	**61,347**	*1.2%*

APPENDIX II: MEDICAL SERVICES AND MEDICAL CONDITIONS

The National Ambulatory Medical Care Survey (NAMCS) defines three categories of diagnostic and screening services: exams, tests, and imaging.

Exams, Tests, and Imaging

Breast exam
Pelvic exam
Rectal exam
Visual acuity exam
Mental status exam
Other exam
Blood pressure test
Urinalysis
TB skin test
Blood lead level test
Cholesterol measure
Prostate screening antigen (PSA) test
HIV serology
Other Blood test
Other test
X-ray
Computerized axial tomography (CAT scan)
Magnetic resonance imaging (MRI)
Ultrasound
Other imaging
Other diagnostic or screening service

The NAMCS defines two categories of therapeutic and preventive services: counseling/education and other therapy.

Counseling/Education

Diet
Exercise
Weight reduction
Cholesterol reduction
HIV transmission
Tobacco use/exposure
Growth/development
Mental health
Other counseling

Other Therapy

Psychotherapy
Corrective lenses
Physiotherapy
Other counseling

REFERENCES

Clement, D.G., S.M. Retchin, R.S. Brown, and M.H. Stegall. Access and Outcomes of Elderly Patients Enrolled in Managed Care. *Journal of the American Medical Association*, v. 271, no. 19, May 18, 1994.

CRS Report 97-482, *Managed Health Care: The Use of Financial Incentives*, by Beth C. Fuchs and Jason S. Lee.

CRS Report 97-913, *Managed Health Care: A Primer*, by Jason S. Lee.

Eddy, D.M. Balancing Cost and Quality in Fee-for-Service Versus Managed Care. *Health Affairs*, v. 16, no. 3, May/June 1997.

Fama, T., P.D. Fox, and L.A. White. Can HMOs Care for the Chronically Ill? *Health Affairs*, v. 14, spring, 1995.

Gabel, J. Ten Ways HMOs Have Changed During the 1990s. *Health Affairs*, v. 16, no. 3, May/June 1997.

Gazmararian, J.A. and J.P. Koplan. Length of Stay After Delivery: Managed Care Versus Fee-for-Service. *Health Affairs*, v. 15, no. 4, winter, 1996.

Hellinger, F.J. Selection Bias in HMOs and PPOs: A Review of the Evidence. *Inquiry*, v. 32, summer, 1995.

Hoechst-Marion-Roussel. *Managed Care Digest Series: HMO-PPO Digest 1996*. Kansan City, MO, 1996.

KPMG Peal Marwick. *The Impact of Managed Care on U.S. Markets*. Washington, DC, 1996.

Mark, T. and C. Mueller. Access to Care in HMO and Traditional Insurance Plans. *Health Affairs*, v. 15, no. 4, winter, 1996.

Miller, R.H. and H.S. Luft. Does Managed Care Lead to Better or Worse Quality of Care? *Health Affairs*, v. 16, no. 5, September/October 1997.

Miller, R.H. and H.S. Luft. Managed Care Plan Performance Since 1980. *Journal of the American Medical Association*, v. 271, no. 19, May 18, 1994.

Robinson, J.C. Decline in Hospital Utilization and Cost Inflation Under Managed Care in California, *Journal of the American Medical Association*, v. 276, no. 13, October 2, 1996.

Safran, D.G., A.R. Tarlov, and W.H. Rogers. Primary Care Performance in Fee-for-Service and Prepaid Health Care Systems. *Journal of the American Medical Association*, v. 271, no. 20, May 25, 1994.

Taylor, A.K., K.M. Beauregard, and J.P. Vistnes. Who Belongs to HMOs: A Comparison of Fee-for-Service Versus HMO Enrollees. *Medical Care Research and Review*, v. 52, no. 3, September 1995.

Ware, J.E., M.S. Bayliss, W.H. Rogers, M. Kosinski, and A.R. Tarlov. Differences in 4-Year Health Outcomes for Elderly and Poor, Chronically Ill Patients Treated in HMO and Fee-for-Service Systems. *Journal of the American Medical Association*, v. 276, no. 13, October 2, 1996.

Weiner, J.P., A. Lyles, D.M. Steinwachs, and K.C. Hall. Impact of Managed Care on Prescription Drug Use. *Health Affairs*, v. 10, spring, 1991.

Wholey, D.R., J.B. Christianson, J. Enberg, and C. Bryce. HMO Market Structure and Performance. *Health Affairs*, v. 16, no. 6, November/December 1997.

Yelin, E.H., L.A. Criswell, and P.G. Feigenbaum. Health Care Utilization and Outcomes Among Persons with Rheumatoid Arthritis in Fee-for-Service and prepaid Group Practice Settings. *Journal of the American Medical Association*, v. 276, no. 13, October 2, 1996.

INDEX

D

E

F

G

H

I

J

K

L

M

Q

R

S

T

U

V

W

Y